THE
HANGING OF
ANGÉLIQUE

THE
HANGING OF
ANGÉLIQUE

THE UNTOLD STORY OF CANADIAN SLAVERY
AND THE BURNING OF OLD MONTRÉAL

AFUA COOPER

The University of Georgia Press
Athens

Published in 2007 by the University of Georgia Press
Athens, Georgia 30602
by arrangement with HarperCollins Publishers Ltd.
© 2006 by Afua Cooper

Printed digitally in the United States of America

Library of Congress Cataloging-in-Publication Data

Cooper, Afua
The hanging of Angélique : the untold story of Canadian slavery
and the burning of Old Montréal / Afua Cooper.
349 p. ; 21 cm. — (Race in the Atlantic World, 1700–1900)
Originally published: Toronto : HarperCollins, 2006.
Includes bibliographical references and index.
ISBN-13: 978-0-8203-2939-0 (alk. paper)
ISBN-10: 0-8203-2939-8 (alk. paper)
ISBN-13: 978-0-8203-2940-6 (pbk. : alk. paper)
ISBN-10: 0-8203-2940-1 (pbk. : alk. paper)
1. Slaves—Québec (Province)—Montréal—Biography.
2. Fires—Québec (Province)—Montréal—History—18th century.
3. Montréal (Québec)—History—18th century. I. Title. II. Series.
HV6248.A55 C66 2007
971.4'28014092—dc22 [B]   2006050180

The original hardcover version of this text was published
in Canada in 2006 by HarperCollins Publishers Ltd.

To my family:
Alpha Diallo, Akil, Lamarana, and Habiba

Contents

Preface 1

I   The Torture and Hanging of Angélique 14

II   Atlantic Origins: The Slave Woman from Portugal . . . 23

III   The Secret of Slavery in Canada 68

IV   Bourgeois Slaveholders: François Poulin de
      Francheville and Thérèse de Couagne 107

V   Angélique's Montréal 141

VI   First Fire, First Flight 175

VII   April's Fire 189

VIII The Aftermath 200

IX   The Trial 214

X   The Verdict 252

XI   The Appeal and Final Judgment 261

XII   The Execution 282

XIII Angélique, the Arsonist 286

Epilogue: A Silenced Voice Heard Again 293

Acknowledgements 307

Notes 311

Sources 327

Index 340

THE
HANGING OF
ANGÉLIQUE

Preface

NOT A SINGLE CLOUD graces this sky of the brightest blue. And the sun that sits at its centre is so hot that vapours rise from the pavement. The beads of sweat that run from my face put me in mind of the Caribbean. Only there have I experienced such intensity of heat. It is the beginning of summer, and the tourist season is on. Almost everyone around me is in a semi-nude state, looking for the "ultimate bronze."

Hot, but feeling inspired, I walk through the few blocks that make up Old Montréal. The modern city of Montréal began here, and grew and developed from its confines. The old city is a tourist attraction, a "living monument," a piece of history promoted by the provincial government. I am here (my fourth time) because of Marie-Joseph Angélique. This was her stomping ground, the place where she lived, was enslaved, and died. It was here that the tragedy of her life unfolded. The boundaries of Old Montréal are the same as they were in the eighteenth century, when Angélique lived here: an irregularly shaped rectangular block. Rue Notre-

Dame still forms the northern boundary, the St. Lawrence River marks the southern limit, rue Berri demarcates the eastern boundary, and boulevard Saint-Laurent the western. The two main thoroughfares in Old Montréal are still, as in the eighteenth century, rues Notre-Dame and Saint-Paul. They run parallel to each other, and to the St. Lawrence River, along an east–west axis.

As one walks throughout the narrow streets of the old town, one is constantly reminded of its colonial history, a history that dates backs to the mid-seventeenth century. There are signs of memorialization everywhere. A monument marks the site where Jeanne Mance, nurse, nun, and colonizer, built the first hospital, in 1642, in the compound of the first habitation. There is a life-size statue of Paul de Chomedey, Sieur de Maisonneuve, first governor of Montréal, at the Place d'Armes, in front of Notre-Dame Basilica. De Chomedey, along with Mance, was one of the French founders of the city. The site of the house of the late-seventeenth-century governor, Louis-Hector de Callière, at Pointe-à-Callière on the western limit of the city, is acknowledged in the form of a museum.

Rue Saint-Paul, "the merchants' street," sits at the heart of the old city. To the north is rue Notre-Dame, to the south, the St. Lawrence. The distinctive house of Huguenot merchant Pierre Du Calvet, built in 1725, is visible at the eastern end of rue Saint-Paul. The house boasts the raised "fire wall" that was designed to contain fire should one arise. Built nearly three hundred years ago, the house is now a high-priced hotel. At the other end of the street is the old marketplace, Marché Bonsecours, now an upscale shopping centre catering to tourists. A short distance away is the home, now a museum, of George-Étienne Cartier, a nineteenth-century premier and the other half of the famous Macdonald-Cartier ministry of 1854.

The old Hôtel-Dieu is gone from rue Saint-Paul. Expensive condominiums and upscale offices stand on the site of the former hospital. The present Hôtel-Dieu is located at avenue des Pins at the foot of Mount Royal in the modern sector of the city. Across the street from the location of the old Hôtel-Dieu is the site of the former Francheville home. Things have changed here since 1734. A low-rise office building sits on the spot. On the ground floor is a high-priced art gallery called Northsud. In the eighteenth century, the south side of rue Saint-Paul backed onto the river. This is no longer the case. The land has been filled in, and a new street, rue de la Commune, separates rue Saint-Paul from the river.

I stand at the spot of the former Francheville home and imagine the place as it was over two and a half centuries ago. The mud from the spring thaw would be hard-packed in the summer heat. Street urchins run about, horse-drawn buggies try to out-speed each other, to the detriment of the passengers. Bourgeois women, dressed in the latest fashion and accompanied by their servants and slaves, walk along the street. Nuns and clerics go about their day. A company of soldiers practise their drill at Place d'Armes...The honking of a passing vehicle wakes me from my reverie and reminds me that this is not 1734 but 2004, and that I must be alert for fast cars, not horse-drawn buggies.

I cross rue Saint-Paul where it intersects with rue Saint-Sulpice and head up the latter street. My destination is rue Notre-Dame. Like rue Saint-Paul, this is an east-west street. Undoubtedly the most remarkable building on this street is the resplendent Church of Notre-Dame. Upgraded and expanded over the centuries, it is now a basilica, an important landmark and a world heritage site. The neo-Gothic basilica is broad and rectangular, with two towers at each end. A statue of a crowned Virgin stands between the two towers. Stars circle the crown. The patron saint of Montréal is the Virgin. In fact, the original name of the city was Ville-Marie (Mary's City), and the church is dedicated to her. The Sulpician fathers built the church, and are still its overseers.

To the immediate west of the basilica is the old seminary of the Sulpicians. The seminary is a grey three-storey sturdy stone building, the oldest building in continuous use in Montréal. It was built in 1684 by the Sulpicians, the original seigneurs of the town. Since 1701, a clock has graced the facade of the seminary; it is reputed to be North America's first clock. Remarkably, it still works.

The Sulpicians, as seigneurs of Montréal, owned the town. They wielded great power and influence, and oversaw the settlement and development of the town. They were everywhere, knew everyone and everything, and could halt or facilitate one's progress. It was a Sulpician, Father Jean-Gabriel-Marie Le Pape Du Lescöat, who officiated at Angélique's baptism.

To the east on rue Notre-Dame, on the south side, is the Château de Ramezay. Built of stone in 1705 by Governor de Ramezay, the château is now a museum. The original structure is still in place, and the structural integrity of the building is maintained. On the other side of the street is the Hôtel de Ville (city hall), an architectural landmark. Built between 1872 and 1878, it stands on the site of the original city hall, built during the French period. The Hôtel de Ville now houses the municipal archives. The more modern Palais de Justice (courthouse), a building of steel and glass, lies to the west of the Hôtel de Ville, on the site of a former prison and courthouse of the French period.

Today, numerous shops and restaurants line the streets of Old Montréal, with diverse souvenirs and culinary treats for tourists and native Montrealers. The old city has also become "gentrified." Developers have built expensive lofts and condos for those with new money and old. But the old city remains a tourist attraction. And we throng its streets. Why are we here? Many come as part of their holiday vacation packages to Montréal. The old city, with its historic buildings, is billed as a "must see." Old Montréal provides the right atmosphere for those who want to "step back in time."

I am here because I want to be in Angélique's environment, however impossible that is now. To walk the same streets she walked. To talk to her ghost. As I walk along rue Saint-Paul, I see Angélique, a scarf on her head, her bleached-out cotton shift trailing in the dust, a basket in one hand, going to the market. I see her crossing the street from her house to Hôtel-Dieu and talking to the soldier named Latreille. Latreille is recuperating from a wound he sustained in a frontier battle. He and Angélique engage in playful banter and share a bottle of syrup. I fast-forward in time and see Angélique running from her house into the street and fixing her gaze on the roof of the house. A short time later, smoke curls from the roof. I hear the screams, the fire alarms, and see the agitated citizenry spilling into the streets.

✳

In April 1734, Montréal burned. A slave woman, Marie-Joseph Angélique, was the main suspect. She was arrested by the police and hauled in front of the court, and she endured a two-month trial. Throughout the trial, however, Angélique maintained her innocence. At the end of the ordeal, she was found guilty and condemned to be tortured, have her right hand cut off, and then be burned alive. Her sentence was appealed in the Conseil Supérieur, the highest court in the land, and the judges of the Conseil modified the grisly sentence—the slave woman was only to be tortured and then hanged. The date for the execution was set for June 21. On that day, the Montréal judge, accompanied by the hangman, who also bore the ghoulish title "master of the means of torture," visited Angélique in her prison cell. The judge intended to get a confession of guilt from the condemned woman; if she refused, then torture would be applied to extract it. Angélique denied setting the fire, and the hangman applied a gruesome torture, in which her legs were squeezed tight between planks of wood and then smashed with a heavy iron. The slave woman broke under the torture and confessed to setting the fire. She was then taken to the gallows, where she was hanged.

The bondswoman was a Portuguese-born Black woman who endured enslavement possibly in Portugal and in other parts of Europe, but certainly in New England and New France. Speaking of New France, I mean *le Canada*, the French colonial settlement in the St. Lawrence Valley.

At the time of her death, Angélique was owned by Thérèse de Couagne de Francheville, the widow of a Montréal merchant, François Poulin de Francheville. In Canada, Angélique endured enslavement for nine years, from 1725 to 1734, but it is the last four years of her life that are well documented in the historical record. Her trial transcripts in particular provide detailed information about her life in Canada. From them we learn that her master had her baptized in the Catholic faith; that she had three children; that she was vocal in expressing her hatred of slavery; that she was rude and disobedient to her mistress; that she detested the French, and all Whites in general; that she had an affair with a White male indentured labourer; and that at least once before the fateful fire she had run away from her servile condition, intent on making it back to Portugal. She never did make it back, but ended her life in the New World, her final moments under a hangman's noose. She was but one of many enslaved Black people who lived and died in colonial Canada.

Yet the story of Angélique, dramatic and extraordinary as it is, is relatively unknown in Canada. Canadian history, insofar as its Black history is concerned, is a drama punctuated with disappearing acts. The erasure of Black people and their history in the examples of the Priceville Cemetery and Africville is consistent with the general behaviour of the official chroniclers of the country's past.[1] Black history is treated as a marginal subject. In truth, it has been bulldozed and ploughed over, slavery in particular.

Slavery has disappeared from Canada's historical chronicles, erased from its memory and banished to the dungeons of its past. This in a country where the enslavement of Black people was institutionalized and practised for the better part of three centuries. Enslaved Africans in Canada (in both the French and English periods) became important to society even as, paradoxically, they were marginalized. Yet many people do not know that slavery existed in Canada and, to be more specific, that an enslaved woman was executed for setting fire to one of the principal colonial settlements. The fire inconvenienced many people. It cost both the local government and that of the mother country tens of thousands of livres (two livres equal about eighty modern-day dollars) to rebuild the city and compensate the victims. But yet we do not this story. How is it that numerous books have been written about New France, French Canada, Montréal, and women in the colony without a reasonable discussion of slavery, of the great fire, and of Angélique? How is it that we know details about the lives of such founding fathers and mothers as Matthew Elliott, Peter Russell, and Marie de l'Incarnation, without knowing that they and other founding parents were some of the most prominent slaveholders? This "little fact" never made it into their official biographies.

In my engagement with African Canadian history, I have come to realize that Black history has less to do with Black people and more with White pride. If Black history narratives make Whites feel good, it is allowed to surface; if not, it is suppressed or buried.[2] That is why slavery has been erased from the collective consciousness. It is about an ignoble and unsavoury past, and because it cast Whites in a "bad" light, they as chroniclers of the country's past, creators and keepers of its traditions and myths, banished this past to the dustbins of history.

The Hanging of Angélique seeks to remedy that situation. It tells a story of slavery in Canada by narrating the tragic life history of Marie-Joseph Angélique. Yet Angélique lived on at least two continents and traversed the ocean between them. In her lifetime, she lived within or under the shadows of four empires: the Portuguese, Dutch, French, and English. An integral part of the story is therefore the miserable wanderings and journeys of Black peoples across the Atlantic world of the eighteenth century. Some have named this experience the "Black Atlantic," others see it as "overlapping diasporas," but by whatever name it is called, it is an experience of woe and sorrow, because the vast majority of these people, deemed subhuman, were violently enslaved and their freedom and sometimes their lives taken from them.

A sister theme of this book is the general topic of Atlantic slavery. It explores how Angélique's birth country, Portugal, initiated the slave trade to Europe and across the Atlantic to the New World; how slavery instituted a new racial hierarchy based on Black subordination and White supremacy in the New World and Europe; and how the slave trade took Angélique to Montréal.

Did Angélique set the fire? Your guess is as good as mine. No one saw her light the spark that started the blaze. All the evidence was circumstantial. But I believe she did set it. She had motive enough. She hated her mistress; she wanted to run away from slavery; and she wanted to leave the American continent altogether. Moreover, she was implicated in another fire, started in February 1734 (two months before the great fire), in the home of Sieur Monière, Madame Francheville's relative. Let us also remember that arson was a tool of resistance commonly used by enslaved Africans throughout the length and breadth of the Americas. If Angélique set the fire, she must have felt she had nothing to lose. And she would have been right. As a slave, she was alienated from society; as a slave, she was the lowest of the low. Perhaps she set the fire to cover her tracks while fleeing and wreak vengeance upon Montréal as a bonus.

Discussions about Euro-Canadian slavery often disconnect Canada from the larger Atlantic and American world of slavery of which it was very much a part. *The Hanging of Angélique* thus links Canada as no work has done before to the Atlantic slave trade and shows Canada's extensive relationship, based mainly on trade and war, to the other imperial powers—the Dutch, Spanish, English, and Portuguese—in the New World.

The Hanging of Angélique is a story that must be told. For one thing, it is not simply "Black" history, but is also a Canadian story. In fact, it is a global narrative, one that belongs to all of us, whether or not we want to claim it, or feel good about it. The story of Angélique provides an opportunity for us to reclaim a hidden past. Since much of the Black past has been deliberately buried, covered over, and demolished, it is our task to unearth, uncover, and piece it together again. This we are called to do because the dead speak to us.

This book is based on fifteen years of extensive research and is the first book of its kind in either English or French. Work was done in public and private archives and research centres mainy in the province of Québec but also in Ontario. I have retrieved, recovered, and reclaimed this story from several sources. The central documents are the trial transcripts recorded by scribes in the high and lower courts. I also culled information from correspondence between colonial and metropolitan officials, and from such eyewitnesses to the fire and its aftermath as Sister Marie-Anne-Véronique Cuillerier, a nursing sister from the Hôtel-Dieu, the city's main hospital. I have likewise examined other sources, such as wills and records of birth, marriage, and death, drawn from the parish archives of Notre-Dame. I perused censuses, hospital records, and seminary documents, especially those of the Sulpician fathers of Montréal and the Hôtel-Dieu, to put flesh on the skeleton of Angelique's life.

In New France, the king's justice was dispensed by a formidable cadre of legally trained administrators. They ensured that the law reached everywhere, encompassed everyone, and regulated every aspect of life. Therefore, I reviewed legal codes, ordinances, edicts, and regulations, of both metropolitan and colonial origins, and read numerous documents drawn up by notaries.

Before 1763, there were no newspapers published in Canada, but news about the colony frequently appeared in American colonial newspapers. I examined several New England, New York, and Pennsylvania newspapers and discovered exciting and crucial news about the fire Angélique was charged with setting. The newspapers also noted the arrival of the ironsmith, Angélique's owner, Sieur Francheville, sent down from Canada to investigate ironworks in Pennsylvania. These early American newspapers provided valuable information on early Canadian colonial history.

Canada was part of the New World, an *American* society. The New World was a slave society, and Canada shared that feature. Therefore, I look at many sources on New World slavery, particularly those relating to slavery in Canada, the thirteen American colonies, the French and Dutch Caribbean, and Dutch New York. For my purposes, records on slavery during French colonization were especially pertinent. Angélique was Portuguese, but during a period of her odyssey a Flemish (or Dutch-speaking) man owned her. For some reason, he took her to New England or New York. In my attempt to piece together Angélique's life, I explore the roles of Portugal, the Netherlands, and British North America in the Atlantic and transatlantic slave trade.

The result is a story that is part slave narrative, part historical analysis, part biography, and part historical archaeology. What I began to intuit as I explored Angélique's fascinating life was that this bondswoman provided a female narrative of what is now called the Black Atlantic.

Angélique did not write this story; neither did she write any of the records that became sources for her life. Elite white men, most of whom were slaveholders, wrote and mediated the records. They also wrote their opinions and gave interpretations of her perceived motives and her assumed guilt. These hegemonic sources are still extremely useful in illuminating this singular tale. Yet I would argue that Angélique, in her own fashion, did write. She did so through her actions. When she ran away from slavery in February 1734, when she told her mistress she was going to "roast" her, the slave woman wrote an oral narrative of resistance.

*

My meandering ends at the square of Place Royale, the site of the old marketplace, the place where punishments and executions took place during the *ancien régime*. I picture the slave woman swinging from the gallows, and I am filled with sadness. The tragedy of it all. I think of the millions of enslaved Africans in the Americas whose lives were broken and destroyed by slavery. Those like Angélique in New France and early Canada who despaired and attempted to break the bonds of their captivity. I am standing in a place filled with monuments for the early explorers, pioneers, and heroic settlers. I cannot help but think that this memorialization is so one-sided, so monolithic, so homogenous. Europeans glorifying and idolizing themselves. Why is there no monument to the slaves? Those who had their lives, labour, and dreams stolen to build up a new colony and satisfy the greed of Whites? Where is Angélique? What plaque or sign attests to her presence and struggle? Is Angélique's story to be thrown to the four winds, as her ashes were?

It has been 271 years since that fateful fire and the subsequent execution of the bondswoman from Portugal. But for me, Angélique's presence in these streets of Old Montréal is still palpable. On rue de la Commune, two ambulances rush by at breakneck speed, their sirens piercing the air with their urgent songs. In the echoes, I hear the wails of Angélique.

I

The Torture and Hanging of Angélique

ON THE MORNING of June 21, 1734, at 7:00 a.m., Pierre
Raimbault, judge of the court for the jurisdiction of
Montréal, and Charles-René Gaudron de Chevremont,
notary and also one of the court assessors, went to the court
chambers in the local prison to pronounce judgment on
Marie-Joseph Angélique, slave woman of Madame Thérèse
de Couagne de Francheville. Angélique had been found
guilty of setting fire to her mistress's house and the subsequent burning of forty-five other buildings. But Raimbault
and Gaudron went to the prison to do more than condemn
the bondswoman; they also wanted to hear Angélique confess
to setting fire to the city, and if she did not confess willingly,
they would torture her until she did. Joseph Benoît, physician
at the convent-hospital Hôtel-Dieu, and Mathieu Leveille,
the hangman and torturer, accompanied Raimbault and
Gaudron. Four armed guards, known as *les archers*, completed
the party. In all likelihood, the Sulpician priest, Father
Navetier, was included in the group, to administer the last

rites to Angélique in case the torture proved too much for her and she expired.

The jailer, one Marchand, brought Angélique before the judge and his party. They sat her down on a chair aptly named "the stool of repentance." The torture instruments—screws, wedges, "wooden boots," and hammer—were ominously displayed on the table in plain view of the accused. Raimbault would cross-examine Angélique one last time. If she confessed to setting the fire and named her accomplices, there would be no need for the torture. But if she did not confess, she would suffer. The judge began.

RAIMBAULT: Tell us your name, age, origin, status, and place of residence.
ANGÉLIQUE: My name is Marie-Joseph Angélique. I am twenty-nine years old. I was born in Portugal. I am the slave of the widow Francheville. I lived with her until the fire.
RAIMBAULT: Who counselled you to set the fire? Did anyone help you?
ANGÉLIQUE: No one told me to set the fire. No one helped me, because I did not do it.

The interrogation was brief. Raimbault wanted a confession. He did not get it, notwithstanding the fact that the instruments of terror were placed before the eyes of the condemned. If Angélique was frightened, she did not show it. She calmly maintained her innocence.

Raimbault now had no other choice but to pronounce the sentence reached by the court and begin the torture. The judge prepared for the forbidding scene that was about to unfold. "Go down on your knees," he commanded the slave woman. She did. The *greffier*, or court recorder, Claude-Cyprien-Jacques Porlier, stood above her and read the sentence handed down by the Conseil Superiéur. Angélique and the others listened in grim silence.

"Marie-Joseph Angélique, you are condemned to make honourable amends [a formal apology], to be hanged and strangled until dead, to have your dead body be attached to a gibbet that will be raised for this purpose. Your body will be then burned and consumed by fire, but beforehand you will be subjected to the *la question ordinaire et extraordinaire* in order to reveal your accomplices."

❊

The manner in which she was to die must have terrified Angélique, but she may have found a little comfort in the fact that this was a modified sentence. On June 4, the court at Montréal had condemned her to have her hands cut off and to be burnt alive. But the prosecutor himself had appealed the sentence to the Conseil Supérieur (the high court) at Québec. The Coutume de Paris, the great legal code promulgated in France and the colonies in 1670, gave the right of appeal to anyone condemned to die. Foucher, in launching the appeal, was simply extending to Angélique her right guaranteed under the Coutume.

The Conseil reduced the savagery of the punishment by calling only for her to be hanged and her body burned. After the *greffier* read the sentence, the judge ordered the torturer to begin his work. The method of torture Raimbault had chosen was the *brodequins*, or the "laced boots." This instrument came out of the torture arsenal of the Middle Ages and was popular in most European countries, in particular France, Germany, and Spain. It was used only on those who had received the death penalty, because many of its victims died while being tortured. The *brodequins* consisted of four boards, about two feet high, placed along each side of each leg, one inside and one outside. The planks were "held tight against the leg by tying them firmly at the knee and above the ankle in such a way that the cords that ran around the boards left enough space to insert wedges. When each of the legs had been dealt with in this way, they were both tied together with heavy ropes."[1]

This "wooden machine" created great pressure on the leg. For the torture of the boots, Raimbault commanded Angélique to sit on "the questioning chair," specifically designed for this torture, and to remove her shoes. Leveille applied the boots. There was a great silence in the chamber. All present knew of the boots, and some had seen them in action. The judge would ask a question, and if the condemned did not answer the way he wanted her to, the torturer would put an iron wedge between the leg and the plank of wood, and then drive it in with a large hammer. This action caused extremely painful pressure on the kneecap, the joints of the knee, and the shinbone. Angélique would endure *la question ordinaire et extraordinaire*. The first part of *la question* comprised four strikes of the hammer; the second segment meant an additional four strikes.

The application of the *brodequins* was not for those with weak stomachs. Only those whose duty demanded it were in the room. Leveille tied Angélique's hands behind her, rendering her completely vulnerable. Once this was done, he stood ready with his heavy hammer. The doctor stood behind

Angélique and held her up in anticipation of her body slumping. Raimbault, once more, demanded that Angélique confess, name accomplices, and spare herself the ordeal. But she only pleaded her innocence.

"No one helped me; I did not set the fire," she insisted. With a nod from the judge, Leveille began his loathsome work. The torturer hammered in the first wedges between the middle planks at knee level and farther down at ankle level; the boards squeezed inward, shooting arrows of pain in the victim's flesh and crushing her bones. Angélique screamed.

"*C'est moi!* It's me and no one else. I want to die. *C'est moi.*"

Leveille hammered a second time, while Raimbault shouted to Angélique to name her accomplices.

"Let me die, monsieur. No one advised me. No one helped me set the fire."

Angélique repeated the same thing on the third strike, and on the fourth shouted, "Hang me! I did it. I did it by myself."

Thus ended *la question ordinaire*. Angélique had broken under torture. She had confessed to setting the fire. Her knees and legs were crushed, and she was at the point of passing out. The doctor gave her medicines to revive her. But the judge would not relent. In Angélique's weak and delirious state, he pounced on her again. "Who helped you set the fire?" he shouted. He wanted to hear the name Claude Thibault. Again, Angélique insisted that she had acted alone. Raimbault signalled to Leveille to continue the torments. The torturer inserted a wedge and smashed it with his hammer on Angélique's knee. Her screams echoed through the halls and rooms of the jail, escaped their confines, and pierced the stillness of the early morning.

"You are killing me."

At the second strike: "I did it by myself."

At the third strike: "Hang me."

And finally on the fourth: "I said it was I who did it, *avec un rechaud*, with a small stove. No one told me to do it, monsieur, a bad thought came to me."

The torture of the boots ended. Leveille had applied *la question ordinaire et extraordinaire*. The slave woman had confessed to setting the fire, though she named no accomplice. We don't know if Angélique's legs had "the marrow of the bones oozing out," as was the case with Urbain Grandier, a seventeenth-century French priest who had the great misfortune to wear the boots[2]; but we do know they were so crushed that she could not stand upright. Angélique was shivering and feverish, with beads of sweat pouring from her body, as the torturer raised her from the chair and placed her on a mat, where he removed the wooden boots from her legs. The doctor, once more, gave her "reviving" medicines.

Yet it was not over. As she lay on the mat, Raimbault, frustrated in his attempts to have her name her accomplices, pounced on her once more. Angélique, in pain and sorrow, and resigned to her fate, repeated to Raimbault and his party that she had acted on her own: "It's me, messieurs, it is I who did it. Put me to death." The application of the *brodequins* was so painful that anyone who underwent it begged for the release of death.

The torture and interrogations ended. At 3:00 p.m., Father Navetier huddled with the slave woman and gave her the last rites and the sacrament of confession.

Having put her soul in order, Navetier released Angélique

to the authorities, who readied her for her journey to the gallows. They placed on her a white chemise that hung to her knees. Embroidered on the back and front was the word "*incendiaire*," arsonist. She was barefoot. A rubbish cart waited in the courtyard of the prison to take Angélique to the hangman's noose. But, before reaching her destination, she would stop at the church of Notre-Dame to make honourable amends, confessing her guilt and begging the pardon of those she had wronged. The guards led her to the cart. Once she was settled in, they placed a burning torch weighing two pounds, the symbol of her crime, in her hands, and tied a length of rope around her neck. Leveille jumped in the vehicle and occupied the driver's seat. The four archers and some members of the constabulary brought up the rear.

The cart rumbled westward from the prison, on rue Notre-Dame, towards the church, which stood on the same street. It was a short journey. Two of the guards helped Angélique from the cart and practically carried her to the portal of the church. She dropped onto her bleeding and bruised knees, and in agony cried three times, in a loud voice, "I beg pardon of God, the king, and justice." Having made honourable amends, she was escorted by the archers back to the cart. Now they embarked on a mournful tour of the lower town—the area blackened and ruined by the fire. They headed east along rue Notre-Dame, turned south on rue Bonsecours, and then went west on rue Saint-Paul. Angélique must see her handiwork: the destroyed homes, shops, warehouses, the hospital and convent.

The inhabitants of the town lined the streets to witness the procession. Some pressed forward from their partially rebuilt homes, others walked behind the cart. A great many crossed themselves as the spectacle passed, while others, outraged that Angélique had caused them so much destitution, cursed her. Angélique passed burnt-out Hôtel-Dieu, where she had visited the sick and chatted with the soldier Latreille. And she passed the site of her former home, the place where she had been enslaved, which now lay in ruins. She surveyed the scene as the cart tumbled along the street, the flames from the torch singeing her cheeks. She must have wept.

The authorities meant to be exacting with the king's justice. Determined to humiliate Angélique and make an example of her, they erected the gallows not in the usual "place of public punishment" but in a space, specially cleared away, in the middle of the devastated area on rue Saint-Paul. The cart arrived at the newly constructed gallows, and the archers once again helped Angélique from it to face her punishment. Leveille, the hangman, himself a Black slave, placed the noose around her neck. Was it the archers or Leveille who released the hatch beneath her feet? In any event, the rope tightened and squeezed her neck, she felt herself gasping for air, her body jerked against the noose. Her neck broke. She found release. The church bells, announcing that a hanging had occurred, began to toll their desolate song. The clock in front of the Sulpician Seminary struck five.

The authorities carried out the king's justice to the letter. The humiliation Angélique endured in the hours before her hanging, and during the execution, continued in her death. Her corpse hung for two hours in a gibbet for all to see. Some of the townspeople who regarded the ghastly scene shuddered and uttered a silent prayer. Others hurried by and refused to look. Dusk gathered, and most of the inhabitants who had come out for the spectacle went indoors for their evening meal. The devout among them hurried to evening mass. At 7:00 p.m., Leveille cut down Angélique's corpse and placed it on the fire that had been prepared. Soon the flames consumed her flesh and bones. Later, when the flames had cooled, the hangman gathered Angélique's ashes and flung them to the four winds.

II

Atlantic Origins: The Slave Woman from Portugal

ON JUNE 21, 1734, Angélique's life ended in a territory on the western side of the Atlantic. Those who saw her life come to a close, however, first heard her stunning narrative of ancestral origin. When Judge Raimbault posed his first questions to Angélique, she stated that she "was born in Portugal and that she had been sold to a Fleming who sold her to the late Sieur Francheville about nine years ago, where she remained ever since." Angélique explained that she had been living in New England before she came up to Montréal to serve Sieur Francheville.[1]

By the time Angélique stood before Raimbault, she had endured an Atlantic odyssey—from Portugal, possibly to the Low Countries (Flanders or the Dutch Republic), to the English possession of either New England or New York, and then to New France. In 1725, when she arrived in Montréal, she was twenty years old. During the course of her young life she had been taken to and had lived at several places on both shores of the Atlantic Ocean, and had been sold at least twice. It seems likely that she was enslaved in Portugal, though she could have been free. However, it seems to have been in Portugal that she was sold to the Fleming, a man named Nichus Block.

If Angélique could talk to us now, what would she tell us about how she ended up on the edge of France's North American empire? Who owned her in Portugal? Who took her across the Atlantic? Was Nichus Block a Flemish merchant living and working in Portugal, and had he purchased her there? What was the link between Portugal, Flanders, and the Dutch-speaking world? Some of these questions cannot be answered with any certainty, but of this we can be sure: Angélique became a bondswoman because of the Atlantic trading complex that centred on the African slave trade, a trade that yoked together several continents. And it was the Portuguese who initiated this Atlantic commerce in human flesh.

In the middle of the fifteenth century, Portugal, a nation of one million people, became the leading maritime power in Europe and, by the end of the century, the world. It established a seaborne empire that took its initial impetus from, and continued to rest upon, a trade in gold, spices, and slaves with Atlantic Africa. How did such a small country become the dominant seafaring nation, with a far-flung maritime empire?

The story of Portugal's maritime triumph usually begins with Prince Henrique, the Infante, dubbed "the Navigator." With little hope of becoming king, this younger son found his calling in the world of navigation. He established a naval college in the Algarve, where he drew "on the most advanced mathematical thinking and map-making of the time."[2] The Infante assembled a large multiracial and multi-ethnic group of experts that included map-makers, shipbuilders, astronomers, mathematicians, scientists, nautical inventors, sailors, and others versed in naval sciences and nautical technology.

Included in Prince Henrique's think-tank were many Moors (Muslims of West and North African descent). Muslim sciences were at the cutting edge in Europe at that time. The Muslims had already invented the astrolabe and the compass, produced maps that showed the world was round, and constructed ships that were swift and reliable. They had also applied trigonometry to the study of astronomy and celestial navigation. Jewish map-makers, one the son of the famous cartographer Abraham Cresques, also worked at Henrique's institute.

From the prince's laboratory came the three-masted caravel. This ship represented the best of current nautical technologies, combining Arabic and European influences. The caravel was small, swift, and manoeuvrable and, unlike most vessels at the time, could sail right into the wind. It was also reliable as it made round trips from the African coast and the Atlantic islands. As important, the caravel could mount cannons on its deck. This ship was destined to become Portugal's vessel of conquest and exploration.

The prince's navigational explorations went in two directions—west into the Atlantic and south along the west coast of Africa. To the west, Henrique conquered and colonized such islands as Madeira and the Azores. Portugal, under Henrique, also conquered the Canary Islands, but lost them to Spain. The Portuguese were familiar with the north and northeast coastlines of Africa, having traded and warred with the nations of these regions for centuries. But the west coast represented a new challenge. As the Atlantic islands developed, they often served as way stations for expeditions setting out for West African shores. In these endeavours the prince had two overriding goals: trade and exploration. His main objective, however, was to find an expedient maritime access to the West African goldfields and in doing so to outflank the Muslims and make the Portuguese Crown wealthy and formidable.

The gold trade—African in origin—was in the hands of Muslims at both the northern and southern reaches of the Sahara Desert. From the south, the gold came from the Muslim-dominated kingdoms of Mali and Songhai. Once the gold crossed the Sahara by camel caravans, it was controlled by the Sharif of Morocco. Europeans were excluded from the gold trade—and they lusted after it. The Portuguese monarchy was perennially short of financial resources, and the national currency was regularly devalued. If the Crown could have a regular supply of gold, the currency would stabilize and prosperity would result. Europe was also excluded from the eastern spice trade—it too was controlled by Muslims, in this case Ottoman Turks, who had a vast and powerful eastern empire. Thus, Prince Henrique's explorations, although they had overtly political and economic motives, also had a religious one: the Christian conquest of the Muslims.

Even if Henrique's expeditions were cloaked in the garb of a crusade, he did enjoy important successes in his step-by-step march along the west coast of Africa. In 1419, he settled Madeira; the Azores and Cape Verde followed some years later. Meanwhile, the explorers inched down the African coastline. In 1434, they rounded Cape Bojador, on the southern coast of Morocco. This was a feat of immense importance. Cape Bojador had long remained a physical and psychological block for mariners sailing down the Atlantic. Most would reach the Cape and then head back north, fearing the "monsters, boiling waters, and intense heat"[3] that they believed lay beyond. In 1444, Henrique's explorers (who would be more accurately described as pirates or conquistadors) reached the mouth of the Senegal River, terrorized a local habitation, and kidnapped some 235 Africans who were then taken back to Portugal, where they were sold on the slave market in the Algarve, but not before Prince Henrique collected his "royal fifth" of the terrified slaves. After 1444, the world would never be the same. The capture and sale of African bodies on the Atlantic coastline had commenced.

In 1448, at Arguim, a coastal town in Mauritania, the prince established a fort and began a lucrative trade in gold, spices, and slaves. In 1460, mariners sponsored by Portugal reached Sierra Leone, where a trading post was built. An active trade in gold commenced in Sierra Leone, and the sale of captured persons gave it an added impetus. Slave raiding, which had been the principal means by which the Portuguese obtained slaves, soon gave way to the more peaceful method of slave trading as they found willing local traders and rulers from whom to buy captured persons. As time went by, however, war became the chief means of acquiring slave captives. The slave trade was becoming almost as important as the trade in gold.

With these expeditions Prince Henrique was killing several birds with one stone. He was assiduously colonizing the Atlantic islands and, at the same time, raiding the African coastline and building up trading connections. Furthermore, he was gaining knowledge of nautical technology and navigation and learning the topography of the region. For every place on the African coast that the Portuguese landed, they drew up maps and determined latitude and longitude. They calculated how far these places were from each other and from Portugal, and thus the length of time required to reach each new point from their homeland. This intimate knowledge of the Atlantic waterways was closely guarded from foreign powers and was one of the main reasons that the Portuguese were able to monopolize the Atlantic trade, and even the Indian Ocean trade, for well over a century.

Prince Henrique died in 1460. Ten years later, the Portuguese arrived at the aptly named Gold Coast, present-day Ghana. In the hinterland were rich goldfields owned and worked by the Akan people. Gold from this region found its way into the trans-Saharan trade and to trade routes in West Africa. In the Gold Coast, the Portuguese built Elmina, a factory-fort, to regulate the trade in gold and captured persons—but not before the leader of the expedition burnt down a neighbouring village and subdued the chief.

Africa had lived up to Henrique's dream as a source of gold. The commerce at Elmina enhanced what was already profitable trade with Arguim (modern Mauritania), Senegambia, and Sierra Leone, and would eventually outstrip all the others. João II, who became king in 1481, inspired by the gold that flowed into Lisbon and the knowledge of the world that the expeditions offered, involved the Crown more directly in these voyages. It was not that the government had not been involved before, as the work of Henrique proved. In fact, the Crown had successfully lobbied the Vatican for recognition of its African "discoveries" and trade, and the pope had issued several bulls that gave Portugal a monopoly on the African trade and "ownership" of the entire continent. (He did the same for Spain in the Americas.) But the previous commercial strategy of the

Crown had been to grant licences to private individuals and companies and let them take most of the risks. When the slaves, gold, and spices arrived at Lisbon, Lagos, Oporto, and other ports, the Crown simply received its percentage of the profits made. The lion's share of the wealth remained in the hands of the merchants and traders, many if not most of whom were foreigners. The king now saw that it was both politically and commercially expedient for the Crown to sponsor a larger percentage of overseas voyages than it hitherto had done. To that end, the Crown set up the Casa dos Escravos, an office designed "to organize the slave traffic to the islands and the Peninsula [Portugal]"[4]; the Crown received a thirty percent royalty on all slave trading. As well, the Crown set up the Casa da Mina, also in Lisbon, to supervise the gold trade and received a one-fifth share on all gold transactions.

Emboldened by their successes and discoveries, the Portuguese—whether native-born or foreigners hired by the Crown—continued to explore and plunder farther down the African coast. In 1482, Diogo Cão reached the Congo. In 1492, Bartolomé Dias arrived at the Cape of Good Hope, the point where the Atlantic and Indian oceans "commingled." Six years later, the explorer-conquistador Vasco da Gama rounded the Cape and sailed up the Indian Ocean to the East African coast and the rich Swahili city states "with an impressive expedition of 2,500 men, its costs underwritten by the profits of the African trade."[5] Da Gama and his crew paused briefly to admire the wealth and splendour of the Swahili cities before they attacked, pillaged, and looted them. The frightened citizens were dragged from their houses and beaten, raped, and murdered. Da Gama planted a cross on a hillside in Malindi, Kenya, then turned eastward and sailed to India. Thus, da

Gama, and other conquistadors who followed him, launched
the Portuguese East African/Asian empire. By 1500, with
Prince Henrique long dead, Portugal, the little nation at the
edge of Europe, had conquered the seas, circumnavigated the
globe, and become wealthy as a result. This was largely due to
the vision of the Infante Prince, the tenacity and ruthlessness
of Portugal's seafarers, and the religious zeal of the Crown.

With these voyages of exploration and conquest, the
Portuguese established an intricate trading system that
encompassed the Atlantic world and beyond. In West Africa,
they exchanged metal goods, horses, salt, and textiles made in
Europe or North Africa for captives, gold, ivory, semi-pre-
cious stones, and spices. From the Atlantic islands of Madeira,
Azores, Principe, and São Tomé came sugar, molasses, cotton,
wheat, and indigo. The East African Swahili cities provided
more gold (East Africa was the principal source of gold for
India and Arabia), and India and China provided tea, silk, and
other exotic goods.

However, as time passed, the slave trade would outstrip the
gold trade and become the leading commercial endeavour
entered into by the Crown. By 1600, close to a million Africans
would have been shipped from West African shores to Iberia
(Portugal and Spain) and the rest of Europe, but primarily to
the newly discovered American colonies across the Atlantic. In
1518, Charles V of Spain gave permission to Portugal to transport captured Africans to his territories in Spanish America.
Charles V's permission was the first *asiento*, a trading licence to
furnish the colonies in the Indies with enslaved Africans. The
asiento would become a valuable piece of paper, fought over
and prized by the major powers in Europe, because it ensured
a consistent source of income for slave-trading nations.

No one at the time was fooled as to the source of Portugal's wealth. João de Barros, a prominent historian, wrote in 1530 that "the African trade was the Crown's most dependable source of revenue."[6] He was right. In 1530, two-thirds of the Crown's wealth came from the African trade.

The Portuguese overseas trade grew by leaps and bounds. Wealth from Africa and India flowed into the country. However, it became evident that Portugal itself was too small to absorb all the goods that arrived there. Further, it did not have the requisite manpower to market the goods through-out Europe. Energetic merchants, traders, and bankers from every corner of Europe responded to the need and flooded into Portugal, the most fabled of the nations. Foreign merchants had more economic resources, more commercial links internationally, and better marketing and distributing techniques than the Portuguese. Italian, German, Dutch, English, French, Scandinavian, German, and Flemish businessmen not only invested in Portugal's overseas voyages but bought up a great share of the goods when they arrived and sold these products in the wider European and Mediterranean market. Through the efforts of these merchants, imported African slaves and Asian tea made their way from Lagos and Lisbon to as far north as Hamburg and Stockholm and as far east as Moscow. Much of the manufactured goods that the Portuguese traders or their agents sold on the African coast were not made in Portugal itself but in Holland and England, brought to the peninsula by merchants from these countries. This was an intrinsic weakness of the Portuguese economy, for which it would later pay—it was heavily dependent on foreign goods and foreign merchants and their capital to stimulate its economy.

The international traders, as long as they played by the rules the Crown outlined, became wealthy and influential as they helped Portugal in its dreams of exploration, conquest, colonization, and trade. Madeira, for instance, was primarily developed with Flemish and Italian capital. In the early fifteenth century, this island was the leading sugar producer in the Atlantic world, until Brazil took the lead. At least two-thirds of the sugar estates in Madeira were owned by Flemish, Genoese, and Portuguese Jews and New Christians (converted Jews). The New Christians were a largely mercantile community, and, because of their financial resources and overseas contacts, they came to play a dominant role in the expansion of Portugal's overseas empire. The Crown, perennially short of cash, often called on the New Christian community of investors for loans and investments.

Along with their activities in Madeira, New Christians were also involved in Asian and African trade and were instrumental in building up the sugar works in the Azores and São Tomé. So successful were these merchants that, beginning in the reign of João II, the country's mercantile wealth would rest largely in their hands. As time went by, there would be a strong identification of Portuguese maritime trade with Jewish and New Christian merchants. As for Portugal's maritime hegemony, it remained unchallenged until well into the seventeenth century, when the Netherlands, Spain, England, Sweden, Denmark, and Brandenburg, Germany, claimed a piece of the African pie.

Angélique's story, of course, is part of the story of Portuguese trade, and particularly its trade in human flesh. Portugal, along with other countries in Europe, had used White slaves since ancient times. Many of these European slaves who circulated around Europe and the Mediterranean came from Germany and the Hanseatic states and the Baltic and Slavic areas. The Vatican sought to discourage the slave trade by issuing papal bull after papal bull that stated it was illegal for Christians to enslave other Christians. But slave trading meant profits for those who bought and sold people, and the Vatican's pronouncements were ignored. It was only with the advent of the African Atlantic trade that the White slave trade declined and eventually died.

Portugal was the first European country to engage in the slave trade in Africa. One scholar estimates that, between 1441 and 1505, close to 151,000 African captives were brought to Portugal and its islands. Some enslaved Africans were absorbed by the domestic economy, but most were resold on the wider European and Mediterranean market.

So active and widespread was the slave trade, and slavery itself, that by 1550, there were close to 33,000 enslaved persons in Portugal, with about 10,000 living in Lisbon, accounting for fully one-tenth of the city's 100,000 inhabitants. The build-up of Portugal's Black population would continue well into the next century, and Portugal would continue its domination of the slave trade for the next century and a half.

This importation of forced West African migrants greatly added to Portugal's and Europe's Black population. During the fifteenth and sixteenth centuries, thousands of Wolof, Mandingo, Guinea, and Congo slaves entered Lisbon and Seville each year and were sold within the Iberian Peninsula. In the city of Évora, Portugal, the Black population exceeded the White.

In Portugal and Spain, slave labour—that of both Black and White slaves—was used primarily in domestic agriculture and household work. In the islands of Madeira, the Azores, the Canaries, and later Principe and São Tomé, enslaved Africans became the dominant agricultural labourers, tied to the sugar plantation system. The demand for slave labour by these economies would probably have remained consistent but moderate if the American conquests had not occurred.

Spain led the way with Columbus and the other conquistadors who came hot on his heels. The New World "discoveries" of the Caribbean islands and Central and South America brought untold wealth into the Spanish treasury, but it came with a price for the "discovered" peoples. Spain's colonization of the "Indies" was a brutal affair that resulted in large-scale genocide of millions of indigenous peoples, especially in the Caribbean and Central America. As the original inhabitants declined, they were replaced by enslaved Africans. France, England, and, to a lesser extent, the Netherlands followed Spain in the establishment of colonies based on the growing of plantation staples and the extraction of mineral wealth.

The plantation and mine owners developed an insatiable appetite for the labour of enslaved Africans, and so the trade on the African coast increased dramatically. Yet "trade" implies a commercial relation between equals. And despite the fact that some coastal African rulers were involved, it was not an equal relationship. The great masses of Africans who were turned into slaves on plantations in the Americas and elsewhere were victims—people kidnapped against their will and brought into slavery. On the African coast and its hinterland, as slaving increased and grew permanent, war became the principal method of procuring people for slavery. The colonization and exploitation of New World territories reoriented the slave routes. The mass of enslaved people would no longer go up the ocean to Europe but across it to the New World.

Portugal had taken the lead in the business of slavery. But other European nations soon joined her in this "odious commerce."[7] Between 1444, when the Atlantic slave trade began in earnest, and the 1860s, when it ended, at least 15 million Africans (and this is a conservative estimate) were forcibly removed from the continent and sold as slaves in the Atlantic world and elsewhere. Another 30 to 40 million died in slave wars, in coffles (human slave caravans), in stinking coastal factories where they were imprisoned, or aboard disease-infected slave ships as they endured a journey of untold agony across the Atlantic, stacked in the bottom of ships like "books on a shelf." By the time slavery was abolished, millions of slaves had died on slave plantations and in mines, farms, factories, and households in the New World—after being terrorized into submission and servitude.

But in the fifteenth and sixteenth centuries, the end of slavery was unthinkable. In the first two and a half centuries of the trade, Portugal dominated it. During this period, Portugal obtained most of its captives from three distinct areas of the West African coastline. The first was the Upper Guinea coast, an area that comprises modern Sierra Leone, Guinea, Guinea Bissau, Senegal, and the Gambia. The other sources were the Gold Coast and central and south-central Africa, today's Congo and Angola. The latter would become Portugal's main source of slaves after the seventeenth century.

For most of the fifteenth century and the first decades of the sixteenth, the majority of the African captives were taken to Lisbon, the capital of Portugal and the centre of its maritime trading activities. Many remained in the capital and were sold to residents there, but others were transported to different parts of the country, filling the demand for African captive labour. Along with Lisbon, the Algarve and Évora were the main centres of Black enslavement in Portugal.

Some Blacks did manage to escape from bondage, and a few bought themselves out or were manumitted by their masters. Most had to wait for freedom until the 1750s, when legislation abolished slavery in Portugal.

Anyone with the means to do so could be a slave owner. A.C. Saunders, one of the authorities on the enslavement of African people in Portugal, puts it this way: "Except for beggars, people of all classes, from labourers to kings, owned black slaves."[8] Even Muslim and Jewish Portuguese, people who faced various proscriptions, could own Black slaves.

The majority of enslaved persons worked as farm and field labourers, or in the household, especially in rural areas. It was common for Black slaves to work alongside White slaves. Men could work as house servants, though this was primarily the province of women. Both women and men worked as nurses, servants, and maids in hospitals. In fact, during periods of infection and plague, they were placed on the front lines.

Men especially worked as retainers in the entourages of the nobility, and both sexes worked in various capacities at Court. Queens and princesses had several slave women as ladies-in-waiting; these slaves apparently had a good life.

Enslaved men worked as shepherds and guarded vineyards and olive fields, monopolizing these occupations that free men found distasteful and monotonous. They also worked as carpenters, masons, goldsmiths, blacksmiths, silversmiths, and in a variety of crafts and as sailors and stevedores. They could work in the latter two occupations as salaried labourers. Their owners usually collected the salaries and gave them a small percentage. However, throughout the sixteenth century, the government sought to restrict slaves from being used in nautical professions because many of them took advantage of their access to the rivers and seas to effect their escape.

Slave women worked as water sellers, coal vendors, midwives, wet nurses, hairdressers, and laundresses. Needless to say, some were taken as concubines by White men. Black women, both enslaved and free, had a monopoly on certain occupations, especially in the urban areas. The distasteful work of removing garbage and excrement from the homes of Whites was one such job. Women also engaged in street vending. Called *regateiras*, these vendors sold stewed plums, cooked beans and pasta, cooked seafood, olive oil, fruits, and vegetables. Enslaved women had to receive their owners' permission to engage in vending, and had to turn over their earnings to them. But the good citizens often complained against these women. In Lisbon, the charge was that the street vendors were "unreasonable" and "insulted" ladies of rank.[9] This was not the first time that White citizens in the Atlantic world hurled such an accusation against Black women. It was not so much that Black women insulted White women of rank, but that they were not, or did not appear, docile and subservient enough to their "betters."

The government responded to the charges levelled against the street vendors. In 1515, King Manuel I passed a law that restricted their freedom of movement: now they could sell their wares only from the doorsteps of their homes. But there was protest from the Black community through the Black religious fraternal order Our Lady of the Rosary. The king modified the restriction by exempting free Black married women or widows. But Black slave women were soon on the streets, hawking their wares. The government turned a blind eye because these women carried out a valuable service to society. They did indispensable work that many free labourers thought was beneath them.

Enslaved and free Africans in Portugal developed an Afro-Portuguese culture that had an impact on mainstream society. There was the *fala de Guiné*, a Creole language that was a fusion of Portuguese, Bini, Kongo, and other African languages. Africans introduced dances that were enjoyed by all levels of society. There was the *mangana*, the *guiné*, the *ye ye*, and the *zarambeque*. The *mangana* is described as a slow, sad dance. Africans also excelled as singers and players of instruments. The music now known as *fado*, Portugal's national music, is said to have its origins in the sorrowful songs enslaved Africans used to sing in bondage in Portugal.

Africans also developed a distinct brand of Catholicism. From the earliest days of the slave trade to Portugal, the monarchs insisted that captives be baptized and taught the rudiments of Christianity if they had not received prior instruction. Manuel I went even further and ruled that captives should be baptized while waiting in coastal factories for embarkment, or while on the ship itself. If this did not happen, then the captives had to be baptized as soon as they landed on Portuguese soil. To make sure this was carried out, in 1513, Manuel erected a font in Lisbon "exclusively for the baptism of slaves."[10] Converting the "heathens" to Christianity was one justification of the slave trade, and this justification would become even more powerful as time went by and more and more Africans were kidnapped into bondage.

The Black Portuguese shaped Christianity according to their own needs. They established Afro-Catholic fraternities and mutual aid organizations. Free Black men ran these associations and used them to press for improvements in the lives of Portuguese Africans, both freed and enslaved. The fraternities buried their members, assisted with marriages and baptisms, and worked to uplift the community. They held dances, rallies, and religious marches and participated in carnivals. When many Black Portuguese made the journey across the Atlantic to become an unwilling part of Portugal's colonizing enterprise in Brazil, they took their brotherhoods and fraternities with them, and helped in the establishment of Catholicism in the New World.

The slave code developed by King Manuel in the early part of the sixteenth century regulated slave life in Portugal. Municipal legislation also contributed. There were many restrictions on the life and free time of the Black population. For example, workmen and slaves were prohibited from playing ball games during the working day—slaves risked a whipping and whites a double fine if they were caught playing with blacks.[11] Free Blacks and their enslaved brethren were categorized as one group under the law and endured the same restrictions and punishments. Enslaved Blacks were entitled to one day of rest per week—Sunday. Of course, many owners ignored this regulation, and the bonded labourers worked, without rest, for the entire seven days. However, New Christians had to be cautious about how hard they worked their slaves on a Sunday because they could be denounced as "fake" Christians for having their slaves break the Christian Sabbath.

Blacks of all categories endured the stigma of the Iberian obsession with "polluted blood," and therefore were restricted from holding government positions. However, some long-time Portuguese Moriscos (converted Muslims) and Jews, people who were also defined as having polluted blood but who had enough resources to manipulate the system, could and did manage to hold government jobs.

Portuguese slavery shared some of the features of New World enslavement. Family members were often sold apart from each other and taken to distant places. Girls and women were vulnerable to sexual attacks from their male owners or other White men and bore undesired children as a result of these forced liaisons. Evidence shows that owners also used enslaved women as breeders. The children born were usually sold in the internal slave trade. As in New World slavery, children of slave women became slaves at birth. Enslaved people endured a host of punishments, ranging from branding and whipping to confinement in jails and prisons to hanging and burning at the stakes of the Inquisition, for offences real and imagined.

However, enslaved people resisted the indignities, humiliations, and degradations that were their daily lot. They fought back in diverse ways and tried to escape from slavery when the opportunity presented itself. On their night watch, male bondsmen burned the olive groves and vineyards they guarded and let loose sheep and cattle to trample the planted fields. So frequent were such fires and animal rampages that the government sought to prevent enslaved men from working in these occupations. There is no doubt that enslaved women spoke back to and "insulted" their White owners, as seen with the charges against the street vendors. Verbal assault was one method enslaved women used to defend themselves and retain a measure of self-worth. Both women and men broke tools and other equipment, "malingered" on the job, and "feigned" illnesses.

Enslaved people also resisted through the various fraternal organizations founded by Portuguese Africans. When King Manuel restricted the movement of the street vendors, it was a fraternal organization that petitioned him to reconsider. He did. Members of fraternities also gave shelter to runaway slaves and assisted them in their escape. It was not long before the fraternities came under government suspicion and legislation was enacted to restrict their activities.

Despite their resistance, the African population still lived lives of "social death."[12] They were socially marginalized, had no identity except that of their owners, and were the most subordinated group in society. They were baptized and corralled into Christianity, had their names changed, were forced to learn a new language and new customs, and had their freedom taken from them. Despite all the contributions they made to society with their skills and labour, they could not hope to advance (notwithstanding the existence of a few Black priests, poets, and painters).

But the Black Portuguese did their best to construct as viable a family life as they could. They often formed marital bonds, though these unions were not recognized by the state. Free Blacks and the enslaved married each other. However, if the woman was a slave, any children born to the couple inherited the status of the mother. Angélique could very well have been born to a slave mother and so entered life as a slave herself.

Blacks remained on the margins of society, despised because of their colour, status, and origin. Free Black people, despite their status, experienced life in much the same way as their slave brethren. They did similar work and often received the same punishments. Free Blacks were usually descended from slaves, and many of them had enslaved relatives. Their colour and origin ensured that their lives would be circumscribed in a colour- and rank-conscious society. To be Black meant that one was at the bottom rung of the ladder.

The Portuguese identity that became manifest during the period of exploration and slavery was firmly based on a tripartite concept of "Whiteness," Catholicism, and descent from Lusitanian stock. The Portuguese were obsessed with the "purity" or "impurity" of the blood of the people within the country (perhaps because so many of them were of mixed blood), and Africans were clearly in the "impure" category. Even biracial Blacks could not claim "Whiteness," nor could they claim Lusitanian descent. And even though many, if not most, of the Africans were Catholic, they were still viewed as "infidels," especially if they originally came from Muslim regions of Africa. The crusading mentality was rife in Portugal, and it was particularly strong among people of rank. The Inquisition became the "arm of punishment of the Church," founded to stamp out all heresies and destroy the unbelievers. Many Blacks, though purporting to be Christians, were nonetheless handcuffed by the Inquisition. The Portuguese Inquisition was said to be worse than the Spanish version.

By 1705, the year Angélique was born, the War of Spanish Succession had begun in earnest. Most of the countries in Europe, including Portugal, engaged in various "grand alliances" to unseat the French duke who had inherited the Spanish throne. This war engulfed Europe for ten years, with the main players—France, Spain, the Dutch Republic, Flanders, Austria, and England (Portugal had made a wise retreat)—shedding the blood of thousands and redrawing the borders of Europe.

While Europe was convulsed with war, Portugal enjoyed a Golden Age. In the early sixteenth century, King Manuel had ushered in Portugal's first Golden Age; now João V welcomed an outpouring of art and culture and an architectural revolution. João V built grand palaces, villas, monasteries, libraries, and gardens. New tastes and ideas—especially French—were introduced at Court and in the country at large as members of the elite returned from their European tours.

The Portuguese Golden Age was literally paid for by Brazilian gold. In the 1690s, gold had been discovered in central Brazil at Minas Gerais (General Mines). African slaves and their owners poured into Minas to mine the gold. By the year of Angélique's birth, the labourers had mined at least 600,000 ounces of gold, which flowed back to Portugal. Brazilian gold did for Portugal in the eighteenth century what African gold had done for it in the sixteenth century. The Brazilian gold that flowed into Lisbon, along with other sources of wealth from the scattered regions of the empire, made the Portuguese royal family the wealthiest in Europe.

The underside of the Golden Age was the expansion of the European slave trade in Africa. The opening of the mines in Brazil led to a huge demand for slave labour. At first, bondsmen were drawn from the plantations of the coastal areas, but that could not continue for long. A "way of death"[13] opened up in Angola and west-central Africa as hundreds of thousands of Africans stepped over the bodies of their fellow victims who had fallen in front of them. These captured Africans were corralled onto slave ships, destined for death-dealing work on sugar plantations and in gold mines. Brazilian gold extraction, like its sugar production, was based on African slavery.

By 1750, Portugal's treasury would be empty, most of the gold having sailed out of the country in English ships. During Angélique's youth, Portugal—even though it had an expansive empire that included Brazil, Angola, countries on the West African coast, and parts of East Africa, India, and China—had become a commercial satellite of England. It imported much of its manufacturing goods from England (and the Dutch Republic and Flanders), as well as meats, cheese, butter, and wheat. Portugal had not developed a strong, indigenous, mercantile, capitalistic class. The wealth that poured in from imperial possessions went to the elite, who were interested not in investing in trade but in consuming luxury goods. Portugal soon developed a payment problem, importing more than it exported and paying for much of its imports with Brazilian and African gold. Because Portugal was an underdeveloped capitalist state, the wealth simply flowed in and flowed out again: as David Birmingham puts it, "the ultimate beneficiary [of Brazil's gold] was neither Brazil nor Portugal but Britain."[14] The English packets, which sailed from Lisbon to the Cornish port of Falmouth with the mail, were responsible for transferring millions of pounds of Brazilian gold out of Brazil into the coffers of the English. Because of its commercial dependency on England, Portugal failed to develop as an industrial nation at a time when many countries in Western Europe were on that path. (Incidentally, the same phenomenon was happening in Spain. The gold and silver that it looted from its American possessions ended up in the hands of foreign merchants and the treasure chests of princes.)

Though Black and poor people, Angélique's friends and relatives, created the Golden Age with their labour, they did not benefit from it. But even ordinary White citizens did not fare well in Portugal's Golden Age. Notwithstanding all the "high culture" and splendid buildings, most of the poor remained poor, or even became poorer. Very little of the nation's wealth trickled down to them. They laboured on their small plots, or fished from the sea, and some who were farmers were locked into an almost feudal relation with the landowners. João V and the kings after him made little or no provision for public education. As elsewhere in Europe, literacy was still confined to the upper classes. Given the general poverty of the masses, the Crown sponsored immigration to Brazil, the Atlantic islands, and elsewhere to get the potentially hostile and rebellious poor out of the country. During the eighteenth century, thousands of Portuguese, facing a hopeless future in Portugal, migrated to Brazil, where they enjoyed great privileges based on their race and origin.

In 1705, when Angélique was born, and during her youth, Black slavery was still a fact of life, and no one thought that it would end or questioned it as the "natural condition" of Africans. Sometime before 1725, Angélique appeared in the New World, and here too, African people lived as enslaved persons. It fact, it was the enslavement of Africans that made this new world possible.

Portugal formed the first chapter in the story of Angélique's life. Flanders, or another Dutch-speaking country, made up a subsequent chapter. What was the link between Portugal and a Dutch-speaking place in the early life of Marie-Joseph Angélique?

Angélique identified Nichus Block as a Fleming—a man from Flanders. A Fleming owning a Portuguese slave is not unusual when we consider the commercial links between historic Flanders and Portugal. Historian Oliveira Marques tells us that in the early sixteenth century the city of Antwerp, in Flanders, was "the final and decisive entrepôt of the Portuguese trade."[15] The main commercial route from Lisbon to northern Europe led to Flanders' two most important cities, Bruges and Antwerp. The latter city was the commercial hub of northwestern Europe and was an intellectual and cultural centre. Flanders played a key role in Portugal's economic life, especially its overseas trade. Flemish merchants distributed Portuguese colonial products to the rest of Europe. Though other towns such as Seville, Augsburg, and Nuremburg were also important depots, Bruges and especially Antwerp were the main centres for Portuguese trade in northern Europe until they were displaced by Amsterdam. Flemish capital, know-how, goods, and other resources were crucial to Portugal's economy. Flemish merchants subcontracted a large part of the African Atlantic slave and gold trades. These merchants or their agents, domiciled in Portugal, re-exported trade goods to other points in Europe, the American colonies, and elsewhere.

What sealed the strong business relationship between Portugal and Flanders was the Portuguese Jewish and New Christian merchant community. Most of the merchants of the "Portuguese nation" in Flanders were of Jewish extraction. Many Jewish families had fled Portugal during the forced conversions commanded by King Manuel in the late fifteenth and early sixteenth centuries. These families still maintained contact with their New Christian relatives in

Portugal, who looked after their trading interests. The Portuguese Flemings, along with their Iberian cousins, developed an intricate business network that stretched from Portugal to the Low Countries, France, Germany, and Spain, and to parts of Africa and the Americas.[16]

At the time of Angélique's birth, Flanders corresponded roughly to what it is today—an area of northern Belgium with linguistic, political, and cultural connections to southern Holland and northwestern France. The region has had a turbulent history. In the early sixteenth century, Flanders was part of the Netherlands; an area of northern France was also part of Flanders. The Netherlands was then divided into seventeen provinces. In the southern part Antwerp emerged as the commercial hub of northwestern Europe, while in the northern portion Amsterdam became hegemonic. Most of the Netherlanders spoke Dutch, but French was also widely spoken.

In 1556, Philip II of Spain inherited the Netherlands from his father, Charles V. By this time, Protestantism was spreading in France, the Netherlands, and elsewhere in Europe. Philip, a fanatical Catholic who saw himself as "God's anointed" and "defender of the true faith," felt it was his divine duty to stamp out the heresy—Protestantism—that was taking root in his empire. He not only cruelly taxed the Netherlands to finance his eternal wars, but he also took steps to suppress their Protestant outpourings. In 1566, the Dutch rebelled against their Spanish overlord in a war of independence that came to be called "The Dutch Revolt." Philip sent the Duke of Alva with his formidable armies to discipline the Dutch. Alva's armies crushed the uprising in the southern Netherlands and, in 1576, sacked and destroyed

Antwerp. The revolt continued in the northern provinces. Tens of thousands of people in the southern provinces, fleeing Spanish rule and subjugation, migrated to Amsterdam and other northern cities, and to France, England, and Germany. It is said that over thirty-three percent of the people living in Amsterdam at this time were Flemish refugees. The figure was even higher for Leiden: sixty-six percent. These refugees, many of whom were from prominent Protestant and Jewish families, brought important skills, expertise, and capital to the northern provinces. The first translation of the Bible into Dutch was done by Flemish migrants into the northern provinces; likewise, it was Flemings who composed the Dutch national anthem. These Flemings played an important role in Dutch intellectual, cultural, and commercial life, and contributed to the rise of the Dutch Republic as a world power.

In 1585, Antwerp was once again occupied by Spanish troops, now under the command of the Duke of Parma. Yet, while Spain dominated the southern region, it could not conquer the north. The Flemings submitted to the Spaniards, and Catholicism remained the official religion. It was during this period that a border between north and south was drawn. The northern provinces signed a truce with Spain in 1609 and emerged as the independent Dutch Republic (what we today call Holland), while the southern provinces became known as the Spanish Netherlands, the South Netherlands, or Flanders.

As the Flemings became part of the Spanish empire, their Dutch cousins to the north took steps to block the economic revival of Flanders. When they signed their truce with Spain, the Dutch won several advantageous concessions that enabled them to exercise economic dominance over

Flanders. For one, the Dutch were able to export much of their goods to Flanders with very low tariffs. Fearing competition from Antwerp, they also blocked the opening of the River Scheldt, thus effectively closing off all maritime traffic to the city. As a result, Antwerp declined. (Of course, the sacking of this once great entrepôt by the Spaniards also contributed to its decline.) The Dutch even maintained a string of forts in Flanders. It became clear that though the southern Netherlands was ruled from Madrid, it was the Dutch, through the economic grip they had over the region, who exercised real hegemony. Flanders, which for centuries had had economic and political independence, now had to content itself with being someone else's colony.

France also had designs on the Spanish Netherlands. Spain had been weakened by its numerous continental wars, and France, seeing Spain's weakness, began to nibble away at its empire. In 1668, Louis XIV invaded Flanders, annexed a large part of it, and redrew its borders. Though Louis was forced by the Dutch Republic to withdraw from Flanders and give up some of the land he had grabbed, he still managed to slice off the ancient Flemish city of Lille and its hinterland and make them part of France.

The rest of Flanders remained part of the Spanish empire until the end of the War of Spanish Succession in 1713. During this conflict, France and Spain fought the "grand alliance" of England, Austria, and the Dutch Republic. Many of the decisive engagements were fought in Flanders and led to much suffering for the Flemings as they were further deprived of their autonomy. In 1706, for example, Anglo-Dutch forces overran Flanders and jointly ruled the Flemish provinces from Brussels. The war ended in a stalemate that maintained the balance of power in Europe, but once again, Flanders was tossed around like a chess piece. The princes who signed the Treaty of Utrecht, which ended the war, gave Flanders to Austria, as part of Austria's land grab. However, the opportunistic Dutch worked out another treaty with Austria (the Austro-Dutch Treaty of Antwerp) "which restored Dutch economic hegemony over southern Netherlands."[17] Though Flanders would remain part of the Austrian empire until 1793, the Dutch were the true rulers. Today, most of the historic Flemish provinces comprise the country of Belgium, a country with a French-speaking region (Wallonia) and a predominantly Dutch-speaking region called Flanders. The Flemings speak a variant of Dutch called Flemish.

The long history of foreign occupation led many of the inhabitants of Flanders, especially the merchants, to move all over Europe. Wherever they went, they took their skills with them. They worked for whatever country or empire was willing to use their expertise. Their loyalty was to the international republic of commerce, not to any particular nation or state. A large number of the most energetic and enterprising merchants migrated to the Dutch Republic and invested their time, money, and energy in the Dutch overseas enterprise.

Under Dutch economic dominance, those merchants who stayed in Flanders accepted the status quo and worked for them. When they were subjects of a foreign power, they used that to their advantage. For example, during the long conflict with Spain, the Dutch found they could trade with Spain only through Flemish agents, who, as subjects of the Spanish king, could trade without restrictions. Their status as Spanish subjects helped the Flemings in their trade pursuits both in Europe and in the New World. In 1580, the crowns of Spain and Portugal united, and Flemish businessmen took advantage of the opportunity this offered.

Nichus Block likely acquired Angélique when she was a young teenager or a child. In the early eighteenth century, the Dutch Republic was the infinitely stronger section of the Netherlands, not only because it had Flanders under its suzerainty, but also because it had become a world maritime power, with plantation and merchant colonies in the New World, and had taken control of a considerable portion of the Atlantic slave trade. Given the historic, linguistic, cultural, commercial, and genealogical bond between the Dutch and the Flemings, if Nichus Block was a man from Flanders and was active in Atlantic commerce, it is very likely that he was working for the Dutch.

The Dutch had become an aggressive and astute nation of businessmen by the middle of the seventeenth century. They had a large navy and men with capital to invest, and in Europe they were the major force in the Baltic trade. Though they had grown important in the Atlantic trade, primarily as middlemen who marketed in northern Europe the tropical produce from Spanish and Portuguese America, Dutch merchants or their agents could be found in every major Iberian city that engaged in trade. And though there was no love lost between them and the Catholic Iberians, each group needed the other. As the century wore on, the Dutch would become even more dominant in Iberian trade, notably in Spanish American silver, Brazilian sugar, and Asian spices. The rise of the Dutch in the Atlantic trade was built on their casting off of Spanish rule, the enormous financial resources they possessed, a growing nationalism, their emergence as "visionary" capitalists, and a sense of their "destiny."

The Dutch became a world and maritime power during the period known as the "second Atlantic system," roughly between 1630 and 1700. One of the defining features of this new era was the Iberian powers' loss of the monopoly they enjoyed in Atlantic commerce. Everyone—the Brandenburg (German) states, England, Scandinavia, France, the Netherlands, even Russia—challenged the Iberians by introducing competition in the slave trade. The English, French, and Dutch had what was, for them, a good reason to want slave labourers: they had colonies in the northern Caribbean and on the North American mainland that they wished to furnish with slave labour. As a result, these nations built slave trading posts along the West African coastline and began engaging in the removal of Africans from their homeland.

However, it was the Dutch who enjoyed the initial success in breaking the Iberian monopoly. Their first attempt at supremacy in the Atlantic was the capture of the Portuguese colony of Pernambuco, Brazil, in 1630. By this time, Brazil had become the leading sugar producer in the world. Its sugar industry was worked by enslaved Africans provided by Portuguese traders. The Netherlands had a stake in the Brazil sugar trade, as some of its merchants were responsible for shipping the sugar to Lisbon and then re-exporting it. The Dutch seizure of Pernambuco launched the beginning of their spectacular Atlantic career.

Not content with capturing the sugar colony and hence the sugar trade, or perhaps flushed by their success, the Dutch dreamed also of controlling the slave trade. After Pernambuco, Dutch expeditions sailed across the Atlantic to the African coast and attacked Portuguese trading posts and possessions at Elmina, Luanda, and Benguela. They were successful. In capturing the African stations, the Dutch ensured that Pernambuco would have a ready supply of enslaved labourers.[18] With the seizure of the slave trade from Portugal, the Dutch had become the world's leading slave dealers. By 1660, when Dutch expeditions captured English trading posts on the African coast, they had taken firm control of the slave trade.

Spain had long waged war in the Netherlands against the Dutch. At the time of the capture of Pernambuco, hostilities continued between the Dutch and the Spanish (the Westphalian Peace Treaty, in which Spain recognized the Dutch Republic's independence, was not signed until 1648). When the Dutch Republic attacked Pernambuco in 1630, the Portuguese were under Spanish rule, even though the Spaniards allowed them to administer their colonial ventures as they saw fit. Nonetheless, by capturing Portuguese sites, the Dutch hoped to strike back and weaken Spanish power, and get rich in the process.

What becomes clear from these European rivalries is the value of African commerce to the economies of Europe. Africa was being hemorrhaged to feed the plantation needs of overseas European colonies.

In 1640, Portugal regained its independence from Spain. Fuelled by this new development, the Brazilians, who had been smarting under Dutch rule, revolted five years later. By 1649, Dutch power had weakened in Brazil, and in that same year Portugal recaptured the African slaving posts. In 1654, the Portuguese finally ejected the Dutch from Brazil. After that, the Dutch had to be content with supplying slaves to the Caribbean and Spanish America and being the innovators in sugar technology. They revolutionized the sugar industry by introducing new sugar technology into Brazil and, in addition, financing the development of the sugar industry in the French and English Caribbean.

The retaking of Brazil by the Portuguese had other repercussions. Prior to the Dutch takeover, many of the plantation owners and settlers in Brazil (some sources say up to one-third) were New Christians and Jews. As Portuguese traders, they also participated in buying captives from the African coast and selling them in Brazil and elsewhere in the New World. Between 1637 and 1644 in Dutch Brazil, Jewish merchants accounted for upwards of sixty percent of purchases of captured Africans landed in Brazil. Jews took the opportunity to travel to Brazil because many of the Protestant Dutch were not enthusiastic about settling in the New World. The Dutch therefore welcomed Jews as colonizers and merchants.[19] Under the Dutch rule in Brazil, Jews enjoyed religious freedom and other advantages. Many New Christians reverted to Judaism and openly practised their faith.

When Portugal regained power, however, the Crown saw the Jewish and New Christian communities as traitorous and imposed many disadvantages upon them. Though some families reconciled themselves to the new order, others, the majority, left with the Dutch when they returned to Europe or went to the colonies of Curaçao, Surinam, and New Netherland (today's New York), where they continued in the various branches of the Atlantic trade, especially the inter-Caribbean slave trade. By the mid-eighteenth century, these colonies would have the largest Jewish communities outside Europe, and in Curaçao and Surinam the communities spoke Portuguese.[20]

However, when Portugal retook Brazil, its economy was

almost ruined by the war with the Netherlands. Its navy was a shadow of its former self, and the Crown was short on capital investments. Portugal needed all the help it could get. To rebuild its fortune, the Crown began hiring and licensing English ships to engage in the Brazil trade. Ironically, it also turned to the Dutch. A Luso-Brazilian Jesuit priest, Father Vieira, travelled to Amsterdam on behalf of the Portuguese government to negotiate with the Dutch government. Father Vieira also took the opportunity to meet with the Jewish community in Amsterdam. He promised to lift some of the prohibitions they suffered in Brazil under the new regime in return for their investment in the Brazilian sugar industry. Father Vieira's meeting with the Jews of Amsterdam points to the significant role that community played in Brazil, during the Dutch occupation and after.[21]

The Dutch enjoyed sweet revenge on the Portuguese when, in 1670, through the West India Company, Spain awarded them the asiento. Slave trading now became their main business. The Dutch Jews (many with roots in Portugal and Brazil) became holders or subcontractors of the asiento and provided the bulk of the slaves to Brazil and the Dutch colonies. The Dutch government would give Jews the opportunity to play "their most tangible role" in the slave trade.[22] At one point, Jewish traders, under the auspices of the Dutch government, were taking the majority of slaves to Portuguese-speaking America. They were also supplying French, Dutch, and English colonies.

Surinam illustrates this nexus of Dutch-Portuguese-Jewish connections. By 1740, Surinamese enslaved Africans owned by Portuguese-speaking Jewish planters had built their own synagogue. These Africans had converted to the religion of their masters. One of the many languages currently spoken in

Surinam, Saramaccan, is a Portuguese-African Creole developed among the slaves owned by Portuguese Jews.

Curaçao became important to the launching of the plantation system in the Caribbean. The Jews in Curaçao were said to be "the second most important element" after the Protestants. Yet their influence in the trade was disproportionate to their numbers. From this island, Jewish traders extended their activities to the French and English islands and the Spanish Main (the northeastern coast of south America and adjoining parts of the Caribbean) by helping to sponsor plantation development. Between 1630 and 1760, Jewish merchants helped land a great many of the 85,000 slaves (about one-sixth of the Dutch slave trade) who arrived in Curaçao. The Caribbean also played an important role in the launching of a North American Jewry: many of the families from the Dutch Caribbean colonies relocated to New Netherland and the colonies of Pennsylvania, New Jersey, and Delaware.[23]

I am by no means saying that the Jews and New Christians were the only traders in slaves. In fact, as time went by, they would participate less and less, especially as the English became the dominant power in the Atlantic slave trade. Throughout the four centuries of Atlantic slave trading, Protestants and Catholics held the upper hand. Slave trading and other Atlantic commercial ventures were sponsored by agents of the state such as the Dutch West India Company, Crown corporations, and government corporations, all of which were officially Christian. But Jews, because of their mercantile skills, capital, and trading diasporas, were allowed by some Crowns to hold certain key positions in overseas trade. Jews engaged in the Atlantic trade not as Jews but as traders.

However, ethnic identifications are sometimes hidden under national terms. When we speak of the "Portuguese" or "Dutch," we usually think in terms of a monolithic identification: White and Christian. This is often misleading, and many of the peculiarities of history get lost in such assumptions.

Some commentators have noted that, though the Dutch failed to become a major colonizing force in the New World (they had been ousted from Brazil and had only a few outposts such as Curaçao, Surinam, and New Netherland), they nonetheless "developed as an awesome maritime and mercantile power."[24] In this second Atlantic system, they ruled the seas and were the greatest traders and capitalists. Their merchant navy (which could be converted into warships), the manufactured goods they produced, their possession of capital, their connections in the global trading diasporas, and their ability to move goods and produce around the Atlantic world and beyond were what made them masters of the Atlantic after 1640. Speaking of the Dutch share in the commerce of the 1680s, one commentator, Ernst Van den Boogaart, estimated that

> the different European traders exchanged goods worth 9.4 million guilders, or £825,000, to acquire African products which were sold in Europe for 19.7 guilders, or £1.7 million. The Dutch accounted for something over a half of the slave trade and Africa commodity trade. In addition, their slave ships will often have been able to pick up a sugar cargo in the West Indies. Thus the Dutch had lost a potentially rich colony [Brazil], and their Atlantic trade was only a little larger than it had been in the 1620s—but it was very probably twice as profitable.[25]

The Dutch would dominate Atlantic commerce until they were supplanted by the English during the first decade of the eighteenth century. The English emerged as a world power after the War of Spanish Succession, when their great armies stopped France and Spain on land and sea. Their Caribbean plantations had taken off, and they were set to become the world largest sugar producers. Likewise, they would outdo the Dutch as the world's greatest slave traders.

Attempts to find Angélique in the Atlantic, in the sea lanes between the Portuguese-speaking world and the Dutch-speaking world, whether in Europe or the New World (or even in Africa), take us in a few directions, one of which is a Sephardic Jewish, or New Christian, route. One could say that this is mere speculation. But I would argue that it is speculation grounded in the specificities of Atlantic history and commerce.

James C. Boyajian, a scholar on the Jews in the Atlantic world, in his discussion of New Christians and Jews in the sugar trade, sheds light upon the tight connections between the worlds of Portuguese-speaking and Dutch-speaking Jews and their role in the sugar trade between European and Brazilian ports. Boyajian notes that sugar founded the fortunes of many Sephardic families in the Netherlands, France, and the Baltic States. He also observes that many of the Portuguese-descended families of Amsterdam still traded with Portugal, using their relatives there as agents. The following example of one such family underscores how easily slaves, servants, and other subordinated persons could pass from one region to another:

Manuel Dias Henriques was among the Sephardi merchants arriving in Amsterdam during the early seventeenth century. Both Manuel and his cousin Miguel Dias de Santiago, who had settled in Antwerp just prior to 1620, had had personal experience in the sugar trade of Brazil between 1595 and 1619. Miguel in Antwerp and Manuel in Amsterdam were able to deal directly with many kinsmen still in Brazil and arrange for shipments of sugar from Brazilian ports directly to Amsterdam. Manuel Dias Henriques was far from alone. Francisco Mendes de Medeiros (alias Isaac Franco Mendes) and Jeronimo Rodrigues de Souza (alias Samuel Abrabanel) were also among the many Sephardi merchants of Amsterdam dealing in sugar in the early seventeenth century with relatives in Brazilian and Portuguese ports.[26]

Here Flanders, the Netherlands, Portugal, and the New World are linked in one Jewish/New Christian family solely through sugar. Though one could argue that much the same was true for Protestant and Catholic merchant families, the Atlantic Jewish/New Christian trading diasporas and the entrenched positions these merchants had in Atlantic trade are too obvious to ignore. Plantation owners or merchants who dealt in sugar and other trade goods, in ports on either side of the Atlantic, had the international contacts that allowed them to move slaves as easily as commodities.

No doubt Nichus Block, like Manuel Dias Henriques, had international connections. That was how he obtained and disposed of Angélique. According to Angélique, she lived in New England before moving on to Montréal. Again, we do not know when she was removed from Europe to New England.

We do know that while she was a bondswoman in New England her Flemish master arranged to have her sold to Sieur Francheville. The year was 1725, and she was twenty years old.

Since her Flemish owner lived in America, he could very well have been a Dutchman or Dutch American. The terms "Flemish" and "Dutch" were used interchangeably in New Netherland, New France, New England, and elsewhere. Both terms really described those who spoke the Dutch language and hailed from the Low Countries (even if they were French-speaking Walloons). In colonial North America, even Germans were sometimes classified as Dutch or Flemish. When the Dutch colonized the Hudson Valley, settlers imported slaves not only from Africa but also from the Dutch West Indies, Holland, and Portugal. Government officials, soldiers, and traders coming out to the New World to take up a new position often had African slaves or servants in their entourage. Trading voyages from Europe usually included Black human cargo. Black Europeans who spoke Dutch, French, and other languages were common enough in the European settlements of the New World.

The slaves who came from the Low Countries to the Americas were either Dutch-speaking or French-speaking if they were from Wallonia (French Flanders). In some cases, they and their owners spoke both Dutch and French. Interestingly, in the early years of New Netherland, more than half of the Dutch settlers were French-speaking Walloons. In fact, in the 1620s and 1630s, there were more French speakers in New Netherland than in New France.

Even with the transformation of New Netherland into New York with the English conquest of 1664, Dutch merchants were still allowed by custom to participate in trade with Africa, and in trade to Europe, although their involvement was now prohibited by law. (New York, as an English colony, had to have all of its overseas trade in the hands of the conquering English). Some Dutch settlers, however, left New York for New England because the English colonial government there treated them better than the one in New York. The cities of Boston, Newport, and Providence thus became important centres of Dutch American life and commerce. Well into the eighteenth century, Dutch American merchants, whether through bribery or connections, managed to clear ships for the overseas trade. The Dutch, having lost their New York colony and hence economic dominance, still exerted strong cultural and linguistic influences in the Hudson Valley region and other areas of central New York. They and their enslaved Africans continued to speak Dutch for more than a hundred years after the English conquest of New York.

At the time that the Dutch still reigned supreme in New Netherland, not a few French Canadians settled among them. Both groups were heavily involved in the fur trade, which led to intense commercial, military, and political activity between New France and New Netherland. New England was drawn into this rivalry, and when New Netherland became New York the French continued their competition with the new settlers. Thus, there was from the very start a trade and social network established between the European colonists in New France, New Netherland/New York, and New England.

Angélique was "sent up" from New England to Sieur Francheville. However, we have to be wary of the term "New England" in mid-eighteenth century Canadian colonial parlance. French officials often referred in a generic way to any of the northern English colonies as New England. Therefore, the name could easily have referred to the area defined geographically today as New York, or even Pennsylvania. As an example, in 1730, the Marquis de Beauharnois, governor general of New France, in a letter to his superior in France, the Comte de Maurepas, minister of marine, described a Dutch-speaking Albany merchant, John Henry (Johann Hendricks) Lidius as "a native of Orange in New England."[27] In 1725, Lidius arrived in Montréal, settled there, took on French citizenship, married a French woman, and in 1730 converted to Roman Catholicism. However, his conversion was false and he turned out to be a notorious fur smuggler. Lidius was subsequently expelled from New France to the Dutch Republic. There are two critical links between Angélique and Lidius. Both arrived in Montréal in the same year, and both were baptized in 1730 by the same priest. It could be that it was Lidius himself, a Dutch New Yorker, who brought Angélique to Montréal. The Dutch connection is intriguing. But the point is that Governor Beauharnois named Orange (Albany) as being in "New England" and not New York. Therefore, when the French authorities stated that Angélique lived in New England before she arrived in Montréal, they could very well have meant that she came from the colony of New York, the Hudson Valley in particular. The fact that her previous owner was a Fleming (a Dutch-speaking man) makes this all the more likely.

There could also have been a Huguenot link to Angélique's wanderings. As a mercantile diaspora, Huguenots were strategically placed to move captive Africans around the Atlantic world. For much of the seventeenth century, the capital of Huguenot businessmen played a crucial role in financing

France's overseas adventures, including the establishment of the colony of Canada. These Protestant bankers and traders also invested heavily in France's internal business. In addition, their money travelled far and wide in Europe. When the Edict of Nantes (which had protected the religious rights of Protestants in France) was revoked in 1685 by Louis XIV, and the persecution of the Huguenots began, many of them fled to more welcoming places in Europe, particularly the Protestant countries of Holland and England. Branches of Huguenot families also moved to the New World, the thirteen American colonies in particular. Like the New Christian merchants, the Huguenot traders developed links with the American colonies, New France, and the Low Countries and bankrolled slave trading voyages.

The connections of the Faneuil family of Boston is but one example of the international outlook of the Huguenot traders. A family patriarch, Benjamin Faneuil fled La Rochelle, France, after 1685 and settled in New York, where he established himself in business. His brother André settled in Boston and during the 1720s traded with Québec merchants while consolidating his links with the Dutch and English in the New York colony. The Faneuil family also invested in the Atlantic slave trade. Even Peter Faneuil, who became a humanitarian and "champion of liberty" (he provided the money for Boston's Faneuil Hall), invested in slaving voyages to Sierra Leone.

The business transactions of the Faneuil family in the Atlantic and American world show how easily an enslaved person like Angélique could move from one port to another. Peter Faneuil conducted an active trade between New England and New France during the French regime. He "sent slaves to Cape Breton [Nova Scotia] in exchange for French goods, instructed ship captain Peter Buckely, in 1738, to buy him a slave in Antigua that was 'a straight Negro lad, 12 or 15 years old, having had the smallpox if possible.'"[28] On several occasions, Peter Faneuil sent enslaved Africans from New England and the West Indies to Nova Scotia.

Faneuil was not the only New England merchant to engage in trade with Acadia and Canada, the West Indies, and Europe. This triangular trade was lucrative, and many merchants of the thirteen colonies participated in it, passing goods and people along its various points.[29] Francheville himself had a direct link with the La Rochelle port, which was formerly a Huguenot stronghold. His agent at La Rochelle, Jean Vaissiere, might very well have been a Huguenot.[30] But even if he was not, the link with Vaissiere tells us that Francheville was connected to a great international mercantile body, and therefore acquiring an enslaved Portuguese woman was not as difficult as it first seems.

I believe we can also understand Angélique's North American wanderings by looking at the colonial fur trade between the French, Dutch, and English. Within this matrix could lie the key of Angélique's early North American life.

In colonial North America, especially in the Great Lakes region, the French, English, and Dutch competed with each other for land and other resources, but they also traded with each other. The item that gave meaning to their trading nexus was fur. The Montréal merchants had the best furs because they controlled a vast fur-bearing hinterland west of Montréal known as *les pays en haut* or the Upper Country. This region extended as far west as present-day Wisconsin, and as far north as Lake Superior. Though, in theory, all furs were to be shipped to France via the port of Québec, Montréal merchants developed a lucrative trade with Dutch-speaking merchants of Albany and the Hudson Valley. The Dutch merchants did obtain furs in the area west of the Alleghenies, but these furs were inferior to those obtained from the Canadians. The main trading route between Montréal and New York was the Lake Champlain/Richelieu Valley corridor. On this route, the Canadian merchants or their agents brought furs to the Albany merchants in exchange for English manufactures and luxury goods, which were better made and cheaper than the French variants. The French kept most of the luxury items for themselves, but they used rum and manufactures in their exchange with the First Nations of the Upper Country, from whom they obtained the furs.

The Montréal-Albany trade was so lucrative that even when the respective governments in New York and Canada outlawed it for whatever reason (usually because of war or other hostilities), the French and Dutch merchants simply used Native people—the Iroquois, or Five Nations, in particular—as their agents and go-betweens. The Iroquois were not bound by the White man's laws, and their ancestral homeland bordered on and included the vast territories that the Whites claimed as their own. The Iroquois possessed a thorough knowledge of their ancestral lands, and often traversed secret routes to Albany in addition to the more public ones like the Lake Champlain/Richelieu Valley corridor. As "Natives of the land," the Iroquois could journey across the New York wilds without fear or restrictions. Furthermore, many Iroquois had removed themselves to one of the several Christian missions close to Montréal. This made them well situated, as Christians and Iroquois, to play an important role in the fur trade, most times legal, sometimes illegal, with Albany.[31]

Manufactures and luxury items were not the only goods that made the return trip to Montréal. Slaves also trekked through the Hudson Valley up to Montréal and other parts of the St. Lawrence Valley. The New York merchants had better access to enslaved labour and they sometimes provided slaves to the French.[32]

Slaves also changed hands through the violence of war. Take the Schenectady Massacre, for example. In 1690, French Canadians attacked the New York village, pillaged, killed, and then took slaves, both Blacks and Natives, back to Canada. Given that most of the settlements in the Hudson Valley, including Schenectady, were still populated mainly by people of Dutch descent, many of the captured slaves were also "Dutch." Even in the early decades of the eighteenth century, the Canadians still obtained slaves, through legal or aggressive means, from the Dutch and English. Those who obtained slaves from the English colonies included soldiers, diplomats, merchants, and *coureurs de bois*, notorious for their illegal trade with Albany.

Angélique was born in 1705. But a veil of silence covers the first twenty years of her life. What we know about her during this period is sketchy. She lies an "unspeaking skeleton" until 1725, when she arrived in Montréal as slave property of Sieur and Madame Francheville. Only the records from 1730 to 1734 provide enough information for us to put flesh on the skeleton's bones.

Unlike many European Whites, Angélique did not come to the New World to seek opportunities, fortune, or adventure.

She came from one Atlantic port to another as an enslaved woman whose life and future were marked by perpetual servitude. Between the time Angélique left Europe and the time she arrived in Montréal, she had been sold at least twice.

Angélique associated the New World with misery and sorrow. In her attempts to flee from Montréal slavery, she had one wish, and that was to reach a New England/New York port and from there board a ship for Portugal. Angélique longed for that corner of Europe that was her birthplace. It was the only home she had ever known.

III

The Secret of Slavery in Canada

SLAVERY IS CANADA's best-kept secret, locked within the national closet. And because it is a secret it is written out of official history. But slavery was an institutionalized practice for over two hundred years. Canada also engaged in the nefarious business of slaving. Stephen Behrendt, a historian and demographer of slavery, reveals that the shipyards of several of the older Canadian colonies constructed ships for use in the British slave trade.[1] Canada might not have been a slave society—that is, a society whose economy was based on slavery—but it was a society with slaves. It shared this feature with virtually all other New World societies. Contrary to popular belief, slavery was common in Canada.

The reluctance to discuss and accept Canada as a place where slavery was institutionalized for 206 years is understandable. In North America, we associate the word "slavery" with the United States, not Canada, because the American economy, especially the southern portion, was fuelled by the labour of millions of African slave captives.

In the story of North American slavery, we associate Canada with "freedom" or "refuge," because during the nineteenth century, especially between 1830 and 1860, the period known as the Underground Railroad era, thousands of American runaway slaves escaped to and found refuge in the British territories to the north. Therefore, the image of Canada as "freedom's land" has lodged itself in the national psyche and become part of our national identity. One result is the assumption that Canada is different from and morally superior to that "slave-holding republic," the United States.

When most people think of slavery, they see a huge cotton or sugar cane plantation worked by hundreds of slaves, with blood dripping down their backs as they endure constant whipping from the slave-drivers. The slaveholder (usually a male) sits on the verandah of his mansion, fanned by docile young slaves. This lurid image is drawn from a southern United States or Caribbean version of slavery, and most people cannot associate it with Canada's early history. Yet the White settlers who colonized Canada during both the French and English periods were indeed slaveholders.

Scholars have painted a pristine picture of Canada's past. It is difficult to find a scholarly or popular publication on the country's past in which images, stories, and analyses of slave life are depicted. We read numerous accounts of pioneer life without learning that some of these pioneers were enslaved people who, like the free White pioneers, built roads and highways, constructed homesteads, fought off bears, caught beavers, established farms from forests, and helped in the defence of the young country.[2] People of African descent, free and enslaved, have vanished from national narratives. It is

possible to complete a graduate degree in Canadian studies
and not know that slavery existed in Canada.

A useful definition of slavery is the robbery of one's freedom and labour by another, usually more powerful person.
Violence and coercion are used to carry out the theft and to
keep the slave captive in the condition of bondage and servitude. This definition applies to slavery in Canada. Laws were
enacted and institutions created to rob persons of their freedom and labour and keep them in perpetual servitude. In the
earliest era of colonial rule in Canada, both Aboriginal peoples and Africans and their descendants were enslaved
(Aboriginal slaves were colloquially termed *Panis*). From 1628
to 1833, slavery was a legal and acceptable institution in both
French and British Canada and was vigorously practised.

The colonists in New France wanted slaves, especially Black
slaves. In all European New World settlements, large percent-
ages of the Native populations were exterminated through
genocide, the harsh conditions of slavery, and the arrival of
new diseases in their midst. In enslavement, the Native populations declined rapidly, which gave Europeans the notion that
Natives could not withstand slavery. In the belief that Blacks
were sturdier people, Europeans began to bring African captives into the colonies to work as slaves. On the whole, Blacks
appeared somewhat better able to withstand the physical
demands of slavery: they lived a little longer than the Native
people. Canada's political and administrative leaders—suave,
urbane, and educated men, some of whom spent time in the
tropical colonies—knew this. They therefore used their power
and influence to bring Black slaves into the country.

The recorded enslavement of Black people in Canada
began with a young boy from Madagascar, an English pirate,

and a Québec clerk. In 1628, when David Kirke, his brother, and other pirates overwhelmed the defence at Québec and seized the feeble French colony for England, Kirke had with him a nine-year-old African boy. Kirke sold the boy, whose African name is unknown, to a Québec clerk. The boy was sold a second time to another clerk, Guillaume Couillard, a friend of Samuel de Champlain. By 1632, the Kirkes had departed the colony, and Québec had reverted to the French. The boy was baptized in 1633 and named Olivier Le Jeune in honour of his godfather, the Jesuit priest Paul Le Jeune. Olivier died in Québec in 1654.

As French colonists settled in Canada and expanded their colonizing ventures, it became clear that the available labour force could not meet the demands created by a burgeoning economy. Thus, New France began its colonial life with a chronic labour shortage. Even though a system of indentureship had been set in place, with contract labourers coming from France to serve out an indenture, it did not solve the problem. Seeing the prosperity of their New England neighbours, a prosperity based on slave labour, *les Canadiens* hit on the idea that slavery was exactly what their colony needed.

In 1663, when the Company of One Hundred Associates relinquished control of New France to the Crown, King Louis XIV determined to make a viable colony out of New France. A new system of administration was set in place, and local colonial officials set about developing the colony. That meant, among other things, exploiting the mines, agricultural base, and fisheries of the region. But the population was small, and there was more work to be done than hands to do it. The Sun King decided to increase the population by sending seven hundred dowried girls and women to New France between 1665 and

1673. Named *les filles du Roi*, or daughters of the king, these women were sent over to marry and produce children.[3]

The action of the king and the fertility of *les filles* did lead to a rapid increase in the population. By 1690, New France had a population of 12,000. But it was not enough. The labour shortage continued. In 1688, bowing to pressure from the settlers, the governor, Marquis de Denonville, and the intendant, Jean Bochart de Champigny, wrote to Louis XIV, requesting permission to introduce Black slaves into the colony. Their letter reflects the concerns of the settlers: "Labourers and servants are so scarce and costly in Canada that those who attempt extensive work are ruined in consequence. We believe that the surest means of obviating this difficulty would be to bring here Negro slaves."[4] Governor and intendant noted that, if the king granted permission, slaves could be obtained from the West Indies and Africa.

The following year the king gave his consent, though he expressed doubts about the effects of the severe Canadian climate on slaves from the tropics. Despite his concerns, enslaved Africans were brought into the colony. Further royal consent was given in 1701, and slavery began to take root. Colonial officials noted that they allowed the settlers to own Black slaves, and thereafter, the word *esclave* became common in the civil register and government documents. However, the colonists still lamented the scarcity of labourers. To be sure, there were enslaved people coming into the colony, but they were coming in insufficient numbers, and they were not arriving fast enough.[5]

In 1716, a new intendant, Michel Bégon, once again appealed to the Crown for help with the labour problem. Like his predecessor, he suggested that the way to improve the situation was to import enslaved Africans. The population of the colony was now only 20,000, and this made labour "expensive and scarce." Bégon added that if New France were to enter the slave trade, independently of France, it would prosper like its English neighbours to the south, New England and New York, both of which had successful economies partially built on the labour of enslaved Africans. And both of which had a population in excess of 100,000.

With or without help from the Crown, New France's colonists were able, with varying degrees of success, to obtain enslaved Africans. One method available to the French was the use of Native allies. The Abenaki and sometimes the Iroquois captured Black slaves from the English to the south and sold them to the French settlers in Canada. However, there were also legal transactions between the French and the English: French colonists bought Black slaves from New York, New England, the Carolinas, and other American colonies. Enslaved Africans also came to New France from the West Indies, from Africa, and from Europe.

In Montréal, which eventually would have the largest slave population in the colony, the first Black person recorded as a slave in the register of the church of Notre-Dame is simply named "Louis." It is noted that he was a native of Madagascar and was twenty-six at the time of his baptism on May 24, 1692. Louis Lecomte-Dupre owned Louis, the slave. On the same day, another slave, Pierre Célestin, age twenty-four, was baptized as well. Also a native of Madagascar, his owner was Pierre Leber. It would seem that both of these slaves received the first names of their owners.[6]

Madagascar featured as a popular place of origin for many of New France's enslaved Blacks. An active slave trade flourished from Madagascar to Asia and the Mediterranean, but many Madagascan captives ended up in the New World, taken there by both French and English slave traders and pirates. Also, Madagascar was a favourite hunting ground for slaves by early colonial American slave traders. But by the end of the seventeenth century, Black captives arriving in Canada were coming from different parts of the world.[7]

The Detroit River frontier, which encapsulates the present Detroit area and the counties of Essex and Kent in Ontario, was also a centre of French habitation and hence slavery. Black slavery in the Detroit River district began when the fur trader and explorer Antoine de La Mothe Cadillac travelled to the region and in 1701 founded Detroit. Cadillac had brought with him several dozen slaves, both Panis and Africans, from Montréal to build a fort at Detroit for the purposes of the fur trade. Among Cadillac's party were potential settlers and colonists. So while the fur traders roamed the Michigan/Ohio countryside, colonists settled on both banks of the Detroit River with their African slaves. These servants for life thus became part of the settlement process and development of the Detroit River district. Black slaves also worked in the fur trade with their owners. Of course, enslaved Native people also made the French colonization of the Detroit River district possible. Acadia (parts of Nova Scotia, New Brunswick, and Prince Edward Island), though not defined administratively as a part of *le Canada*, was also a French colony in which enslaved Africans lived, worked, and died.

The French empire in the West Indies was built on sugar production and the labour of enslaved Africans. The Code Noir, a French legal code, regulated slavery in the West Indies. Though it was never made law in Canada, New

France's slaveholders applied the Code Noir when they thought it necessary. In 1685, when the Code was applied to the French West Indies, the governor of New France, the Marquis de Denonville, thought it might as well be applied in New France. Canada's colonial officials therefore used the Code Noir to give legal foundation to slavery. Under the Code Noir, slaves were declared "movable," that is, personal property, in the same category as livestock, furniture, and trade goods. The Code Noir regulated other aspects of slave life, such as relations between master and slave, the status of slave children, slave marriages, and so forth.[8]

An important clause of the Code was that all slaves were to be baptized and instructed in the Catholic faith. As with the case of Olivier Le Jeune, Louis, and Pierre Célestin, many owners followed this instruction and baptized their slaves. Yet this was more symbolic than anything else, since baptism did not mean that slaves would be liberated from their servitude or enjoy social equality with Whites. Father Paul Le Jeune reported that the young Madagascan boy who received his name rebuked the priest when he baptized him and proclaimed that all who accepted Christianity became of one blood, united in Christ. The priest wrote that the boy said, "You say that by baptism I shall be like you; I am black and you are white, I must have my skin taken off then in order to be like you."[9] The act of baptism did not fool young Olivier.

Imperial edicts and local laws also consolidated, regularized, and protected slavery in New France and enshrined the rights of colonists to own slaves. In 1701, Louis XIV gave his full consent to Black slavery in Canada, authorizing "its colonists to own slaves. . . in full proprietorship."[10] This consent was merely academic, because Canadians had already been doing so. In 1709, Intendant Jacques Raudot made into law a bill that sought to confirm the servile status of Panis and enslaved Africans. This bill was prompted by the frequency of slave escapes, with slaves claiming to be free people. Raudot's bill announced that "all the Panis and Negroes who have been purchased and who will be purchased, shall be the property of those who have purchased them and will be their slaves."[11] The intendant made it a criminal offence to induce slaves to run away. Anyone who did so and was found out would be arrested and made to pay 50 livres. The fact that the intendant felt the need to pronounce upon the responsibilities of owners demonstrates that slavery was established in the colony.

Between 1706 and 1736—the time when Angélique would have come to live in New France—the number of slaves increased in the colony. As a result, many slaves were running away from their owners and insisting they were free, in spite of Raudot's 1709 bill. In addition, some Whites were encouraging slaves to escape, telling them that they were free. This prompted Intendant Gilles Hocquart, in 1736, to issue an ordinance regulating manumission: only those slaves manumitted through a formal, notarized agreement would be considered legally free.[12]

Black slavery in Canada was patriarchal, meaning that the male slaveholder was the head of an extended family that included people he was related to by marriage and blood (his wife and children) and enslaved persons. Slaves often lived in the same houses as their owners, ate the same food, were baptized by their owners, and had owners or their close relatives as godparents, and sometimes they received the name of the owners' family.

The paternalistic nature of slavery in New France had much to do with the scarcity of labour in a growing colony: slaves were a valuable resource. Yet the economy, largely based on the fur trade, did not demand large gangs of labourers in the way that an agriculturally based economy would have. True, in Canada, agriculture was an important secondary economic activity, and many of the White colonists were farmers who did use slaves as farm labourers. Canada's economic model made for a form of slavery that was, to some degree, different from the slavery seen across the southern United States. It was more in line with the type of slavery found in colonial New England and New York.

Slaves in Canada engaged in a variety of occupations—from rat catcher to hangman—but most worked as house servants, as farm labourers, or in skilled occupations. In New France, and later in British Canada, slaves were owned by a variety of individuals and corporations. The Church, the nobility, merchants, lawyers, government officials, gentry, soldiers, seigneurs, tavern-keepers, farmers, business people, and artisans all held slaves. The merchant elite, as a group, held the largest number of enslaved people.

Angélique lived in Montréal, an urban centre, and that reflected the residential pattern of most of the enslaved people. The majority of this population lived in the three main centres of the colony: Montréal, Trois-Rivières, and the capital, Québec. This made slavery in New France a more or less urban phenomenon. By the end of the French period, in 1760, seventy-seven percent of all enslaved people lived in urban areas, with fifty-two percent of this group residing in Montréal alone.[13] Living in cities, the enslaved had some mobility and so became acquainted with the geography of their locale. This knowledge, in many instances, accounted for their frequent escapes.

Generally speaking, the kind of work enslaved people did ensured close proximity to their owners. Even if relationships between owners and slaves were hostile, the two parties nonetheless maintained physical domestic closeness. Enslaved people could legally marry, with the permission of their owners, and upon death were usually given a Christian burial. New France's slaves also had certain rights typically reserved for free persons in the rest of the New World. For example, they could serve as witnesses at religious functions and could petition against free persons.[14]

But not all enslaved persons lived in town, worked as domestics, or laboured on farms. The case of Louis Lepage, a slave boatman, reveals the multidimensional nature of Canadian slavery. On December 27, 1744, in the office of two Québec notaries, a contract was drawn up between Jean-Baptiste Vallée, a Québec "bourgeois," and François de Chalet, inspector general of the Company of the West Indies, in charge of the French trading posts at Cataraqui (Kingston) and Niagara. Vallée hired out his slave Louis Lepage to de Chalet "to serve as a sailor on the boats of the ports." De Chalet agreed to pay Vallée 25 livres per month for the services of his enslaved man. De Chalet was also to provide the sailor with "a jug of brandy and a pound of tobacco a month, and for his food, two pounds of bread and a half a pound of pork a day."[15]

As a boatman in the Company's employ, Lepage would do the backbreaking work of loading and unloading trade goods and furs into canoes and rowing the lakes and great rivers of the colony. He would also spend a lot of time in

The Hanging of Angélique   79

the woods. But there was an upside to his work: Lepage would labour under loose supervision, and the location of his job would ensure that he enjoyed relative independence and freedom. And though Vallée described Lepage as "faithful and well-behaved,"[16] there is no reason to think that the sailor would not see the ample opportunities for freedom his work provided and escape into the wilderness of New York.

Enslaved Africans were hired out, as in the case of Lepage, and they were also sold and bought. On September 25, 1743, Charles Réaume drew up a contract in the office of a Québec notary to sell five enslaved Africans to Louis Cureux:

> Appearing in front of the royal notary in the precinct of Québec, sieur Charles Réaume, merchant, residing in the seigneury of Isle Jésus, near Montréal, and now present in this city to sell to sieur Louis Cureux dit St.-Germain, bourgeois of this city...five Negro slaves, two men and three women and children.[17]

The entire slave party was sold for 3,000 livres.

The French colonists and rulers also gave away slave children as gifts:

> In July, 1748, Jean-Pierre Roma, Commandant for the King at the Island of St. Jean [Prince Edward Island]...on his passage to Québec, made a singular Gift to his friend, Fleury de la Gorgendière....He gave him a mulatto Girl, five months old and named Marie.
>
> The child was born at Québec, February 20, 1848; she was baptized the following day, and her godfather and

godmother were M. Perrault, a merchant, and Marie-Anne Roma, daughter of Commandant Roma.

The gift made to M. Fleury de la Gorgendière is explained by the fact that the mother of the child, the slave of Roma, died in giving it birth. Roma, not being able to charge himself with raising the orphan, preferred to give it to M. Fleury de la Gorgendière.

The deed is drawn up by the Notary, Jean-Claude Panet, July 15, 1748; and it is the stipulation that in case of the death of Fleury and his wife, the mulatto will return to Mdlle [Mademoiselle] Roma (her godmother). If she cannot take her, it is stipulated that she will receive her freedom.[18]

This sad story hides as much as it reveals. The slave mother died giving birth to her child, and her owner gave the baby away because he felt he could not raise her himself. The child, described as a mulatto, was called an "orphan." But for a child to be created, a father had to be involved. Who was the child's father? Was it Roma himself? Was that why he felt so obliged to find a home for the child, and why he gave her away to his trusted friend instead of selling her? A veil of semi-protectiveness was drawn around the slave baby. Not only was she given to someone whom Roma believed would care for her, but Roma's daughter was the baby's godmother and a stand-in parent if that became necessary. The baby's mother remained nameless, but we know a few things about her: she was a Black woman; she was Roma's slave; and she died in childbirth.

Enslaved Africans in Canada reacted to slavery in much the same way that slaves did in other New World societies and took steps to wreak revenge on their owners. They ran away, talked back, broke tools, were disobedient, threatened their owners, organized slave uprisings, and in two cases allegedly set major fires that devastated colonial towns.

Slaves also died young. The average age of death for Panis was 17.7 years, and for Blacks, 25.2. Only a few Blacks lived to be 80.[19]

During the French period, enslaved Panis were more numerous than enslaved Africans because Panis were easier to obtain. This situation would be reversed with the Conquest of Canada.

In 1760, at the end of the Seven Years War between Britain and France, Britain conquered Canada. Three years later, by the Treaty of Paris, France ceded Canada to Britain. New France ceased to be, and the Canadian territory seized by the British was renamed and transformed into the colony of Québec. By the time of the conquest, over 1,500 Black slaves had landed in Canada.

With the 47th article of the treaty of capitulation, signed between the victorious British and the defeated French, the British confirmed the rights of the French colonists to own and retain their slaves. The governor general of New France, the Marquis de Vaudreuil, who surrendered to the British, inserted this clause into the treaty, and General Jeffrey Amherst accepted it as part of the terms of surrender for the British.

> The Negroes and Panis of both sexes shall remain, in their quality of slaves, in the possession of the French and Canadians to whom they belong; they shall be at liberty to keep them in their service in the colony or sell them; and they may also continue to bring them up in the Roman religion.[20]

Thus, the slave question was an important treaty issue, and one supported by the British. British law colluded with French law to further the enslavement of African people in Canada. The same clause was incorporated into the peace treaty signed in Paris in 1763. With the Treaty of Paris, Britain introduced English criminal and civil law into the newly conquered territory. One pernicious effect of this new development for the enslaved people was that it deprived them "of those few protections provided by the…Code Noir."[21] Under French laws, modelled on Roman law, the enslaved were recognized as human beings, and this apparently tempered their enslavement. Under English laws, they were regarded as mere chattel, to be bought and sold as one would a horse or a chair. Some historians feel that the introduction and retention of English criminal law had a harmful effect on enslaved Blacks.[22]

I believe this point is debatable; I also believe it is merely academic. There is no evidence to prove that the French were more humane to their captive Africans than the English were. The Code Noir did make provision for the baptism and marriage of enslaved Blacks, but it also regulated their lives in harsh and brutal ways. San Domingue, a French colony run under the auspices of the Code, was "hell on earth" for enslaved Africans. Their treatment in Guadeloupe, Martinique, and other French tropical colonies was the same. In Canada, owners could brutalize their slaves any way they wished. And as historian Kenneth Donovan informs us, in Île Royale (Acadia), quite a few slaveholders ignored the more positive aspects of the Code Noir. For example, many did not baptize their slaves, while some did so on a slave's deathbed.[23] The issue is not the specific code of law but how slaves on an individual basis experience slavery. Put another way, treatment of enslaved people depended on the character of individual owners. English laws might have recognized slaves only as chattel, but that did not mean the treatment of slaves under the English dispensation was any worse (as one would imagine, given the nature of the law) or any better than under the French regime.

With its successes in the Seven Years War, Britain became the strongest power in the world. By this time, it was also the most powerful slave trading nation. During the first decade of the eighteenth century, after the signing of the treaty that ended the War of Spanish Succession, Britain gained certain concessions that gave it an edge over its rivals, especially France. It also gained the asiento, the slave trading contract given by Spain to bring slave captives to New World colonies. The asiento ensured a steady source of income for whichever country held it. By the time of the Conquest of Canada, Britain had transported hundreds of thousands of captive Africans to the New World in numerous slave ships. Britain also had a large slave empire centred in the West Indies and the United States, with slave colonies in southern India and south Africa.

If the enslaved Canadian Blacks and Panis thought the Conquest would deliver a chance for freedom, they were wrong. The British conquest led to the intensification of slavery in Canada. Britain had the resources to pump slaves into Canada; however, no large-scale shipments of slaves were required to provide the Canadian colonists with slave labour. With Canada now a British possession, land-hungry British-American colonists to the south began migrating in large numbers to the new territory. The post-Conquest immigrants brought their Black slave labourers with them, thus increasing the slave population in Canada.

The British preferred Black slaves to enslaved Panis, and, having the resources, ensured that more Black bondspeople would enter the colony. As a result, under the British regime, Black enslaved labourers became more numerous than Panis. Consequently, enslavement gradually became identified solely with Africans.

The British governor himself, James Murray, whether or not he was a slaveholder before he took up his post in Québec, certainly wanted to become one. His preference for Black slaves reveals how, in the minds of Whites, Blacks were closely identified with slavery.

Murray assessed the labour situation in the new colony of Québec and determined that there was a shortage. Echoing the view of his French predecessors, he believed the best solution to the labour problem lay in the importation of enslaved Africans. In November 1763, he wrote to a New York colleague, bemoaning the shortage of labour in Québec. Murray noted that "Canadians will work for nobody but themselves" and that "Black slaves are certainly the only people to be depended upon." He requested that his colleague buy for him "two stout young fellows, who have been accustomed to country business...and buy for each a clean young wife, who can wash and do the female offices about a farm."[24]

Murray wanted strong young men, but he was concerned about their sexual needs, so he also sought young women as companions for each. These women would not only satisfy the emotional needs of the male slaves, but would also be useful as domestic machines. Murray's letter reveals the gendered nature of slavery: both men and women performed heavy labour, but women had the additional task of taking on domestic and wifely duties.

The British conquerors introduced the printing press and the newspaper to the newly acquired territory. From these papers we learn that slaves in the new dispensation, as in the old regime, continued to run away. Throughout the colonial period, English-language newspapers regularly announced slave flight. These advertisements give us insight into the enslaved people, their condition, and their responses to slavery. A couple of examples will suffice.

Quebec Gazette, July 29, 1769

Joseph Negrie, a young man of about 22 years of age, of brown complexion, slim made, 5 feet 3 inches high, small legs, speaks French and English tolerably well, ran away in the night between 7th and 8th instant....The public is desired not to employ the said Negrie, and all captains of vessels who may take him on board are forewarned from carrying him out of the province, as they will be pursued to the utmost rigour of the law. Whoever shall discover said Negrie is desired to inform his master, Peter [Pierre] Du Calvet, esquire of Montréal.

Pierre Du Calvet was a successful Huguenot merchant who lived under both the French and English regimes. He acted as a translator for the English during and after the Conquest. Du Calvet suspected that his slave would try to escape on a ship, since Montréal was a river town, a port centre, and vessels were one likely means of escape.

Another runaway was the slave woman Cash.

Quebec Gazette, October 19, 1769

On Sunday morning…a Negro wench named Cash, twenty-six years old…speaks English and French very fluently, carried with her a considerable quantity of linen and other valuable effects not her own; and as she has also taken with her a large bundle of wearing apparel belonging to herself, consisting of a black satin cloak, caps, bonnets, ruffles, ribbons, six or seven petticoats, a pair of old stays, and many other articles of value which cannot be ascertained, it is likely that she may change her dress.

Cash absconded with a large portion of her owner's wardrobe and must have thought of using these clothes as a means of disguise. Or, quite likely, she felt that her owner owed her all that she took.

From these ads, we learn that many slaves were bilingual, sometimes multi-lingual. We often learn of a slave's knowledge of skills and trades. For example, one Pompey was noted to be a sailor. And we get a description of the kind of clothes the runaways wore.

Where would slaves run? Slave runaways could take refuge with sympathetic Natives in the Upper Country or disappear into some frontier communities. Escaping to land held by a foreign power was another possibility, as was escaping via ship to the West Indies or Florida. But it is likely that slaves like Cash and others who came with their owners from places such as New England and New York were running *back* to these places—places they knew and where they may have had relatives. When going back to the thirteen colonies, escapees traversed a reverse Underground Railroad.

The fact that these slaves were fleeing their enslavement reveals that, even if Canadian slavery has been considered to be "mild" by some historians, the victims found it harsh enough.[25] Lorenzo Greene, an expert on slavery in colonial New England, stresses the point: "Although the slaves were generally well treated in New England, slavery was so unbearable to some Negroes that, rather than remain in bondage, they committed suicide..."[26] Comments on the "mildness" of Canadian slavery trivialize the lives of the enslaved and rob them of their humanity.[27]

Marronage, the act of running away, could be either temporary or permanent. With temporary (or *petit*) *marronage*, enslaved persons ran away for a few days or weeks because they were upset and angry with their owners. However, they intended to go back. Temporary *marronage* was a weapon enslaved Africans used to show their owners that they did not have to "put up with it." It also showed that slaveholders did not have complete ownership over the bodies of their slave property. Permanent *marronage* meant that the captives escaped and lived in freedom in hard-to-reach places such as forests, wildernesses, swamps, and mountain strongholds.[28]

Newspapers in the colony of Québec were not the only ones that broadcasted the flight of slaves. In the forty years after the Conquest, and in the early years of the nineteenth century, ads for runaway and missing slaves also graced the pages of colonial newspapers in New Brunswick, Nova Scotia, and Upper Canada.

The sale of slaves was another feature of life in Canada. The value of slave property depended on physical health (acquired immunity from smallpox was an asset), special aptitudes, age, and sex, among other factors. Olivier Le Jeune was sold for 50 livres in 1628. Marie-Joseph Angélique was sold for a barrel of gunpowder. In 1738, in Montréal,

Catherine Raimbault sold two of her Black male slaves, Laramee, aged thirty, and Charles, aged ten, for 200 and 570 livres respectively. That a ten-year-old child fetched more than a thirty-year-old man is not strange, given that slaves died so young in the colony. The seller and purchaser probably knew that Laramee did not have long to live, while the boy could potentially render fifteen more years of service.

In the post-Conquest period, a woman skilled in housework could fetch between £30 and £50. The woman described in this ad would likely have commanded a good price:

> *Quebec Gazette*, February 23, 1769
>
> Mr. Prenties has to sell a negro woman, aged 25 years, with a mulatto male child, 9 months old. She was formerly the property of General Murray; she can be well recommended for a good house servant; handles milk well and makes butter to perfection.

Remember General Murray, the first British governor of the newly conquered colony who wanted to buy slaves? Well, he certainly acquired "a negro woman" after taking up his post in 1763. By 1766, Murray had departed the province, obviously not taking this particular slave with him. His slave woman and her child were now the property of Prenties, who wished to sell them. This nameless slave woman is but one example of an enslaved African passing through the hands of successive owners—another common feature of the life of the enslaved.

The Hanging of Angélique 89

May 10, 1785

A gentleman going to England has for sale a negro wench, with her child...she understands thoroughly every kind of house-work, particularly washing and cookery. And a stout negro boy 13 years old. Also a good horse, cariole and harness. For particulars enquire at Mr. William Roxburgh's, Upper Town, Quebec.

The above two ads and others reveal, certainly, that slaves were seen as chattel, like horses or harnesses. They also tell us that women's primary occupation was that of domestic. Black women laboured in the homes of their owners doing all manner of housework, including childcare. The image of the Black woman who "understands thoroughly every kind of house-work," the tireless domestic, has persisted throughout the centuries. Little is gleaned about the fathers of their children. That the child of Mr. Prenties's slave is a mulatto testifies that a White man, possibly Prenties himself, was the father.

Sale of slaves was usually a transaction between two parties, but sometimes slaves were sold publicly. The same Mr. Prenties who advertised in February 1769 was not successful in selling his slaves. Six months later, he chose to do so at a public market. "To be sold at public vendue...a negro woman aged 25, with a mulatto child, male..."[29]

Slave ads pertaining to women and children often indicate that children were sold with their mothers. Some of these children are described as mulattoes, the fathers of whom are "unknown." The relatively large mulatto population at the time of the Conquest reveals that White men often sired the children of Black women, most of whom were enslaved women. This fact must be placed in the context of the power relationships in slave societies. White men owned Black women's bodies and what came out of those bodies. Black women were regularly subjected to sexual assaults by their owners and other White men. If the women were impregnated and had children, these children inherited the status of their mothers and were enslaved. It mattered little that the children's fathers were White men, sometimes very prominent White men; what mattered was that their mothers were enslaved and Black. One of the most dehumanizing aspects of slavery was the loss of control that Black people, especially women, experienced over their bodies.[30]

One commentator on Canadian slavery makes light of the sexual abuse that Black women faced when he casts them as seducers whose charms (hapless) White men cannot resist.[31] Slaveholders who sexually abused Black women, kept them as concubines, and impregnated them may have subscribed to this sentiment. It is a common attitude of those in power. Refusing to take responsibility for their offence, they blame the victim.

The American Revolutionary War (1776–1783) produced a further expansion of slavery in Canada. Many Americans who remained loyal to the Crown fled to Canada, with their enslaved chattel, on the heel of British defeat by the American forces. At least 35,000 of these Loyalists fled to Nova Scotia. Five thousand were Black, both slave and free; however, the majority were free. The expansion of Nova Scotia's population led, in 1784, to the province being divided to create New Brunswick. This new province got its share of free and enslaved Black Loyalists. Likewise, some Black Loyalists made it into Prince Edward Island.

About 10,000 Loyalists—White, Black, and Native—came

to the province of Québec. However, unlike in the Maritime provinces, most of the Québec Black Loyalists were enslaved. They came with their White owners from New York, New England, Virginia, the Carolinas, and other parts of the thirteen colonies. Some of the enslaved Blacks were also in the parties of members of the Iroquois Confederacy.

In English and Loyalist Canada, slavery was given legal foundation and institutionalized through a series of treaty clauses, acts, and statutes. Recall the capitulation treaty and the Treaty of Paris, in which Canadians were given the right to own slaves. The British Parliament passed the Quebec Act in 1774, returning the colony to French civil law; this act also reaffirmed the right of the colonists to own, buy, and sell slaves. Slavery was further buttressed by the passing of the Imperial Act of 1790. This act, directed at British citizens living in the United States, was designed to encourage their immigration to Canada with the hope of increasing the English-speaking population. Britain permitted the introduction, duty free, into Canada (now called British North America) of all "Negroes, household furniture, utensils of husbandry or clothing."[32] The "Negroes" mentioned were enslaved Africans—free Blacks were discouraged from immigrating to British North America. Though this act would be challenged three years later by a naive lieutenant governor of Upper Canada, it gave further legal protection to the institution of slavery.

In 1791, the western portion of Québec was hived off to create the province of Upper Canada, today's Ontario. Upper Canada was established to satisfy the needs of the English-speaking White Loyalists who chafed under French civil laws and customs. The French landholding system and agricultural practices irked these Anglo-American immigrants. Their xenophobia inspired them to clamour for a province of their own, where they could establish "British" institutions. The British government, feeling that Québec was large enough to accommodate the "two founding races," gave Upper Canada to the fractious Loyalists. The new province covered a huge expanse of land stretching west from Cornwall to the Detroit River frontier, and south from the lower Great Lakes to the far reaches of James Bay.

European settlements clung to the more southerly parts of the province. Loyalists built along the banks of the St. Lawrence in the eastern portion of the province, and on the Niagara and Detroit River frontiers.

In Upper Canada and Québec (renamed Lower Canada after 1791), though many Blacks were free people, the majority were enslaved. The enslaved population, brought to Canada mainly by White Loyalists (members of the Mohawk elite also held Black slaves), came with a variety of skills, which they used in the founding and development of the colonies. Slaves worked as millwrights, blacksmiths, coopers, printers, and tinsmiths. They felled trees, made roads, opened highways, and worked as domestics, nannies, and farm labourers. James Walker insists that "we cannot understand early pioneer history unless we acknowledge that slavery existed..."[33] By 1793, it is estimated that there were five hundred slaves in Upper Canada.

Like many of the families of the old French regime, most of Upper Canada's leading families, including many of the province's founding fathers and mothers, were slaveholders. The list of slaveholders in the colony reads like a "who's who" of Upper Canadian society. Among the prominent men and women who owned slaves were Colonel Matthew Elliott of Sandwich and Amherstburg, who owned more than fifty slaves; William Jarvis, secretary of the province, and his wife, Hannah; Robert I.D. Gray, the solicitor general; Peter Russell, provincial administrator, and his sister, Elizabeth Russell; Mohawk Chief Joseph Brant; Colonel John Butler of Butler's Rangers fame; Sieur Jacques Baby *dit* Dupéron, scion of an old Windsor French family; and Reverend John Stuart of Kingston.[34]

Robert I.D. Gray, for example, had a family of slaves in his house in Cornwall: a woman named Dorinda Baker, her two mulatto sons, and her mother. The Gray arrangement reeked of paternalism. The Gray family had owned Dorinda and her sons when they lived in New York State. Having fled to Canada after the Revolutionary War, the family took the slaves with them. But Dorinda's mother was not in the flight party. Gray travelled back to New York, bought Dorinda's mother from another slaveholder, and reunited her with her daughter and grandchildren. After Gray's untimely death, his will revealed that he had generously provided for Dorinda and her sons. It is more than likely that Dorinda was the mistress of Gray's father, and that her sons belonged to him. The sons and the younger Gray were in the same age group.[35]

The court records for the Town of York provide information on William Jarvis's slaves. On March 11, 1811, Jarvis imprisoned two of his slaves, a young boy and girl, for allegedly stealing gold and silver from his desk. Jarvis also requested that Coachly, a free Black, be arrested "on suspicion of having advised and aided" the two slaves.[36]

Peter Russell, a member of the Executive Council and future provincial administrator, held at least five slaves, four of whom comprised one family: a woman named Peggy and her three children. Peggy and her family lived with Russell and his sister Elizabeth in their town home in York (now part of Toronto).[37]

Those who have written our history books up to now would not have chosen to include Peggy. Although she was a pioneer, she was not a gentlewoman, nor was she White, and so she would not be included in a book dealing with the history of non-Native women in Canada. And although slavery was an important institution on the frontier, slavery has been expunged from our national narrative, so Peggy would not make it into a book about the early history of Canada.

Peggy, the mother of three children, Milly, Amy, and Jupiter, and the wife of a free Black man named Pompadour, was a disobedient and recalcitrant slave who bucked the Russells' authority by talking back to them and running away whenever she felt like it. On more than one occasion, her master had her confined to the town's jail. Jupiter, her son, was also a runaway and "disobedient"; he too was lodged in jail for his rudeness and "saucy ways." Peter Russell determined to get Peggy off his hands by selling her to another member of the colonial elite, slaveholder Matthew Elliott, then living in Sandwich. In a letter to Elliott, Russell states,

My slave Peggy, whom you were so good to promise to assist getting rid of, has remained in prison ever since you left this (in expectation of your sending for her) at an expence of above Ten pounds Halifax, which I was obliged to pay to the gaoler [to] release her last week by order of the Chief Justice. She is now at large, being not permitted by my sister to enter this house, and shows a disposition at times to be very troublesome, which may perhaps compel me to commit her to again to prison.

Russell entreats Elliott to take Peggy off his hands.

> I shall Therefore be glad that you would either take her
> away Immediately, or return to me the Bill of sale I gave
> you to enable you to do so. For tho I have received no
> money from you for her, my property in her is gone
> from me while you Hold the bill of sale; and I cannot
> consequently give a valid title to any other who may be
> inclined to take her off my hands. I beg to hear from
> you soon.[38]

Peter Russell, an Anglo-Irish man, accepted the institution of slavery in Upper Canada even though in Britain
itself slavery was on the decline. He behaved like a typical
American slaveholder: he separated families if he saw fit, he
punished and imprisoned his slaves, and when they would
not "obey" he sold them. He was not going to put Peggy
on the auction block; rather, he was selling her through a
more "genteel" method. Nevertheless, the result would be
the same: Peggy would be separated from her husband and
children.

Yet, contrary to a once-popular belief that slave masters
had "absolute authority" over their slaves, Russell was not in
total control. If conditions were not to their liking, slaves
often tried in subtle and not so subtle ways to live within the
bounds of the institution on their own terms, to change the
frame of reference. Peggy was doing just that when she left
the Russell household to live "at large."

Peggy's way of dealing with her enslavement paralleled that
of enslaved people throughout the Americas and Canada.
American slave Henry Bibb often ran away from his owners

for a few days or weeks. Marie-Joseph Angélique made a habit of running away until she made her final escape. Peggy may not have tried to make a permanent bid for her freedom because she had young children and wanted to remain with her family. What Peggy engaged in was *petit marronage*, running away temporarily to protest one's enslavement, or taking a vacation of sorts to escape the vagaries of slave life.

The deal with Matthew Elliott fell through. Elliott, it turned out, wanted to sell Peggy to Mohawk leader Joseph Brant. That did not occur, and the Russells were stuck with her. Elizabeth had to renege on her earlier decision and allow Peggy back into the house. But two years later, Peggy again absented herself from the Russell household. Russell gave notice of this in the September 2, 1803, issue of the *York Gazette*. Russell warned that whoever was "hiding or putting up" his slave would be dealt with by the law.

Even though York was a small town, others would employ and harbour Peggy while knowing she belonged to someone else. Because there was a labour shortage, Peggy could find sympathizers who would take her in. Who knows what was going on in the Russell household that led Peggy to run from it. Was she sexually abused by either owner? It seems that her relationship with Elizabeth Russell, in particular, was strained. Peter Russell, in his letter to Elliott, said that Peggy showed a "disposition at times to be very troublesome," revealing that Peggy was an incorrigible slave. She would not behave.

Jupiter also kept the Russells busy. On January 25, 1806, Elizabeth Russell wrote in her diary that Jupiter had been released from jail. He had been lodged there for verbally abusing the Denisons, a prominent York family.

. . . Jupiter was released from Prison today and contrary to orders was brought into the house, but was sent off home with Pompodore who was very drunk today and impertinent to Peter who was very angry at Jupiter's being brought into the house. He behaved so ill when he was here that I am determined he shall not come at all to the house which Peter is so good as to comply with. He is a thief and everything that is bad, and since he has been in jail he is overrun with lice. He has also behaved so ill at the Farm that Mrs. Denison objects to his going there so he is to remain at Pompy's till he is sold.[39]

By 1806, Peter Russell, who by this time was no longer the provincial administrator, was at the point of desperation. He wanted to rid himself of Peggy and her son, Jupiter. He advertised in the *York Gazette*:

February 19, 1806, To Be Sold:
   A Black woman named Peggy, aged forty years, and a Black boy, her son, named Jupiter, aged about fifteen years, both of them the property of the subscriber. The woman is a tolerable cook and washerwoman, and perfectly understands making soap and candles. The boy is tall and strong for his age, and has been employed in the country business, but brought up principally as a house servant. They are each of them servants for life. The price of the woman is one hundred and fifty dollars. For the boy two hundred dollars, payable in three years, with interest from the day of sale, and to be secured by bond, &c. But one-fourth less will be taken for ready money.

If the Russells seem to have been "reluctant" masters, Peggy and her family were "irresolute" slaves. What is quite clear is that Peggy and her family pushed and pulled at slavery and sought to effect their freedom or gain concessions. Like Angélique before them, they would not willingly accept their bondage.

Common people also bought, held, and sold slaves. In the *Niagara Herald*, on January 2, 1802, we find "for sale, a negro slave, 18 years of age, stout and healthy, has had the smallpox and is capable of service either in the house of out of doors." In the same paper, on January 18: "For sale, negro man and woman, the property of Mrs. Widow Clement. They have been bred to the work of the farm; will be sold on highly advantageous terms for cash or lands. Apply to Mrs. Clement."

Colonists could also place ads when they wished to buy slaves. The *Niagara Gazette* and *Oracle* of January 11, 1797, ran the following: "Wanted to purchase, a negro girl from seven to twelve years of age of good disposition. For full particulars, apply to…W.J. Cooke, West Niagara."

How were enslaved people treated? Some masters baptized their slaves, married them, and remembered them in their wills. One salient example of a "good and paternalistic master" is Robert I.D. Gray. He apparently treated his slave family well, and provided generously for them in his will, manumitting them and setting up a trust fund for them. Yet not even he could free the slaves while he lived. They had to wait until he died, and therefore had no further use of their time and labour, to get their freedom. Another slaveholder, Isaac Bennett, made provision in his will for the education and freedom of his two slave boys. But, for every humane master, there was a brutal one to match. Again, we have to question the claims of some authors regarding the supposed mildness of Canadian slavery. Describing the Canadian form of enslavement as mild denies the humanity of the enslaved and further compounds their degradation. Kenneth Donovan hits the nail squarely on the head when he writes: "Slavery perpetuated a culture of oppression. Owners might be cruel or kind, but whatever the treatment accorded them, the shared experience of slaves was usually oppressive and humiliating."[40]

Slaveholders may have thought they were "good masters," but the slaves themselves thought otherwise, as amply demonstrated by those who ran away. Even masters who treated their slaves well still exercised ownership over their bodies and had the legal right to manage their lives as they saw fit. And some owners were cruel. Matthew Elliott whipped his slaves in the manner of a Southern slave master. William Vrooman tied up his slave woman Chloe Cooley and threw her in a boat (he likely beat her too). A master in Nova Scotia punished his recaptured slave by tying a rope through his earlobe and dragging him to his death. Madame Francheville regularly whipped her slave Marie-Joseph Angélique. Owners could and did draw upon the coercive resources of the state when they disciplined their enslaved property. Peter Russell exercised his power over his slaves Peggy and Jupiter by confining them to prison when he felt they were not "obedient" enough. Slaves could also be deported as a form of punishment. The Panis Charles, after leading a slave mutiny at the Niagara garrison, was transported to Martinique with full instructions that he be used as a slave.[41]

*

Black people, then, throughout the length and breadth of British North America, were owned, bought, and sold by White colonists. The lives of the Black enslaved people and their offspring were regulated and circumscribed by those who owned them and the legal resources they could access. Slavery was as Canadian as it was American or West Indian. It is important to note, though, that in this period of the mid- to late eighteenth century, there were also free Black communities in British North America. In Nova Scotia and New Brunswick, Black people of Loyalist origin built free villages and towns in such places as Preston, Shelburne, Birchtown, and Saint John. In fact, these and others became the first free Black communities in North America. However, the residents of these communities faced extreme hostility from Whites. For example, in 1783, White mobs composed mainly of dis- banded soldiers attacked the community of Birchtown, destroying homes, property, and livestock. Other Black com- munities were also penalized one way or another. In 1792, at least 1,200 free Black Nova Scotians and New Brunswickers, fed up with the treatment they were receiving in their respec- tive provinces and feeling that there "was little hope for the advancement of their race" in British North America, decid- ed to migrate to Sierra Leone in search of a better life.[42]

Slavery did not remain unchallenged. And the enslaved were always the first to challenge the conditions of their servitude. We have seen that they ran away and performed other hostile acts against their owners. However, the first offi- cial challenge to slavery came from the top down and occurred in the colony of Upper Canada. Colonel John

Graves Simcoe, veteran of the Revolutionary War, arrived in Canada in 1792 to take up the post of lieutenant governor of the new province of Upper Canada. Simcoe had been a member of the British Parliament and supported antislavery measures in its House. On arriving in Canada (he came by way of Montréal), Simcoe realized the extent of slaveholding among the White population and is reputed to have said that, under his governorship, he would not discriminate "between the natives of Africa, America, or Europe."[43] On reaching Upper Canada, Simcoe was determined to abolish slavery.

He had his chance in March 1793, when he heard of the case of Chloe Cooley, a slave woman who was manhandled, tied up with ropes, and thrown in a boat by her owner, William Vrooman of Queenston in the Niagara district. Vrooman then rowed the boat to the New York side of the Niagara River and sold his slave to someone on the American side. Eyewitnesses related that Cooley "screamed violently and made resistance."[44] Simcoe decided to prosecute Vrooman, but his chief justice told him he did not have a leg to stand on, since slavery was legal in the British empire and Vrooman was well within his rights to dispose of his slave in any manner he wished. Simcoe then decided to prosecute Vrooman for disturbing the peace.

Later, Simcoe gathered enough support in the legislative and executive councils and the assembly to push for a bill on the immediate abolition of slavery in the province. But it was not to be. The slaveholders inside his parliament and those outside were outraged at his audacity and fought him. They claimed that slave labour was essential for the economic life of the colony and that Simcoe would ruin them if he abolished slavery. In a letter to Henry Dundas, his superior in England,

Simcoe noted the chief complaints of those who opposed him: "the greatest resistance was to the Slave Bill, many plausible arguments of the dearness of labour and the difficulty of obtaining servants to cultivate lands were brought forward."[45] The legislators, merchants, and others who favoured the retention of slavery insisted (and they were right) that the 1790 act confirmed their right to hold slaves. So Simcoe backed off, and he and his advisers worked out a compromise. In July 1793, "An act to prevent the further introduction of slaves and to limit the term of contracts for servitude within this province" was pushed through the legislature.[46] The title of the act tells us that it was a compromise indeed. Nothing was said about abolition, because that was not the act's intent. The act did not free a single slave.

It did accomplish other things. First, it confirmed that current slaves would remain slaves. Slaveholders had pushed for this, and they got it. Now they could breathe a sigh of relief. Second, the act banned the introduction of new slaves. Third, the children of current slaves would gain their freedom upon reaching twenty-five, and if they had children before they reached that magic number, their children would be automatically free.

Interestingly, the act did not prevent the sale of slaves across international borders. Many slaveholders saw this loophole and, like Vrooman, sold their slaves into New York.

Upper Canadian slaves who were hoping to be freed by Simcoe's bill had to look for their freedom elsewhere. In 1787, the Northwest Territory (Michigan, Indiana, Ohio, Illinois, Wisconsin, and part of Minnesota) issued an ordinance prohibiting slavery. Vermont and other parts of New England had also abolished slavery by this date. And, in 1799, New York made provisions for the gradual abolition of slavery. As a result, many Upper Canadian enslaved Blacks escaped into these free territories.[47] So numerous were some of these former Canadians in Americans cities that, in Detroit, for example, a group of former Upper Canadian slaves formed a militia in 1806 for the defence of the city against the Canadians. They also fought against Canada in the War of 1812.

If Simcoe's bill had a redeeming feature, it was the article that prohibited the importation of new slaves into the province. This meant, in effect, that slavery would decline, as it could not be expanded through importation. Perhaps more important, it also meant that any foreign slaves would be immediately freed upon reaching the soil of Upper Canada. That was what began the Underground Railroad for enslaved Americans. By the War of 1812, they had heard of this novel situation and many began making the trek northward. The paradox is inescapable: at the same time, many Upper Canadian slaves were making the trek southward to freedom in Michigan and New England.

Simcoe has come down in the literature and in popular imagination as the hero of the antislavery movement in Canada. Indeed, he enacted the first antislavery legislation in the British empire, and for that he must be commended. As a White, powerful, and elite male, he was reserved a grand place in history. But what of Chloe Cooley, the woman whose fate brought about the antislavery legislation and made Upper Canada a refuge for oppressed American Blacks? The woman who made Simcoe Upper Canada's, indeed Canada's, antislavery champion? The different fates of Cooley and Simcoe in the writing of the history of Canada are telling.

Cooley, as an enslaved Black woman, was at the lowest end

of the totem pole and hence an outcast in history. Until recently, the historical experiences of enslaved Black women were not deemed important enough to write about or study. We know very little about Cooley. We do not know her age, her marital status, or even if she had children. She remains in the shadows, silenced. But in March 1793, as Vrooman threw the slave woman in the boat, she "screamed violently and made resistance." Let us therefore, for a moment, take Simcoe out of the centre of the drama and put in that space Chloe Cooley, the woman whose voice and action led to Simcoe's timid but important antislavery bill.

In the other provinces, there was some movement against slavery. A few legislators in Lower Canada tried to copy Simcoe's bill, but they were roundly defeated by the slave-holding interests in the House. One such proslavery legisla-tor, a slaveholder himself, was none other than Québec nationalist Joseph Papineau. It would be the courts in Lower Canada, not the government, that would move against slav-ery. Some Québec slaves took their masters to court, claim-ing that their masters were holding them illegally. In 1797, the courts began to rule in favour of the enslaved. In some instances in Nova Soctia and New Brunswick, local courts also freed some slaves who petitioned for their freedom. The slaveholders of Prince Edward Island, on the other hand, held fast to their right to own enslaved property. Slaves there did not even bother to present their case in court. Gradually, over time, slavery declined in the five colonies that made up British North America. It would eventually come to an end in 1834, when the British Parliament outlawed and abolished it in all its territories.

Though the story of slavery in Canada has been silenced,

those who owned slaves and those whose actions impinged directly on the lives of the enslaved did not adopt a secretive pose in their dealings with their slave property. Government officials deliberated slavery as a public issue. Various statutes and acts concerning Black enslavement came from the imperial and provincial parliaments. The courts also documented the presence of slaves and their concerns. Further, census takers counted enslaved Blacks among the general population. In fact, in the years following the Revolutionary War, there were at least two censuses done to count the number of slaves in the populations of Upper and Lower Canada.[48] As important, enslaved people bore witness to their own presence through flight and other subversive actions.

Slaveholders have left for posterity records of their transactions in the buying and selling of slaves. They recorded the births, baptisms, marriages, and deaths of their slaves. They wrote in their journals and to each other about their slaves; petitioned the courts concerning the Africans they enslaved; in their wills, passed on their slave property to their heirs—and sometimes made provisions for their slaves' freedom. When slaves committed criminal acts, the state chronicled these acts through the writings of notaries, attorneys, scribes, jailers, and judges. Angélique's trial transcripts are salient examples of powerful men recording the lives and actions of those whom they subordinated.

Slaveholders as a group were literate, and it is because of their literacy that we are able to bring to light much of the story of Canadian slavery. Marie-Joseph Angélique's owners, François Poulin de Francheville and his wife, Thérèse de Couagne de Francheville, were upstanding and well-placed members of Montréal's mercantile elite. In addition to the records left by the authorities, they too (here I am referring to the Franchevilles) left records documenting the lives of their enslaved property, most notably Angélique. Who were the Franchevilles? Who and why did they become slaveholders? What was the relationship between them and their bondswoman? To learn more about Angélique's story, we must turn to theirs.

IV

Bourgeois Slaveholders: François Poulin de Francheville and Thérèse de Couagne

FRANÇOIS POULIN DE FRANCHEVILLE and his wife, Thérèse de Couagne, Angélique's owners, saw themselves as bourgeois, persons with refined tastes belonging to a social and economic group whose *raison d'être* was commerce. Bourgeois then (as now) also meant a social class of middle standing—between the aristocracy and the lower classes. And because of their social and economic position, the Franchevilles had ties to other prominent groups such as the clergy, the judiciary, and the military.

But commerce was the lifeblood of Montréal, and during the 1720s and 1730s Sieur Francheville emerged as one of its leading merchants. His business was the fur trade, which involved organizing expeditions to the hinterland to gather furs, supplying troops stationed at garrisoned posts around the Great Lakes, and financing voyages of exploration, primarily to discover new fur resources. He also advanced credit to other merchants involved in the trade and so established himself as a leading moneylender.

In addition to his direct business in fur, Francheville owned a farm in Saint-Michel, a village in the suburbs of Montréal, and a vast estate, or seigneury, called Saint-Maurice, in the Trois-Rivières district. Francheville was ambitious and energetic, and was determined to advance even higher on the social ladder. In Montréal, Francheville and his wife lived in a two-storey stone house on rue Saint-Paul in the merchant quarter of the town.

Born François Poulin (he later adopted the title de Francheville) in 1692 to Michel Poulin and Marie Jutra, Francheville came from a mercantile, landholding, and judicial family that had its roots in the Trois-Rivières and Mauricie region of the colony. His grandfather, the French-born Maurice Poulin de la Fontaine, was a fur trader and judicial officer for the Trois-Rivières jurisdiction. Maurice Poulin began the family tree in Canada and was the first seigneur of Saint-Maurice. In this capacity, he set about bringing settlers to populate and develop the land. The seigneurial system in Canada was a pattern of land ownership instituted by the French in which large tracts of land were granted by the Crown to seigneurs. Seigneurs constituted a definite social class. Most were nobles, military officers, members of the clergy, or high-ranking government officials. It was the responsibility of the seigneur to bring settler-tenants, called *censitaires*, to the land, parcel out lots to them, and have them develop the land. Censitaires paid a range of fees to the seigneurs for the use of the land.

Maurice Poulin's son, Michel, not only inherited his father's seigneury but also became a judicial official in the service of the Crown. When Michel Poulin died, his sons, François Poulin de Francheville and Pierre Poulin, inherited the seigneury. Thus, almost from the beginning of the colony, the Poulin men were faithful servants of the Crown, exercising tremendous power and authority.

Further, the Poulin family was involved in the fur trade from a very early period. Francheville was also related, on his mother's side, to the renowned explorer and fur trader Pierre-Esprit Radisson. On both sides of his family, he was marked by the spirit of commerce and adventure.

Francheville was born and grew up in the right social milieu. His grandfather and his parents were among the powerful, influential, and privileged, and this social network would later serve to advance his career and standing. He grew up in Trois-Rivières but sometime in his early manhood moved to Montréal. This move may have been influenced by the fact that Montréal had become the hub of the western trade in the second decade of the eighteenth century. All the convoys leaving for the Upper Country set out from there, and the bulk of the furs also arrived in Montréal, so if Francheville wanted to have a chance of success in the trade, he had to be stationed in the city. Between 1710 and 1720, there was a steady migration of merchants, traders, and artisans from other parts of the colony to Montréal.

Francheville was likely already involved in the western trade while he was living in Trois-Rivières. His grandfather had laid the foundation for the family business in fur, and many others in Francheville's familial circle were involved.

Numerous notarial acts from 1722 to 1733 testify to Francheville's direct involvement in several facets of the trade. And from all indications, he was a successful fur merchant.

Francheville entered the trade at an auspicious moment. French, that is to say Canadian, trade with the western Great Lake Indians, after a lull caused by the Treaty of Utrecht in 1713, resumed in full swing by 1720. The treaty, which closed the War of Spanish Succession between England and France, curtailed France's right to trade directly with the western tribes and confirmed England's claim to Hudson Bay. This was a blow to France's trade and imperial ambitions in the far west and the country north of the Great Lakes. The French had seen the west and its vast resources as "belonging" to them, and the Natives as "their Indians." For at least seventy years, the French had traded with the western Natives, established alliances with them, and counted on their cooperation to help the west remain "French" by cold-shouldering the English. From France's point of view, perhaps the most insidious result of the Treaty of Utrecht in regard to North America was that it empowered the English to elbow their way into areas previously dominated by the French, to take over the Natives, and to push France out of the fur trade.

The cutting off of France from Hudson Bay and the western Great Lakes meant there was a shortage of fur on the Parisian/French market, and concomitantly, a rising demand there for it. Given the ramifications of Utrecht, the colonists in New France were unable to meet that demand. They therefore sought to change the status quo. Backed by the colonial and imperial governments, the colonists, at least the merchant sector, decided to challenge the treaty. Canada had, during this period, two imperial-minded governors who ignored some of the treaty clauses and pressed France's claim in the far west. Phillipe de Rigaud de Vaudreuil ended his governorship in 1725, and the following year, the Marquis de

Beauharnois arrived as governor. These two men laid the basis for France's reclamation of the west, using both aggressive and diplomatic means to re-establish French influence among the western tribes.

The governments in Québec and Versailles accepted the loss of Hudson Bay but were determined not to give up the west. The key to gaining back their ground was to revive trade and re-establish alliances with the First Nations in the area west of Lake Michigan, in the Upper Mississippi River Valley, and west and north of Lake Superior. The "country of the Sioux" on the Upper Mississippi (Wisconsin/Minnesota) was a particularly attractive prize. Why the attraction to the Sioux (Dakota) country? The colonial government (and it persuaded the imperial government to accept the idea) felt that France's imperial expansion in the west lay in acquiring the fur-wealthy Sioux region and the lands beyond. Thus, by 1716, the government began a campaign of building and rebuilding trading posts and forts in the Great Lakes region. Posts in the eastern lakes were strengthened, and several were garrisoned. But the hub of activity was in the western lakes. Garrisoned posts rose up in the region of Lake Michigan and Lake Superior, in the Green Bay area and the Upper Mississippi in particular. The post at Michilimackinac was regarrisoned, and overtures were made to the neighbouring Natives to regain their loyalty. These posts were established with three main objectives in mind: to use them as bases for future exploration, to shut off the Natives' routes to Hudson Bay (the French did not want them to take furs to the English), and to protect routes to the Sioux country. To stimulate trade, Vaudreuil began issuing *congés*, or trading permits, to the Montréal merchants.

These aggressive moves from the French brought many western nations, such as the Illinois, Fox, Chactas, Sioux, and Cree, into the trade. The Ojibway, a "friend" of the Sioux, already had a long history of trade with the French. Beauharnois, when he became governor, continued Vaudreuil's practice of issuing trading permits to Canadian merchants. He also authorized the selling of liquor to the Natives. The king had prohibited this controversial practice because of the disastrous effect alcohol had on Native people, but Canadian merchants continued to sell liquor to them. The merchants argued that, if they did not sell alcohol to their trading partners, they would lose the trade to the English, because the English had no qualms about selling rum to the Natives. The merchants noted that many Natives would not broker trade deals unless liquor was part of the goods. Beauharnois, wanting to win the west, acquiesced to the merchants' demands.

Thanks to the strategies pursued by Vaudreuil and Beauharnois, the trade recovered. By 1717, the French had regained the loyalty of many First Nations, with the result that numerous pelts poured into Montréal. Two years later, the Compagnie des Indes Occidentales (Company of the West Indies) was formed and given a monopoly in the export of furs to France and Europe.

When Beauharnois took the reins of colonial administration in 1726, he continued Vaudreuil's strategies of expansionism through diplomacy. But he also took war to the western tribes when he felt they stood in the way of France's ambitions. In 1728 and 1730, when the Fox, middlemen in the fur trade from their home in Green Bay, tried to protect their role by attempting to restrain France's march into the

Sioux country, Beauharnois sought their extermination. He was nearly successful. In 1730, Beauharnois sent a force of 1,400 men against the Fox. They killed several hundred. Defeated, the Fox begged for mercy. Beauharnois responded by rounding up most of the survivors and selling them into slavery in the West Indies. Several tribes, even former enemies of the Fox, took pity on them and offered refuge to the few survivors who had escaped death and slavery. Even those tribes who were friendly to the French took a lesson from the Fox's demise: if they did not dance to the tune of the French, they too could be crushed. That is the lesser-told story of the French (and English) campaigns in the west.

In spite of the losses sustained with the Treaty of Utrecht and rising English opportunism, the policies pursued by determined French governors enabled the French in North America to continue their dominance in the fur trade. Manpower, business acumen, capital, and initiative were all needed in this age of expansion.

Francheville was in the right place at the right time. By 1720, the fur trade, of which Montréal was the unchallenged centre, was growing by leaps and bounds. And he was there to help nurture it and ensure its ascendancy. He sent out supply convoys to various garrisoned posts and acted in conjunction with their commandants to supply his voyageurs with fur on their return trip to Montréal. For example, in 1722, as recorded in one of the earliest notarial acts about Francheville's involvement in the trade, he hired Jean Pomainville to take foodstuff and trade goods to Sieur Beaujeu, commandant of the post at Michilimackinac. On his return trip, Pomainville brought furs to Montréal. In the summer of 1724, Francheville hired four voyageurs—Pierre

Voyne, Jacques Chapu, Pierre Baron, and Joseph Dubois—
and sent them to Sieur Lignery, another commandant at
Michilimackinac.

Michilimackinac was the largest and most important post
in the Upper Lakes. It also had a religious mission, and a
Native settlement grew rapidly around it. The post was garrisoned, and it supervised the fur trade in the Upper Lakes.
Given its strategic location and importance, it was a popular
destination for voyageurs from Montreal.

A fort and trading post at Detroit supervised trade with the
surrounding region. Francheville also sent convoys to
Detroit. In 1729, for example, he went into partnership with
one Madame Deschaillons and sent a five-man canoe to the
post there.

Throughout the 1720s, Francheville sent annual convoys to
the forts of the Upper Lakes, especially those at
Michilimackinac and Detroit, supplying them with goods
and getting furs in return. Francheville must have had a close
relationship with commandants Lignery and Beaujeu at
Michilimackinac, because he was one of the main suppliers
of goods to that post. The most important fur was that of the
beaver, but there was also a market for the pelts of the
"moose, deer, bear and mink."[1]

By 1725, a typical fur brigade to the hinterland consisted of
several canoes, each holding four to five men, and carried
blankets, clothing, mirrors, beads, guns, gunpowder, scissors,
pins, needles, kitchen utensils, pots, kettles, and tobacco.
Alcohol, especially brandy, became an indispensable trade
item. Though merchants like Francheville sent out goods to
be exchanged with the Native people for fur, they also supplied the forts and trading posts with needed cargo.

Garrisoned posts and missions had soldiers and priests who had to be fed and maintained. Every convoy leaving Montréal carried foodstuffs, including sugar, coffee, tea, wines, flour, beans, and peas, and kitchen and work tools for the White workers at the posts and missions. Without support from Montréal, these posts and missions would not have been able to maintain themselves, and the claims of the French in the region would have been meaningless.

Different segments of colonial society were drawn into the trade and made it their life's business. The trade was the pivot upon which most other affairs, especially politics, religion, and war, spun. Politicians and priests, Natives and French, merchants and voyageurs, soldiers and kings, architects and engineers all had careers made, enhanced, or unmade by the fur trade. It is therefore no exaggeration when scholars call the fur trade "the lifeblood of the colony."

Francheville was firmly ensconced at the centre of the fur business. He had many contacts and advantages. Given his relations and alliances, he was also able to engage in the business of exploration and further Canada's and France's imperial ambitions in the west. The Sioux country was a chief target. In 1727, the governor general, the Marquis de Beauharnois, himself involved in the fur trade, formed a company in Montréal. Named the First Sioux Trading Company, it had among its founders some of the colony's most influential men, such as Longueuil, Youville, Campeau, and Boucher de Montbrun. The company was to be a trading initiative meant to open up trade with the Sioux by building a fort among them. A number of men, including Francheville, were hired for the *poste des Sioux*. In the party were also soldiers and two Jesuit priests. The company had received a three-year trade monopoly with the Sioux. They arrived on the west shore of Lake Pepin (on the Upper Mississippi) on September 4 and began the construction of Fort Beauharnois. The expedition built an enclosure and three buildings. A chapel named St. Michael the Archangel was also constructed. Fort Beauharnois was a trading post, a garrison, and a missionary post all in one.

It was the building of this fort, and moves by the French to take over the Sioux fur trade, that so angered the Fox, who themselves had a big part in the trade. Less than a year after the completion of Fort Beauharnois, hostilities broke out between the Fox and the French that led to the near extermination of the former. As with most trading sites in North America and the rest of the colonial world, Fort Beauharnois encapsulated the ideology of Europeans on the frontier: commerce, Christianity, and civilization. The third part of this trinity almost always included war.

Francheville, then, should not be seen as a naive merchant from Montréal; rather, he was very conscious of the fact that he could further his own ambitions by supporting imperialistic objectives. He was sent to the post not as a common voyageur but as a trade agent. His role was to help in the supervision of the trade with the Natives and to scout out other fur resources. That he was hired by the governor general of the colony of Canada for such an important mission illustrates that he was well connected to the trading and bureaucratic elite. Francheville's ties to the extreme western trade and to one of the richest fur-bearing areas secured his position as one of the most important merchants in Montréal and the colony.

By 1731, there was a Second Sioux Company. And in this

venture, Francheville was the one doing the hiring. In July 1731, he hired Augustin Mouet de Langlade for a "voyage to the country of the Sioux." Langlade was Francheville's cousin on his mother's side and was also related to Pierre-Esprit Radisson. It appears that Francheville did not go on this second voyage, because by this date he was immersed in mining activities at the Saint-Maurice forges. Though Francheville was involved in the fur trade in all areas along the Great Lakes, the trade relations on the extreme western portion was his newest and potentially his most profitable venture.

Sieur Francheville was also a farmer and seigneur. He had a farm at Saint-Michel, on the outskirts of Montréal. The farm had over fifteen acres under cultivation, in which he grew wheat, hay, flax, and vegetables. He also kept a variety of farm animals. Much of the wheat he grew was sent directly into the fur trade. The seigneury at Saint-Maurice was another focus of Francheville's energy. Being seigneur, he was embedded in a web of social and economic relationships with the censitaires on his land. Like all seigneurs, he supervised the concessions already granted and parcelled fresh plots to new censitaires. Though the censitaires owned the hectares of land they worked, they still had to pay an annual fee to Francheville. They were obliged to give bushels of wheat to the seigneur and to pay fees for milling rights, since only the seigneurs could own mills. If the censitaires sold their land, they had to pay a sales tax.

Seigneuries were usually wealthy in natural resources, and the one at Saint-Maurice was no exception. The Saint-Maurice River, teeming with all kinds of fish, flowed south through the land into the St. Lawrence and was deep enough to carry barges. Timber abounded, and well into the nineteenth century barges sailed down the river carrying their burden of timber. Yet the censitaires could not use the resources of the seigneury. According to the laws that governed the operation of seigneuries, the wealth of a seigneury was reserved for those who owned it. Thus, only Francheville, his brother, Pierre, their families, or their representatives could exploit the resources of wood, fish, game, and minerals.

In the village that grew within a seigneury, the seigneur was the local lord and, with the local priest, exercised power and authority. The seigneur owned a manor house and was given the title "sieur." As seigneur, he sometimes acted as the local judge, settling disputes among his habitants and dispensing justice. There is no indication that Francheville ever became a judge on his seigneury. He may have left the day-to-day running of the seigneury to his brother, Pierre, who lived in the area and was a notary and seigneurial judge. Like many seigneurs, Francheville was an absentee landlord who lived in Montréal and engaged in the fur trade.

Yet there was one activity in the Saint-Maurice seigneury that drew Francheville time and again to the region. Iron ore had been discovered there, and Francheville, ever the entrepreneur, wanted to develop this resource. Iron deposits had been known to exist in Trois-Rivières and neighbouring regions since the mid-seventeenth century. In 1663, Intendant Jean Talon wanted to exploit this resource, but Jean-Baptiste Colbert, the imperial minister responsible for the colonies, frowned on the idea and in effect killed it. Colbert, one of the strongest promoters of the mercantilist ideology, saw any kind of industrial development in the colonies as harming the mother country. From the mercantilist's point of view, the colony existed to supply the mother

country with natural resources; the mother country recipro-
cated by sending manufactured goods to her child, the
colony. The colony was not to compete in the area of industry and manufacturing with the mother country. In 1716, for
example, when it appeared that Versailles would look with
favour upon an appeal from Intendant Bégon to establish a
foundry in Canada, the new king, Louis XV (he was still a
minor), responded by stating that "there was enough iron in
France to supply all of New France." Successive intendants
wrote about this resource of iron deposits and sadly remarked
that it was going to waste. But the intendants were persistent.
Again, in 1727, Intendant Claude-Thomas Dupuy wrote to
France with a proposal for the development of ironworks in
Canada. As usual, his appeal fell on deaf years. Francheville
planned to change all that. The principal iron deposits were
located on his seigneury, and he knew that when the colonial administrators wrote to France about the iron resource,
they were talking about his land. Francheville must have rea-
soned that it was only a matter of time until Versailles would
look favourably upon the idea of an iron industry in Canada.

As she had with the fur trade, Lady Luck smiled on
Francheville. A confluence of factors worked in his favour in
getting the support he needed to mine the iron ore on his
seigneury. The three men who headed the colonial and imperial governments were of like mind: they wanted to diversify
the colonial economy. In 1723, Jean-Frédéric Phélypeaux,
Comte de Maurepas, became secretary of state for the colonies
(his title was minister of marine). The minister looked with
favour upon strengthening the colonial economy by promoting
development and allowing free enterprise, if only for the benefit of the mother country. The Marquis de Beauharnois

became governor general of Canada in 1726, and he too had enlightened views on colonial development. (Beauharnois was Maurepas's cousin; in fact, Maurepas had secured the Canadian appointment for him.) Gilles Hocquart, an intendant as energetic as Jean Talon, took the post in 1729, and he too supported colonial economic diversification. Hocquart saw in the Saint-Maurice iron deposits a way for that to happen.

Hocquart paved the way for Francheville. He wrote to Maurepas (Beauharnois also signed his name to the letter), informing him of the iron ore discovered at Saint-Maurice and urging him to give Francheville a twenty-year monopoly to exploit it. For any expensive colonial venture to be successful, it had to receive financial support from France. Fortunately for the Canadians, by the time Maurepas became minister, mercantilist ideology did not hold the powerful sway it once had under his predecessors. To sweeten the deal, Hocquart told Maurepas that the iron ore could be shipped to France and used in shipbuilding.[2] Urged on by Hocquart, in 1729, Francheville wrote to the minister to request a twenty-year monopoly to mine the iron deposits. Francheville's letter was attached to the one sent by Hocquart and Beauharnois.

> My Lord, The Count of Maurepas
>
> François Poulin de Francheville, merchant in Montreal, very humbly represents that he is the owner of the St. Maurice estate…which he owns, and which is rich in iron deposits, the exploitation of which would be a considerable advantage to the colony, where a large quantity of iron is consumed both for the building of sea ships as well as for other duties which are expensive, in case we had to, by necessity, import from France.

He offers to make the necessary advances for the exploitation of mines if it would please your Majesty to grant him the concession for twenty years of iron deposits which are found all over the country…and which includes the D'yamachiche estate up to and comprising the Cap de la Madeleine estate, at the following conditions.

That he could alone, with the exclusion of all other, open and exploit all iron deposits which are found throughout the country, as mentioned above, which would be the only one capable of producing iron from the exploitation of all mines, and produce all types of iron, and engage in commerce.

Your very humble and obedient servant,
Francheville[3]

Francheville offered to develop the iron works at his own expense, thus not burdening the king with financial costs. How could the Crown refuse his offer? In a letter dated April 4, 1730, the minister wrote back, giving Francheville the twenty-year monopoly to exploit the iron resources in the Trois-Rivières area.[4]

In April 1731, Francheville recruited through his factor in the city of La Rochelle two professional miners. The men were thirty-two-year-old François Trébuchet and twenty-two-year-old Jean Godard. Maurepas gave permission for these men to leave France. He paid their passage and sent with them two pieces of mining equipment. The men arrived at the Québec port on the ship *Les Héros* and from there travelled on to the site of the forges at Saint-Maurice, where they signed a four-year contract with Francheville.[5] In another missive to Maurepas, Francheville thanked him for paying the way of the two labourers and told him that several buildings at the forge were near completion and that "the labourers have found that the mine is abundant, and produces very soft iron."[6]

Maurepas and Hocquart, wanting to get the forges off to a good start, had one Sieur La Brèche, a master forger, sent over from France to oversee mining operations at Saint-Maurice. Even though La Brèche was already a master forger, Francheville immediately sent him to the English colonies "in order to examine all the iron forges established in the said land and...obtain all the knowledge necessary for the exploitation of the said Forges at St. Maurice."[7] For La Brèche, this meant learning the process of *direct reduction*, used by the foundries in the English colonies to the south.[8] In Europe, iron was made from iron ore through the process of *indirect reduction*. Francheville was modelling his forges on the American variant, so the French iron master needed to learn the American method. Francheville also sent along two other iron men, quite likely Trébuchet and Godard, with La Brèche.[9]

By this time (late October 1732), Francheville had spent over 10,000 livres on the project. It had been an individual investment, and he was finding it difficult to fork out the necessary expenses that such an enterprise demanded. Again urged on by Hocquart and Beauharnois—with both men paving the way with yet another letter to the minister, pleading Francheville's cause—Francheville wrote Maurepas and "humbly begged" for a loan of 10,000 livres, the exact amount he had spent on the enterprise so far. He informed the minister that he had sent men to the English colonies to learn English iron working, and that the quality of the Saint-Maurice iron ore was as good as that of Spain.[10]

Francheville, in the meantime, did not sit idly and wait for

Maurepas's response. He took action. In January 1733, he formed a company with his brother Pierre Poulin, fellow Montrealer and business associate Ignace Gamelin Jr., Louis-Frédéric Bricault de Valmur, and François-Étienne Cugnet. These men took out shares in the company and would help Francheville stand the cost of developing the forges.[11]

The members of Francheville's company were the *crème de la crème* of Canadian society. Cugnet was a member of the highest judicial body in the colony and was also director of the "king's domain" (royal resources of fish, fur, and timber). Valmur was secretary to the intendant, giving Francheville direct access to the Crown. Pierre Poulin was a notary and seigneur, while Gamelin was a leading Montréal merchant. Francheville and Company represented a collaboration between merchants and officers of the Crown. Though the Saint-Maurice ironworks got off to a very rocky start, it stood a chance of success because it had the backing of several powerful men.

In March 1733, Francheville hired another iron master, Christophe Janson *dit* Lapalme, a Montrealer. Lapalme was also a maker of edge tools and a mason. He was quickly packed off with La Brèche for another tour of "New England" mines.[12] Lapalme was hired for three years and was to provide his own tools. A month later, Francheville heard from Maurepas. The minister found favour with Francheville's request for a loan and told him that "the king granted him the loan of 10,000 livres."[13]

France, always at war with some foreign enemy, was in need of iron for several of its war industries. Maurepas decided that the Saint-Maurice forges would be valuable in providing iron for use in naval construction and in making military equipment such as guns, cannons, bullets, and the like. He would later support the construction of several warships at Québec. Maurepas also promoted the idea of intercolonial trade between Canada and the West Indies and saw the development of a Canadian iron industry as a way to achieve this. Moreover, having been told by both Francheville and Hocquart that the iron was "of a good quality, similar to the type found in Spain," Maurepas felt that, if the Saint-Maurice ironworks were developed, France would be less dependent on Spain and Sweden, two of its traditional iron suppliers. From the minister's point of view, the Saint-Maurice forges would aid the king in achieving glory for France.

The money for the loan came out of the colonial treasury and was given to Francheville at Québec in October 1733. The loan was interest-free and was to be repaid within three years. But getting the loan was not as easy as it seemed. Francheville had to mortgage his house in Montréal and all his movable and immovable goods in both Montréal and the forges at Saint-Maurice.[14] Enslaved people were counted as movable goods, so Francheville's slave Angélique was undoubtedly part of the mortgage.

The same month Francheville received the loan, he wrote to Maurepas, thanking him for the loan and giving him details about the evolution of the forges.

Monseigneur,

I have the honour to offer Your Highness my most humble thanks for the grace that His Highness has kindly accorded to me in consideration of the enterprise of the iron forges at St. Maurice. I have received from the Treasurer the sum of 10,000 livres that Your Highness has ordered to be remitted to me, I have given my receipt for the reimbursement following His orders.

All the buildings necessary for the exploitation of the forges are completed and the forges are ready to receive the ore. I have six hundred barrels of iron ore, of which two hundred have been delivered to the forge, and four hundred barrels of coal have also been delivered to the forge. I had hoped, Monseigneur, to send Your Highness the first piece of iron that would have been produced in said forges, but the continual rains that we have had for a month have increased greatly the amount of water in the mines, and this has caused the collapse of fourteen wall supports in the mills, and the work that had to be undertaken in order to rebuild the walls has delayed the casting by several days; but I anticipate to be able to commence the casting in eight days or a bit later. I have attached myself to this enterprise with so much more hope ever since we have recognized the excellence of the iron that this mine produces. It makes steel just after the first refining process; and we have manufactured from it some axes and knives which cut as well as the tools of this type....All makes me hope, Monseigneur, that the success [of the mine] will meet our expectations, and that Your Highness will have the satisfaction of having honoured with his protection an enterprise that is advantageous to the colony.

I am, with a very deep respect, Monsiegneur, the very humble and very obedient servant of Your Highness.

Francheville[15]

This letter makes plain how connected Francheville was to power and prestige. He had direct access to one of Louis XV's most powerful ministers! Francheville had requested and received from Maurepas a 10,000-livres loan for the development of his mine, at a time when the imperial government was miserly in its dealings with the colonies. The letter also shows the progress (or lack thereof) of the endeavour and the owner's zeal. That Francheville was enthusiastic, despite setbacks, about the forges and the role they could play in the development of the colony was clear. The letter reveals his ambition and presents him as an enterprising and forward-thinking bourgeois, one who knew how to network. Though not appearing overly obsequious, Francheville noted that he (and the mine) were under Maurepas's "protection." In a follow-up letter to Maurepas, Francheville observed that because of the loan "the success of this establishment will be certain."[16]

The forges at Saint-Maurice became a "company town." Francheville hired French and Canadian carpenters, masons, welders, forgers, and other skilled workers to get the forges underway. Specialized buildings, including a blast furnace, were constructed. As important, houses were built for the workers and their families, and land was cleared for food production. In the early stages, Francheville sent wheat to the forges for the workers' upkeep, but he also sent wheat seeds so the workers could grow their own food.[17] From the letters Francheville sent to Maurepas, and extant records of the forge, it appears that by October 1733, the forges had produced such utensils as "axes and knives."

Francheville was an entrepreneur who saw the value of the colony becoming self-sufficient in making its own iron goods. He also saw the potential profit. As a fur trader, he knew that goods made of iron, especially cooking utensils and farming implements, were the mainstay of the trade.

Francheville hoped to produce these items (such as the knives and axes he mentioned in his letter) at his forges and funnel them into the trade in beaver skins. In this way, he would personally connect the diverse strands of the trade, making himself rich in the process.

Francheville died in November 1733, just as the mines were about to take off. He nonetheless left his mark on Canadian industrial history by establishing the iron industry. Because of his persistence, the Saint-Maurice ironworks became a reality that lasted until 1883. By 1741, under new management, the forges were producing an annual output of 400,000 pounds of iron. Though most of this was consumed by France, some was also exported to the West Indies and Acadia, and some was used by the St. Lawrence colony itself. The ironworks also fulfilled Francheville's dream of producing manufactured goods—items ranging from stoves to sewing needles—for the local and fur trade markets.[18]

Clearly, Francheville was a leader in society, a "mover and shaker," and a social climber. His social and economic status and milieu necessitated that he be a slaveholder—even though New France's economy was not dependent on slave labour. The main business was collecting furs, and a few hundred voyageurs and Native partners satisfied the demands of this low-labour activity. But the slaves in the colony formed an intrinsic part of the social and economic ladder. They were definitely a social "necessity," since they were visible proof of wealth and status. Yet New France's slave owners were not simply acquiring slaves to show off. Enslaved persons did not stand around in livery fanning their owners, nor were they high-priced retainers. They performed a variety of roles, from the back-breaking work of rowing goods-laden canoes upstream to meeting the unrelenting domestic demands of mistresses and masters. The tasks that slaves performed freed up their owners to engage in economic pursuits: their free labour subsidized the colonial economy, making them an economic as well as social necessity.[19]

It has already been mentioned that, though almost everyone in colonial society owned slaves, merchants as a group owned the most. By 1731, Francheville, whether driven by social necessity or not, had three slaves in his household in Montréal. Two were Panis, and one, Marie-Joseph Angélique, was Black. It was not difficult to acquire Panis slaves, since the various inter-tribal and European-Native wars on the frontier had reduced many Aboriginal people to slavery. One wonders if Francheville's two Native slaves were survivors of the Fox-French wars.

We have a portrait of Francheville as a businessman and entrepreneur, but what kind of a slave master was he? Except for Angélique's baptismal paper, no record showing Francheville as a slave master has come to light. Documentation indicating his purchase of Angélique may have been lost in the fire. Naturally, Sieur Francheville accepted the hierarchical society in which he lived—a settler society ordered according to rank, status, gender, and race. Patriarchy sanctioned by Church and state was a prevailing ideology. We know he performed masterly duties such as baptizing his slaves and renaming them, but did he also avail himself of some of the privileges that White male slaveholders felt they had over the bodies of the Black women in their charge? Did he sexually assault Angélique? Was she his concubine? It was immediately after Francheville's death that the slave woman began "acting up" and asking for her freedom. In Angélique's trial documents she notes that since the death of

Francheville her mistress had stopped mistreating her. We may wonder if the cessation occurred because the source of conflict between servant and mistress was removed from the house.

It is unlikely that Francheville questioned the social order and conventions. Men had authority over women and children, masters had authority over their slaves, and Whites ruled Blacks. He went through what must have been a tremendous effort to acquire Angélique all the way from the English colonies. And though he was to be disappointed, he may have hoped to increase his slave stock through Angélique's fertility. Francheville revealed two traits as a slaveholder: determination and conscientiousness. He was determined to get slaves, even if that meant going beyond the borders of New France, and he carried out his legal and religious duties by baptizing his slaves.

If Francheville is shadowy as a slaveholder, can we discover more about him as a husband? When he married Thérèse de Couagne in December 1718, the charmed circle in which he had been moving expanded. His wife came from a wealthy and influential Montréal mercantile family with connections to the military, the Church, and the judiciary. Charles de Couagne, Thérèse's father, was one of the wealthiest Montréal merchants. He was a large outfitter in the fur trade, loaned money to other merchants, had business accounts with French merchants, and invested heavily in real estate. At his death in 1706, his gross assets were worth 224,058 livres. Once widowed, Thérèse's mother, Marie Gaudé, married a military officer, Pierre Derivon de Budemon. This military marriage paved the way for her sons, by her late husband, to pursue careers in the army.

The marriage contract of Francheville and Thérèse was

signed in the presence of members of the Montréal elite on November 26, 1718.[20] Among the witnesses was Claude de Ramezay, the governor of Montréal; this gives an indication of the social standing of the couple. The marriage was celebrated a day later at the church of Notre-Dame. Given Francheville'a background, it is clear that the marriage was mutually beneficial.

Less than a year after the marriage, Madame Francheville gave birth to a daughter, who was named Marie-Angélique.[21] But the child lived only a few months, and after her death no more children were born to the couple. No doubt the Franchevilles mourned the loss of their infant daughter. Colonists at all levels and ranks equated children with wealth, and children in eighteenth-century Canada were a vital part of any household. If they were from humble origins, they helped around the house and the farm. As they grew, their parents sometimes sent them out to learn a trade by apprenticing them to a master. Children of wealthier parents went to school, were tutored in their homes, or were sent to France for an education. Upper-class girls in Montréal and Québec often went to convent schools, where they learned academic subjects and "refinements." Such girls were destined for marriage to important men. Likewise, elite boys were taught by clerics, and many entered the army as officers or went on to hold civil and bureaucratic positions. Children were greatly desired in a colony with a shortage of colonizers. Yet in eighteenth-century Canada, child mortality was high. One in four children died before reaching their first birthday.

Two years after the marriage, Francheville bought a piece of property on rue Saint-Paul in the lower portion of the town. The property was situated between rue Saint-Joseph and rue Saint-Amable. Rue Saint-Paul was one of the two principal thoroughfares of the town and was at the heart of the merchants' district. The property, on the south side of the street, backed onto the St. Lawrence River. Francheville and his wife hired a Paris-born stonemason to build a stone house on their land. Immediate neighbours were François de Béréy and his wife, Jeanne, Étienne Radisson, Joseph Guyon, Jean-Baptiste Tétreau, Marguerite César, René Chorel de Saint-Romain, and François-Lucien Gatien. Sieur de Béréy was a military officer; Étienne Radisson was a colonel in the local militia, a small trader, and a storekeeper; and Joseph Guyon was a butcher.

The Francheville home was typical of most houses in the merchant district. It was two storeys high, with a kitchen, pantry, parlour, hearth, and storeroom on the ground floor. Upstairs were the bedrooms and the attic. There was also a basement typically used as a store or shop. Like most merchants, Francheville conducted his business from home. In the storeroom he kept his furs and trade goods. The house would have been full of activity, with voyageurs coming and going, Francheville meeting with his business associates and writing letters to persons in high and low society, and Madame Francheville supervising the household and organizing dinners for her husband's colleagues and friends.

The *donation mutuelle*, or gift, Thérèse and François gave to each other in 1727 offers a picture of their relationship. On February 24 of that year, several notaries, including Michel Lepailleur and Charles Gervaise, drew up a contract for the spouses that specified in certain terms the gift they gave to each other in the event of the death of one.

Before the royal notary of the island of Montréal...François
Poulin, sieur de Francheville, merchant bourgeois of this
town, and demoiselle Thérèse de Couagne, his spouse,
whom he authorizes for the effect of the present contract,
both of whom being in perfect health...and considering
that they have no children born of their marriage...and
that they are capable of giving each other some indication
of the reciprocal affection that they have for one another
by leaving the surviving spouse the means to live more
comfortably for the remainder of his/her days, and that
they have voluntarily stated and by this present contract
state their wish to have a mutual and reciprocal donation
between the two of them, and [by consequence] to the
surviving spouse, wilfully accepting all and every part of
the moveable possessions, and possessions acquired during
the marriage, and immovable possessions that will be
found in the possession of the one who expires first, on the
day of his/her departure, in whatever localities and places
that the said possessions will be found.[22]

The *donation* provided for the material well-being and
security of the surviving spouse. However, the Franchevilles
drew up a clause that if children should be born the existing
contract would be annulled, as according to law the bulk of
the estate would go to children born to the couple. The document for the *donation* read like a will, giving each spouse
rights of ownership to the goods obtained during the marriage. The *donation* also spelled out that whatever goods,
property, and possessions each party brought to the marriage
(for example, a dowry) belonged to the party that brought
these goods.[23]

In the document drawn up by the notaries, the couple expressed their "reciprocal affection" and their desire for the surviving spouse "to live more comfortably for the remainder of his/her days." Though the *donation* was a standard practice that bourgeois and elite couples engaged in, the act nonetheless indicates that Francheville and his wife cared enough about each other to ensure that the surviving spouse would be taken care of upon the demise of the other. New France was a patriarchal society, and though Francheville stood to benefit from this mutual gift, its principal beneficiary was his wife. Many women in New France were left destitute on the death of their husbands because husbands often squandered a couple's assets.[24] The *donation* ensured that Madame Francheville would not be denied house and home if Francheville were to die before her.

This arrangement was made nine years after their marriage. No more children had been born to them after the death of Marie-Angélique, and the couple may have felt that they would remain childless. If there were not going to be any children, then the wise thing to do was to make each the heir of the other. They may also have felt that death could happen at any time. And indeed it could, given the vagaries of life in the eighteenth-century Atlantic world.

There was probably yet another reason to create the *donation*. In June of the same year, Francheville set out on an expedition to the country of the Sioux. Everyone knew that many dangers could befall the White French traveller who journeyed west. He could drown in any one of the numerous rivers and lakes of the western country, succumb to disease, be killed by a Native, be captured and killed by the English, or be overtaken by a frigid and deadly winter.

Francheville was likely the one to suggest the *donation* because he was planning a journey of over six hundred miles and would not have been sure he would return to his wife alive. And he had good reason to fear. Eleven of the men who were part of the western expedition left Fort Beauharnois in the spring of 1728 to return east. However, they were taken prisoner by the Fox and did not make it home until 1730. (It is not possible that Francheville was part of this group: he was home by 1729, writing to Maurepas about the iron deposits on his seigneury.)

On November 28, 1733, within six years of signing the *donation*, Francheville became ill and died. Records show that he got sick in October on a journey to Québec. His health did not improve upon his arrival in the capital. He later returned to Montréal, where he died.[25] No indication is given as to the cause of his death, but smallpox could have been the culprit, because in that year the deadly disease ravaged Montréal and the colony. An entry in the Notre-Dame parish records indicates that two Sulpician priests, Jean Bouffandeau and Jean-Jacques Talbot, officiated at Francheville's funeral on November 30. He was buried in the Saint-Amable Chapel in Notre-Dame. Francheville was only forty-one when he died, in his prime and at the peak of his career as a businessman. Given Francheville's work and his role as an entrepreneur, his death has been seen by some as a loss to the fledgling colony.

His death also caused serious repercussions in the household. Thérèse was now a widow. Francheville left her his material possessions: the house on rue Saint-Paul, his shares in the Saint-Maurice ironworks, the seigneury, "and a small annual income derived from his having contributed these lands as capital asset." Francheville was gone, but he left his wife comfortable and cared for, at least financially. Because Thérèse de Couagne was her husband's heir, she came into full possession of the slaves in the household.

Even before her husband's death, Madame Francheville was quite involved in his business dealings. She helped her husband hire and pay his voyageurs, and she arranged business deals with her numerous relatives and friends. It also appears that she spent more time than her husband at the farm in Saint-Michel. Here, Madame Francheville supervised the workers, inspected the crops and farm animals, and ensured that business was carried on smoothly, since much of the produce of the farm was funnelled into the fur trade. Like her husband, she was enterprising and energetic.

When her husband died, she took control of his business and emerged as the redoubtable Canadian widow of popular imagination. She took his place on the board of the mining company he had formed and less than one month after his death drew up a loan contract with the objective of paying off her husband's debt to the Crown. This shows that Thérèse was not ignorant of her husband's affairs, but a knowledgeable partner.

> Before the royal notaries in the jurisdiction of Montréal, residing there the undersigned, demoiselle Thérèse de Couagne, widow of the late sieur Francheville...of her own free will accepts responsibility to the King to pay 10,000 livres which was advanced from the coffers of His Majesty to the said late sieur, her husband.[26]

However, the state looked favourably on Madame Francheville and discharged her of the 10,000-livres debt in

October 1735.[27] The determined widow continued her husband's practice of lending money to merchants involved in the fur trade, and ran her household in Montréal. She even acquired more slaves. By 1741—long after the fire and Angélique's execution—Madame Francheville owned seven slaves. Perhaps she had expanded her farm production and needed more labour, or perhaps she needed more hands to handle the pelts brought to Montréal.

Thérèse de Couagne de Francheville did not remarry. That seemes to have been her choice. She was a wealthy widow, came from the elite classes, and no doubt had eligible men interested in her. She was thirty-six when her husband died and was still of child-bearing age. But as a wealthy widow and a bourgeois, she exercised power and may not have wanted a man to limit her horizons.

Widow Francheville was also very religious and could have decided to "dedicate herself to God" by joining a convent. But she continued living at the house on rue Saint-Paul, rebuilding it after the 1734 fire. The will she dictated to notary Pierre Panet the day before her death speaks to her comfortable material position and the life she carved for herself following the death of her husband.

On February 25, 1764, Madame Francheville lay ill and dying in the women's wing of Hôtel-Dieu. She knew her time was drawing near. At 9:00 in the morning, she was surrounded by Pierre Panet, the priest Henry de Vallières, and one Sieur Joseph Sarquint. She dictated her will to Panet. Noting that she was "healthy in mind, and memory," she named her testator (Charles Hery, a Montréal merchant) and, as was customary, advised that her debts be paid upon her demise. She then put her soul in order with her God:

...as a good Christian member of the Roman Catholic and Apostolic Church, she commends her soul to God...supplicating him through the infinite merit of the Passion of Jesus Christ his son to have mercy on her and to place her among the Blessed, for this effect calling the intercession of the Most Blessed Virgin Mary and all the saints of Paradise, particularly Saint Theresa, her patron saint.[28]

Her next wish was that she be buried in the parish church, Notre-Dame, beside her husband in the chapel, and that "three hundred low requiem masses, be celebrated as soon as possible after her death." The three hundred masses were meant to speed her soul from purgatory to heaven.

The next section of the will indicates that Thérèse had rented her house to sieurs Landuiere and Sarquint (perhaps the same witness standing at her bed) for one year, the anniversary of their tenancy being June and July 1764. She had rented the house to the two men for 500 livres each. She noted that she had not yet received the yearly rent from either man, but that "she desires that the said tenants finish their tenure for the said year accepting her intention to leave it to them." That she had rented her house to tenants suggests that she may have been a patient at Hôtel-Dieu for most of 1763.

The will also gives an indication of Thérèse's involvement in business, especially that of advancing credit. She stated that one Dame Sonnusault had owed her 327 livres since 1757. Perhaps thinking that it was unlikely she would be repaid, she noted that if the dame was unable to pay she should be discharged of the loan. She also clarified a loan agreement between her late husband and one Sieur Charly, noting that a certain Madame La Noue should be the beneficiary of the 2,000-livres loan.

She dictated to Panet that her sister should be given 400 livres, and her niece Louise de Couagne (the wife of Sieur Baby) 300 livres. The dying woman then turned her attention to Hôtel-Dieu and the nuns who looked after her. To the hospital she gave her silverware, half her clothing, serviettes, bedsheets, and tablecloths, "in consideration of the good care that she has received from them." Thérèse expressed the hope that the nuns of Hôtel-Dieu would "not forget her in their prayers." To the destitute patients of the hospital, she gave her mattress and pillow. She gave part of her possessions (movable and immovable) to two young girls—the minor daughters of one Monsieur de Cargueville and the late Monsieur Godefroy.

Widow Francheville's will reveals her web of relationships, her business acumen, and her religiosity. She had no children, so her heirs were close relatives and close friends. The will also hints at the relationship between her and Hôtel-Dieu. One of her sisters, Anne de Couagne, had become a nun at the hospital-convent in 1725; thus, there was a direct tie between Madame Francheville and the hospital. Moreover, her husband had loaned money to the convent-hospital during its many times of need.

A day later, on February 26, the widow died at the hospital. She was buried beside her husband in Saint-Amable Chapel. Perhaps the nuns did say the three hundred requiem masses for her and her soul sped to heaven.

Thérèse de Couagne outlived her husband by some twenty-nine years. She lived to see the conquest of Canada by the British, dying less than four years after the French army surrendered to the British, and five months after the Treaty of Paris was signed, the treaty that confirmed France's defeat and England's triumph by ceding New France to England

and causing the name to be changed to the British province of Québec.

Madame Francheville, like many Canadian colonists, must have been shocked and heartbroken by the Conquest, and likely found it difficult to reconcile herself to the new order. Perhaps the fact of the Conquest weakened her system and made her vulnerable to illness. She was a devout Catholic, and the British rulers, all Protestants, were staunchly anti-Catholic. Thérèse lived under the British military regime for at least three years, but her business did not seem to suffer. When she died, she was still a wealthy widow.

There is no mention in her will of slaves. She did talk about her "moveable and immovable property." Since slaves were classified as movable possessions, if Widow Francheville owned any at the time of her death, she may have left them to her heirs. Though the world was turned upside down with the Conquest, she had no reason to fear that the new rulers would take away the slaves of the conquered French. The English (owners of the largest and most profitable slave empire in the world) were pro-slavery, and in this regard dealt favourably with the French. With the 47th article of capitulation, signed by the new English ruler, General Amherst, and the French governor, Vaudreuil de Cavagnial, England confirmed the right of the newly conquered people to continue to buy, hold, and sell slaves. For Blacks and Panis slaves, the new order did not change their status.

Affluent people owned Angélique. But did this make her life any easier? It appears not. At the end of her time with the Franchevilles, she was uncontrollable, angry, and vengeful. Her hatred of her mistress, at least, must have stemmed from mistreatment. The Franchevilles' wealth did not prevent tensions from building up between slave and mistress. This tension caused Angélique to desire to light the spark that would destroy much of the Franchevilles' world.

Thérèse de Couagne de Francheville died in 1764, thirty years after the disastrous fire that changed her life and sent Angélique to the gallows. As she lay dying in the women's wing at Hôtel-Dieu, did she think at least once about Angélique? Did she cast her mind to that day on June 21 when the rubbish cart took her slave woman to her death? For all her religiosity, Madame Francheville treated Angélique harshly. There was no love lost between her and her bondswoman.

V

Angélique's Montréal

MONTRÉAL WAS FOUNDED as a religious mission under the auspices of the French-based Société de Notre-Dame. In 1642, a small band of missionaries led by soldier-mystic Paul de Chomedey de Maisonneuve and nursing nun Jeanne Mance arrived in Montréal to found a City of God. The missionaries' goal was to bring the word of Christ to the Native people and convert them to Christianity. However, the missionaries soon found themselves administering to the needs of the small local French population because the Natives were more interested in trading with the Europeans than in acquiring their religion. By the time the Société de Notre-Dame became defunct in 1657, trade had come to overshadow the original purpose for which the settlement was established.

The piece of land on which Montréal was built and grew was an island. To the south lay the St. Lawrence River; to the north, the Rivière des Prairies; to the west, the Lake of the Two Mountains; and to the east, the confluence of the St. Lawrence and Rivière des Prairies. However, the settlement (first called

Ville Marie de Montréal and then simply Montréal) that was established did not occupy this entire island space but grew within an irregular rectangular block that was bordered to the west by today's rue McGill, to the north by rue Saint-Jacques, to the east by rue Berri, and to the south by the St. Lawrence River. The most southerly street was rue Saint-Paul and the land of the houses on the south side of that street backed onto the river. The two principal streets were Notre-Dame and Saint-Paul, and these were cut at right angles by several narrower streets, including rues Saint-Amable, Saint-Joseph, and Sainte-Anne. The town was small but had plenty of room outside its borders for expansion. Beyond the northern border was a hill (it was called a mountain) named Mont Royal, after which the city got its name. Around and beyond Mont Royal were several suburbs and farms. At least two roads led from the city to Mont Royal and beyond.

In 1721, the French Jesuit historian Pierre-François-Xavier de Charlevoix visited New France. In the writings he left behind, he provides a description of the physical layout of Montréal. He notes that the town was "a long square, situated on the bank of the river" and was divided into an "upper town" and a "lower town" without any clear line between each sector. The "Hôtel-Dieu, the king's storehouses, and the Place d'Armes are in the lower town, as well as almost all the merchants." In the upper town were to be found "the seminary and the parish church, the Récollets, the Jesuits, the Ladies of the Congregation, the Governor and the majority of high-ranking military personnel."[1] Charlevoix could have added that the prison, courthouse, and town hall were also in the upper town. The cemeteries—including the Native one—lay outside the immediate northern boundary of the upper town.

Well before Charlevoix's visit, a wooden wall surrounded Montréal. In 1716, the king sent engineer Gaspard-Joseph Chaussegros de Léry to Canada to oversee the defence of the colony. De Léry began a campaign of constructing forts, fortifications, and stone walls. One of the first projects to which de Léry turned his attention was the fortification of Montréal. A wooden palisade already surrounded the town, but it was not sturdy enough to provide the protection that the colonists desired and needed. Therefore, in 1717, de Léry began the stone fortifications along the street boundaries that framed the original city. A wall, thirteen feet high, would eventually encircle the town; five city gates, one opening onto the St. Lawrence, punctuated the wall and allowed communications with the town. Six or seven bell towers were part of the fortifications. The wall was completed in 1741.[2]

In 1725, when Angélique came to Montréal, the stone wall was not complete and parts of the wooden palisade remained. The fortifications, both wooden and stone, were constructed to protect the citizens and keep out enemies. In the late seventeenth century, when the wooden fence was built around the town, the enemies were the Iroquois of the Five Nations; by 1725, the French had come to a peace agreement with the Iroquois, and the enemies were and would continue to be the English, even though the French and English worked out a truce from 1713 to 1745.

The census of 1731 for Montréal (carried out by the Sulpician fathers) revealed that it had a population of 2,980 out of a total colonial population of 34,850. Soldiers were enumerated separately from the civilian population; there were about 200 soldiers quartered in barracks or living with the civilians. The servile class consisted of 142 slaves, both Panis and African, and domestic labourers formed about one-fifth of the town's population. There were 129 children under fifteen, and "913 adults, with females and males equally represented." There were about 380 houses, fifty-six percent of which were wooden and single-storied, the rest of which were stone. A quarter of all houses had two stories. The town witnessed a growth spurt in the first three decades of the eighteenth century. Many demobilized soldiers settled in Montréal, and craftsmen, traders, and labourers from Québec and Trois-Rivières migrated there.[3]

Angélique's Montréal contained several distinct classes based on a strict hierarchy, with each group conscious of its rank and status, or lack thereof. Comprising the first estate were royal officials, military personnel, and members of the clergy. Several of this group were nobles, French-born or ennobled in the colony. As time passed, the colonial aristocracy became more and more Canadianized. According to historian Marcel Trudel, in his book *Introduction to New France*, the Canadian noble had "really one privilege…that of carrying a sword and bearing the title of knight."[4] Trudel, of course, is exaggerating. Though the Canadian noble class had to work hard to earn a living because it was not independently wealthy, its members had other privileges than those described by Trudel. Most of the upper administrative positions were reserved for them; in addition, they received the bulk of the military commissions from which they earned an income. Moreover, most engaged in trade—the fur trade. Nobles received a fair share of the fur trading licences and, in their roles as military commandants in far-flung posts, controlled a good portion of the trade. In Canada, unlike in France, there was no stigma attached to trade for the aristocratic class.

Montréal was a fortified town with a permanent military garrison. Domiciled in the city were several regiments of soldiers and their commanding officers. By the end of the French period, there were upwards of three hundred men serving as officers in these regiments. These officers were usually aristocrats, and they and their families composed "the bulwark of [the] colonial aristocracy."[5] This subcaste was a tightly knit group connected by blood and group interest. Military officers maintained their position as an aristocratic elite by marrying into each other's families, and military command became hereditary as sons and nephews followed their male elders into the profession.

Members of the clergy comprised a separate arm of the elite. Montréal had begun as a religious mission, and by 1731 it had about one hundred nuns and forty clerics. There were five convents, and five chapels and churches.[6] Cloistered nuns ran the Hôtel-Dieu hospital, and lay nuns ran the Congregation of Notre-Dame schools. The Sulpicians also had a seminary. Many of the clerics were French-born and came from noble families. Nobles, whether soldiers, clerics, or officials of the Crown, dominated society and set the tone. As elites, they enjoyed a higher standard of living than the masses.

Nobles might have dominated society, but Montréal was "an island of merchants." The town was the centre of the fur trade, and merchants were indispensable to this venture. Truth be told, merchants were the single most important community in the town. The merchant class was clannish, connected by ties of blood and business. Merchants' daughters married merchants' sons; often, a member of the mercantile class married into the nobility. Further, important merchants like Francheville and his friend and neighbour Ignace Gamelin Jr. had close ties with the military aristocracy. Francheville, for example, partnered with at least two commandants serving at the posts in Detroit and Michilimackinac; from these men he received the furs he sold. Madame Francheville's stepfather was also a military officer. Gamelin underwrote the western exploratory and fur trade expeditions of Sieur de La Vérendrye, a military officer, who happened to be his wife's uncle. Links with the colonial elite served to extend the influence of the bourgeois class.

Merchants also engaged in the supply side of commerce. They provided the colonists with such diverse goods as dried fish and other maritime foods from Acadia, "rum and molasses and coffee from France's Caribbean colonies," and "luxurious textiles and clothes, jewellery, wines and spirits, even books and art from France."[7]

The mercantile community as a group was very self-conscious. Its members sought, through their ties of marriage, to influence policies that directly affected them. By 1717, the merchants of Montréal and Québec had established chambers of commerce to expand their commercial influence and widen their social and economic network.

Voyageurs were also part of the mercantile community. They were the men, employed by the merchants, who actually travelled to fur country and obtained fur from the Native people or military commandants. In Montréal, voyageur families were as important as merchant families in helping to make the town the centre of the fur trade. Some voyageurs, such as Alexis Lemoine *dit* Monière, made the transition to merchant and moved up the social ladder.

Artisans, small traders, and other service providers formed the third layer of society. Montréal was large enough to support a vital cadre of housebuilders, carpenters, locksmiths, masons, cabinetmakers, silversmiths, blacksmiths, bakers, butchers, tavern- and innkeepers, goldsmiths, dressmakers, tailors, coopers, weavers, and wigmakers. There was some fluidity among and between the lower classes. An artisan down on his luck or a young farmer tired of tilling the soil might sign up for seasonal work as a voyageur.

All three groups employed domestic workers. But domestics were by no means at the bottom of society. Below them were the enslaved people, Aboriginal and African, who were owned and used by the nobles, merchants, and artisans. Slaves were social outcasts whose *raison d'être* was to serve others.

In Angélique's Montréal, there might have been social distance, but this was mediated by physical closeness. The three groups—nobles, merchants, and artisans—and their servile workers lived in close proximity to each other. The "upper town"/"lower town" division described by Charlevoix was artificial. A narrow ridge demarcated these spaces, and in some spaces the division wasn't even present: upper town merged into lower town without an obvious border. The layout of the town, and its small size, meant that each social group jostled against each other. The denseness of the city would assist the rapid spread of the fire that Angélique was hanged for setting.

From a modern perspective, Montréal was a small place. However, this did not prevent it from being a hierarchical society, with each group conscious of its rank and standing. Rich merchants and nobles, in particular, sought to maintain their rights, privileges, and prejudices. The titles "sieur" and "madame" were reserved for members of the bourgeoisie, and a bourgeois man or woman considered it an insult not to be called by the proper title. Rich merchants and nobles, in particular, had the right to "drub" their social inferiors if the latter did not show them sufficient deference.

But Montrealers, at least the free ones, seemed bent on enjoying life. Historian Gustave Lanctot describes them as a people constantly on the go: visiting each other, playing games, having parties, and engaging in all kinds of frolic.[8]

During the fall season, when the fur brigades returned from the hinterland, the population increased by several hundred. The arrival of the brigades could be called the highlight of the year for the city. There was much celebration as voyageurs reunited with families they had not seen in months or even years. The merchants who employed the voyageurs, ever concerned about money, were thrilled that the furs had arrived safely. Tavern-keepers were also happy, as were the prostitutes whose incomes rocketed with arrival of the voyageurs and their fur-laden canoes.

But fall was also a time of work. Montréal buzzed with noise and activity as merchants gathered their furs, paid the voyageurs, and sold the furs (for a low price, they would argue) to the king's agents from the Compagnie des Indes Occidentales, who prepared the furs for shipment to Europe. For merchants like François Poulin de Francheville, this was a busy time. He and his wife constantly checked their account books, settled their accounts with voyageurs, received payments from other merchants to whom they had loaned money, and learned if they had made a profit from their investments. The return of the fur brigades also meant increased work for servants and slaves like Angélique, who would help to unload, sort, and pack the furs, run numerous errands, and prepare meals for the transient voyageurs.

In the winter, Montrealers went sleighing on the river, if it was frozen hard enough. They also sleighed in the streets, especially the young men. This group caused so much mischief and racket that one intendant, Jacques Raudot, issued an ordinance banning sleighing in the streets. Soldiers stationed in the town cavorted with servant girls (and sometimes with married women whose husbands were away), got drunk and disorderly, and at times beat up innocent bystanders.

Balls, parties, gambling sessions, and other kinds of "debauchery" were a part of life in this frontier town. Balls were the preserve of the nobility and the richest merchants. Bewigged and perfumed noblewomen and noblemen, imitating cosmopolitan fashion, dressed in their finest. Low-cut gowns for women were in vogue. (In the late seventeenth century and throughout the eighteenth, bishops preached sermons against women who showed "too much of their arms and bosoms.") Of course, the poor also had their fun. They too went sleighing and celebrated baptisms, marriages, and important Christian holidays. Montrealers also took part in carnival, or *Mardi gras*. Just before Lent, townspeople in costumes took to the streets and participated in the "farewell to the flesh." This was a time of revelry, dance, drunkenness, boisterousness, and feasting. Every sector of society, even the slaves, as Angélique's trial transcripts tell us, joined in this event.

But if Montrealers were a fun-loving bunch, contemporary evidence, as outlined in ordinances, suggests that theirs was a dirty and unhygienic city. The conditions of the streets were "shocking." Long walks posed a challenge because "the eyes and nose of the pedestrian [were] constantly assailed by the foul sights and smells; his feet and his clothing wet, dirty, and spattered by the mud and the melting snow and ice; in dry weather, choked by the clouds of dust; his personal safety endangered by the reckless drivers, who monopolized the roads, even mounting the pavement at times."[9]

Religion was an important part of life, and though the Crown sought to limit the power of the clergy whenever it could, the Church in Canada was a formidable institution. The clerics in Montréal kept a watchful eye on the towns-people, monitoring their ways and intervening if they saw them drifting from the straight and narrow. Never was the Church more watchful than in the case of witchcraft. Sorcery was a crime and sometimes carried the death penalty. Several colonists were dragged before the courts on charges of sorcery and were humiliatingly punished.

But religious groups also provided vital social and educational services. Religious sisters such as the Hospitalier nuns attended to patients at the Hôpital Général, a hospital for the poor, indigent, and mentally ill and for unwed mothers. In 1742, the hospital took on added responsibility by constructing a wing for the confinement of female criminal offenders. The nuns of Hôtel-Dieu administered to rich, poor, slave, and soldier. The sisters of the Congregation of Notre-Dame taught the girls of the wealthier classes. The Sulpicians, the Jesuits, and the Récollets attended to the souls and morals of the settlers; the Sulpicians also taught students in their seminary.

Significant changes occurred for Montréal during the period of the "long peace," the era from 1713, when the Treaty of Utrecht ended hostilities between Britain and

France, to 1745, when hostilities resumed. (Though Britain and France were at peace, France was still warring with many of the Native groups in the west. It was during the long peace, for example, that Governor Beauharnois launched his campaign of extermination against the Fox.)

In 1721, a fire devastated the settlement, and Intendant Bégon stepped in to regulate the construction of new buildings. The intendant passed an ordinance that called for the rebuilding of the town in stone, as opposed to wood, which was too flammable. The ordinance also required the street to be widened and straightened as a fire-prevention measure and to enable speedy communication. Bégon further embarked on a street-cleaning campaign designed to improve the sanitary conditions of the settlement. This was also an age of civic progress. A postal service was installed between Montréal and Québec in 1721, and by 1730 a highway was established between the two towns.[10]

In 1724, King Louis XV, through his colonial representatives, continued his attempts to regulate the fur trade and bring it firmly under royal control. He moved against the illegal trade with New England and New York. Canadian merchants visiting the English colonies, on returning to Montréal, had to give an account to the governor of the quality and the quantity of goods they brought back with them into New France. In the same year, the governor of Montréal, Claude de Ramezay, died and Charles Le Moyne, first Baron de Longueuil, succeeded him.

Throughout the 1720s, the royal government continually sought to regulate every aspect of trade in the colony. In 1727, the king sent out a special edict that "strangers, even naturalized citizens, cannot be merchants, brokers, or commercial agents under any form."[11] Not only was the Crown limiting the growth of the colonial economy by its protectionist policies, it was also limiting the development of the merchant class. The "strangers" who were targeted were English and Dutch traders from the colonies of New England and New York, or their factors. The Crown had good reason to believe that many of these men came to Montréal (and some became naturalized Frenchmen) solely to engage in smuggling activities with their Canadian counterparts.

The banning of foreigners in commerce also pertained to the overseas trade. Earlier, Louis XIV had banned Huguenots from entering the colony, but his successor gave them permission to trade with the colonies, so long as they did not settle there, bring their families, or marry. However, this was difficult to enforce, and by 1730 a significant portion of the overseas trade to Canada was done by Huguenots and their agents, operating from several French ports and the city of Québec.

Native people frequented the city mainly as traders. But there was also a resident Native population. Those who had been Christianized were attached to one of the religious bodies, but the non-Christian Natives maintained their independence and continued to adhere to some of their traditional ways. It affronted the White citizens of Montréal that many of these Natives went around almost naked.[12] Some French authorities were also concerned that alcohol "debauched" the Natives, and in 1725, the Crown banned the selling of alcohol in and outside Montréal. This ban, of course, was very difficult to enforce, given the important role liquor played in the fur trade.

In the early years the colony of Canada was run by several fur trading outfits, the most important being the Company of One Hundred Associates. The Company gained control of the colony in 1627 and ran it as its personal fiefdom. Though one of the Company's mandates was to bring in several hundred settlers a year, it saw Canada only as a huge fur trade business and was bent on making a profit. Therefore, it brought in few settlers and devoted few resources to the development of the colony. By 1663, when, wracked with internal dissent, the One Hundred Associates lost control of Canada, there were only about three thousand settlers in the entire colony.

The French Crown came to the rescue. Louis XIV took personal responsibility for the development of Canada and established a system of royal government. At the head of the government was the governor general, who was installed at Québec, the capital of the colony. He was responsible for all military and political matters, including defence and diplomacy. The governor general also served as the local governor of Québec. An intendant assisted the governor general in the running of the colony and took control of all domestic matters, including justice, finances, and public order. Local governors were installed in the two other major Canadian settlements—Trois-Rivières and Montréal. Religion was to be overseen by an archbishop sent over from France. The Conseil Souverain, ensconced in the capital, was the highest court in the land and functioned as the court of appeal. The Conseil consisted of the governor general, the intendant, the bishop, the attorney general, and eight councillors. The Conseil Souverain later evolved into the Conseil Supérieur, and the number of councillors increased to twelve. Below the high court were the lower courts installed in each of the three major settlements. Québec also had an admiralty court that oversaw all matters relating to the marine. Some seigneuries had their own courts, presided over by the local seigneurs. A judicial system modelled on the French legal code, namely the Coutume de Paris, was adopted in the royal courts.

Royal government meant that the colony would have a permanent system of defence. A militia system was organized, and a permanent army, composed of 1,400 men and their officers, arrived in the colony in 1665. The wars with the Five Nations and the British colonies to the south necessitated a permanent garrison in Montréal. The billeting of soldiers in the town meant an increase in the population and hardships for civilians, who had to assist in feeding the soldiers. By 1731, however, some soldiers were quartered in barracks.

As seats of royal government, the three major settlements in the St. Lawrence Valley provided employment for a number of civil servants and bureaucrats, including judges, notaries, clerks of the court, scribes, royal officials, military officers, police officers, tax collectors, and bailiffs. This corps of men and the activities they performed touched the lives of everyone, both high-born and low-born, free people and slaves.

The government of the colony was autocratic, and power and authority were invested in the king's representatives. The governor general and the intendant answered to the minister of marine (domiciled in France), who was also responsible for the marine and overseas colonies. The minister of marine answered to the king. And the king's authority was absolute and his decision final. There was no concept of democracy as we understand it today. The common people had little or no say in their own affairs. People could not meet in groups or call an assembly without the permission of the authorities. The poor bowed to the prevailing authority, and the habitants often took their grievances to the seigneurial courts within the boundaries of their seigneuries.

Though Montréal, like Trois-Rivieres and Québec, was a royal settlement, its history and evolution differentiated it from the other royal seats. Montréal was a seigneury. In 1657, the Company of One Hundred Associates, on the brink of collapse, gave up the administration of the colony. The Sulpicians who arrived at this date became the *curés* of the settlement, and soon acquired Montréal. The new seigneurs embarked on its development. They set up courts and constructed mills, new streets, bridges, and civic buildings. In addition, they brought over settlers and skilled workers from France, parcelled out land to new censitaires, and collected rents and other duties owed to them. They also built a seminary. When royal rule was established in 1663, the Sulpicians influenced the appointment of officials. In regard to the administration of justice, the clerics had control over issues pertaining to religion. They had an ecclesiastic court for delinquent clerics and laypersons who committed crimes against religion. They also disciplined their own workers. The Sulpicians were powerful seigneurs whose influence in Montréal could still be felt even after the British Conquest.

This, then, was the Montréal into which Angélique came. It was to be the scene of perhaps the greatest drama of her life. In this world, White subordinated Black, men had power over women, and those of high rank wielded authority over the less fortunate. Angélique was disadvantaged on all three counts of race, gender, and social status. She chafed under such oppression and had little respect for this world in which she found herself. Alienated from it, she would attempt to destroy it.

*

From somewhere in the Hudson Valley or the New England colonies, in the year 1725, Angélique arrived in Montréal. If she travelled by sea, she would have come up the coast to Acadia, then proceeded upriver on the St. Lawrence to Montréal. If she came by land, she likely travelled via the Lake Champlain/Richelieu Valley route. If she arrived in the spring, she would have witnessed the hustle and bustle of the departure of the fur expeditions. In the summer, she would have seen the marches of the soldiers as they did their daily drills. In the fall, she would have witnessed the intense activity surrounding the arrival of the canoes laden with beaver pelts. It is unlikely that she came in winter because long-distance travel during this season was severely restricted. Most of the rivers would have been frozen, and strong maritime gales made sea travel dangerous. If Angélique arrived in Montréal by land and entered through one of the land-bound gates, she would have had a lateral view of the city. Descending from a bateau on the St. Lawrence and coming through the port gate, she would have beheld Mont Royal rising behind the town, the steeples of the churches, and the visible three-storey building that was Hôtel-Dieu.

Angélique entered the Francheville household on rue Saint-Paul as a domestic slave. The number of servants a family could employ depended on its economic standing. And the Franchevilles were economically well placed. They used

Black, Native, and White domestic labour. Marie-Françoise Thomellete and Marie-Louise Poirier, two White women, worked as domestic labourers for the Franchevilles during the 1730s. There were also two adult male labourers, and, before 1734, one Panis slave, a boy named François, in the household. Angélique was the only Black worker.

As a domestic, Angélique engaged in an unrelenting round of tasks that included cooking, cleaning, serving, washing, and other household chores. These activities were time-consuming. Take food preparation, for example. The food had to be obtained, fires made and maintained, pots and cauldrons cleaned, and the food prepared and cooked. "Soups, stews, roasts, and bread were standard fare and were cooked mostly in open fireplaces."[13] In the fall, fruits and vegetables were harvested and some were preserved for the upcoming and long winter months.

Being a domestic slave did not mean that Angélique worked only within the household. She also did agricultural labour at the Franchevilles' farm in Saint-Michel, planting and attending to a variety of food crops and vegetables that included barley and wheat, carrots, onions, squash, and beans.

Letters by colonial officials and newspaper reports documenting the sale and flight of female slaves in colonial Canada confirm that Black enslaved women were exploited as both household workers and agricultural labourers. In 1763, General Murray wrote from Québec to a colleague in New York. He asked his friend to purchase for him two female slaves who can "wash and do the female offices about a farm."[14] The January 2, 1802, issue of the *Niagara Herald* advertised the slave of a slave "who is capable of service either in the house or out of doors." And in the same paper, two weeks later, one Widow Clement told prospective buyers that the slave couple she had for sale "have been bred to the work of the farm." When Peter Russell advertised the sale of his slave woman in the *York Gazette* on February 19, 1806, he described her as a "tolerable cook and washerwoman," who "understands making soaps and candles." Likewise, another York slaveowner explained to the readers of the December 20, 1800, issue of the *York Gazette* that the female slave he had for sale "understands cooking, laundrying and the care of poultry" and "can also dress ladies' hair." These accounts and numerous others reveal that enslaved Black women's work in early Canada ran the gamut from cooking to washing to looking after chickens, milking cows, tending crops, making soap, and fixing women's hair.

It used to be a common belief that domestic slaves had an "easier" time than slaves who laboured in the fields, especially in the plantation economies of the Caribbean, South America, and the American South. The reasoning goes like this: because house slaves lived within their master's house, they ate more and better food, were better clothed, and did lighter work than their field brethren. Also, it was believed that, since domestic slaves lived with Whites, they were readily acculturated to White norms and adjusted better than the field workers to their bondage. Such views have led some modern commentators to make the specious argument that, because this form of slavery was domestic and familial, the work household slaves did was "easy" and their bondage "mild."[15]

Yet, in several respects, enslaved domestics had a harder time. Unlike field slaves, they were under the constant gaze of their masters and could be routinely punished for the slightest infraction. Additionally, they were at the beck and call of the slaveholders and attended their every whim. On call twenty-four hours a day, domestic slaves were tired workers. Moreover, because domestics tended to be contained with the households of their masters, they had fewer opportunities to develop a sense of community, unlike field slaves, who laboured and lived with others of their kind, away from the constant surveillance of masters and overseers. Further, enslaved household workers, especially females, were vulnerable to predatory sexual assaults from the slaveholders; indeed, numerous enslaved Black women were raped by White owners and overseers.

Still, even as Angélique engaged in a routine of hard and constant toil, she had some free time. From her trial records we learn that Angélique often took walks along the banks of the river and in the meadows outside the city walls. She spoke with the soldiers, drank with neighbours, visited the sick in the hospital, engaged in frolic with the slave girl of a neighbour, and conducted at least two love affairs. These "perks" that Angélique enjoyed had to do with the nature of slaveholding in New France. Most of the enslaved people, especially the females, lived in close proximity to their owners. And though some members of the elite owned numerous slaves, most settlers owned only a few bondspeople and so "remained confident of their hegemony." In these conditions, slaveowners were willing to give their slaves "a certain degree of autonomy."[16] However, for Angélique, these free-time activities no doubt brought her bondage into sharp relief and failed to reconcile her to her servile condition. She yearned to break the bonds of her enslavement.

We have no physical description of Angélique. There is no mention of her height, weight, colour, or other vital statistics in the records. We know that she was an "esclave de la nation negresse." A Black slave woman. We also know that she was young, and that she was baptized on June 28, 1730, as required by the Code Noir.[17] Marie-Joseph Angélique was her baptismal name. Her godmother was Marie-Josephe de Couagne, sister of Thérèse Francheville and wife of Alexis Lemoine *dit* Monière; Sieur Francheville, her master, was her godfather. The officiating priest was the Sulpician Father Le Pape Du Lescöat.

Why did Angélique's owners baptize her? She came from Portugal, a Catholic country whose laws ensured that enslaved people were baptized upon entering its borders. Children born to enslaved persons were baptized as a matter of course. Angélique was Portuguese-born, so it's likely that she was baptized at birth. But perhaps not. I can think of three possibilities that could account for Angélique not being baptized in Portugal. The first is that she had a non-observant owner who allowed her to grow up as a "pagan." Not a few slave masters were lax in attending to their Christian duty with regard to their enslaved property. They were fined or pressured by the authorities to baptize their slaves. It was also not uncommon for neighbours to report a lax master to the authorities.

Another possibility is that Angélique was owned by or grew up in the household of a non-Christian, either a Muslim or Jew, but more likely a Jew. By 1705, the year of Angélique's birth, there were officially no Jews or Muslims in Portugal. Jews had been transformed into New Christians or expelled, and Muslims, likewise, had been removed or converted. But many Jewish New Christians still practised the old faith in secret, and some who owned slaves may have been deliberately lax masters who simply "forgot" to baptize their slaves in the Catholic faith. Moreover, if Angélique was owned by a New Christian or Jew who took her outside Portugal, perhaps to the Netherlands, where he had religious freedom, then there would not have been any incentive to baptize her in the Catholic faith.

A third possibility is that, before her arrival in New France, Angélique was owned by a Protestant—a Huguenot or member of the Dutch Reform Church. The very Catholic name she received upon baptism suggests that she was anything but a Catholic prior to her arrival in Montréal. The name Marie-Joseph Angélique, a popular female slave name, symbolized her transformation from non-Catholic unbeliever to Catholic believer.

Yet this ritual of enslavement occurred five years after she came to Montréal. Was she called Marie-Joseph Angélique in the five years before the baptismal ceremony? Or did Sieur Francheville carry out the ritual simply to adhere to the Code Noir? The long interval between Angélique's arrival in Montréal and the date of her baptism indicates that owners baptized their slaves not always out of Christian conviction but more often than not for pragmatic reasons. Frequently, it was an impending death that motivated slaveowners to baptize their slaves.

Another reason for the long delay might be that Angélique herself resisted baptism. Trial records indicate that the bondswoman was no wilting flower; she constantly challenged her mistress and spoke back to her. Could it be that Angélique at first refused baptism? Did she later consent only because she thought that she could gain some benefit from it? Angélique may have felt that if she accepted Catholic baptism there was a chance she might attain her freedom. Her owners may have been the ones to dangle this carrot. Conversion to Christianity or Catholicism in some colonies was occasionally used as a prerequisite for manumission. Indeed, some slaveholders deliberately prevented their enslaved property from becoming Christianized because they felt, based on Middle Ages jurisprudence, that they had to free slaves who embraced Christianity.[18]

Obviously the slave woman's name was not Marie-Joseph Angélique when she came to Montréal. She might have had an English name (having come from the English colonies) or a Portuguese name (having been born in Portugal) or even a French or Flemish name (having been previously owned by a man from Flanders). She might also at some point have had an African name.

The ritual of baptism clearly illustrated the power Francheville as master had over his slave woman. As her owner, he determined how her lineage would be formed and expressed. He decided what his slave's name would be and whether she would have a surname. Whatever lineage Angélique was connected to in Portugal, New England/New York, or Flanders was cut when he renamed her. And that was the intent of the ritual: to detach her from "any other time, place, culture, or family she had known."[19] The renaming aspect of baptism symbolized and reinforced Angélique's status as chattel. Francheville could deal with her thus because as a slave woman she was "natally alienated," that is, without a legitimate heritage; as chattel she was a social non-entity.[20]

Baptism also served an integrative function: through this

act, it was hoped that the slave would be assimilated within the household, society, and the Christian community. But slaveholders also hoped it would make enslavement more bearable for their slaves, producing servile workers who were less "hostile" and "uncivilized," and more "cooperative" and "docile." Whatever the motives of Angélique and her owners for engaging in baptism, the act did not seem to make the bondswoman a "better" slave.

Angélique became a mother in January 1731. This means that when she was baptized she was already two months' pregnant, which could be why she was baptized. She gave birth to a son, who was named Eustache.[21] She named Jacques César, a fellow slave, as the father. The population of Black slaves in Montréal was small, and the enslaved people were united by bonds of servitude, race, and origin. Angélique and César were around the same age and thus had much in common.

Sieur Francheville may have forced Angélique to be intimate with César. It was common enough for slave owners in all parts of the Americas—particularly the American South and the Caribbean—to engage in the "breeding" of their slaves to increase their slave population. But Angélique and César might simply have been attracted to each other.

Jacques César came from Madagascar, an island in the Indian Ocean, off the coast of East Africa. Slave hunting was as much a fact of life in East Africa as it was in West Africa. César, to get to New France, had to cross two oceans, on a journey that took twice as long as that from the Atlantic coast of Africa. Yet many Madagascan captives, from the young boy Olivier Le Jeune to César, eventually found themselves in bondage in New France.

César's owner, Ignace Gamelin Jr., was a leading Montréal merchant and a close friend, neighbour, and business associate of the Franchevilles. When Francheville set up the Saint-Maurice ironworks, Gamelin sat on the board of directors. Gamelin and Francheville also partnered in importing goods from Acadia, the West Indies, and France. An enterprising bourgeois, Gamelin built several ships for use in his commercial ventures. He used Jacques César as his coachman, body servant, and man Friday. It is likely that Angélique's affair with César was encouraged by their owners, given the close relations between them. The affair bore fruit, and Eustache was born.

Eustache lived for only one month. There is no reason listed for his death.[22] But Angélique was fertile. In May 1732, she gave birth again—this time to twins. At their baptism they were named Louis and Marie-Françoise. Louis lived for only two days; the girl lived until October.[23] If Francheville had bought Angélique with the intention of increasing his stock of slaves, he must have been disappointed.

In any event, the children that Angélique and César produced did not belong to them. Slave children belonged to their mothers' owners. This was sanctioned by law in all slave societies in the New World. From the moment a slave woman conceived, she lost all rights to the child that grew in her body. Because Whites owned the Black slave woman's body, they also owned whatever issued from it in the present and had rights to any children she might produce in the future.

Was Jacques César the only one visiting Angélique's bed? Angélique's last child died in October 1732. On the baptismal record of this child, the father was listed as "unknown." This was strange, because the child was a twin, and the father of her twin brother was listed as Jacques César. This puzzle could be explained simply by noting that owners affirmed the link between child and mother and not between child and father. The father was simply not of consequence. Or it could be that the child was a mulatto, fathered by a White man, possibly Francheville himself, and different answers relating to their paternity were given. The phrase "father unknown" on the baptismal records of slave children was often used as a cover-up to hide the fact that the father was a White male, usually the owner of the mother.[24] This White owner usually had a legal White wife. And the slave mother who gave birth to a child fathered by her master had to bear the brunt of his wife's jealous rage.

André Lachance, in *Vivre, Aimer, et Mourir en Nouvelle-France*, tells us that in early Canada childbirth was a communal female affair. During her labour, the expectant woman, taken to and ensconced in her mother's house, was surrounded by close female relatives, and even neighbours, along with the midwife. These women gave the labouring woman moral and psychological support and encouragement as she went through the pains of giving birth. They also provided physical support, holding her up, massaging her, and putting poultices on particular areas of her body. Surrounded as the woman was by kith and kin, the ordeal was made less difficult. Males were not allowed inside the birthing room, though a priest hovered close by in case he had to baptize the newborn if it appeared that the child's life was in danger. In this atmosphere, the (White) woman gave birth with the sure knowledge that she and her husband would own, love, nurture, and raise their child. Therefore, in spite of the dangers surrounding childbirth, and the pain the woman endured, the successful delivery of a child was a time of rejoicing.[25]

As a Black bondswoman in New France, could Angélique have claimed such a positive birthing environment as the one described by Lachance? Scholars of New World slavery speak of a "female slave network"[26] that shored up enslaved women, especially in times of pregnancy, delivery, convalescence, and childrearing. The Black midwife was central to this community because, in addition to her midwifery skills and duties, she also functioned as a healer and doctor well-versed in the field of female health.

Though a midwife certainly delivered Angélique's children, we do not know if the slave woman's births were communal female affairs. Madame Francheville might have been present, as might Marie-Manon, the slave woman owned by the de Béréy neighbours. But what other female community would come together to support the slave woman at this trying time? She had no mother or close female relatives to attend to her. She was giving birth far from those who might have loved her. And even if other slave women were present, the atmosphere would certainly have been different from that surrounding a White woman's labour. Angélique, as an enslaved Black woman, must have been painfully aware that her body was reproducing future labourers for the slave system and that she had no claim to her children. The sad reality of her bondage must have made the ordeal of her labour and delivery more intense. She would not have been rejoicing, though her owners might have been.

When a slave woman became pregnant, the tensions, cruelties, and contradictions inherent in slavery must have become paramount. A woman slows down as her pregnancy advances.

She often experiences ill health. It is a time when she is most vulnerable, and needs as much care and nurturing as she can get, for her own benefit and that of the fetus. Slave women did not have such comforts. Slaveholders still expected as much labour from a slave woman, never mind that she might not be physically and emotionally able to satisfy his wish. If a pregnant slave woman was forced to work at the same level as she did when she wasn't pregnant, her health and that of the fetus were more than likely compromised.[27]

During Angélique's pregnancies, on whom could she depend for help and nurturance? As her pregnancies advanced, did the Franchevilles lighten her workload? Did her food intake increase? Who cared for her and her children after birth? How soon after each birth was she sent back to her regular duties? Did she receive adequate medical care during her pregnancies, births, and convalescences? And when she returned to her duties, who watched and cared for the children? We cannot answer these questions in any precise way. But research done on other slave societies reveals that enslaved pregnant women and nursing mothers had to attend to their regular duties in spite of the demands of pregnancy and motherhood. Slave women were put back to work two to three weeks after giving birth, and often got a whipping if they did not finish their work on account of childminding. It was, after all, the slave owners who determined the kind of care enslaved pregnant women and nursing mothers received. By all indications, the care received by these women was substandard.[28]

In New France, though the mortality rate for Whites was high enough, that of Black slaves was higher. That the life expectancy of enslaved people was short was undoubtedly because of the harsh conditions of their bondage. The average age of death for enslaved Blacks during the period of French colonization was twenty-five. Very few Blacks lived to see their fifties.[29] Angélique's babies could have died quickly because of lack of attention, inadequate nutrition, or disease, all sufferings that Black babies endured during slavery. Angélique herself could have been overworked and malnourished. These factors would have diminished her chances of giving birth to healthy children.[30]

The reproductive story of enslaved Black women shows that slavery was as much a system of sexual bondage as it was one of racial bondage. Because of the gender "disadvantages" faced by women, they experienced slavery differently from men. And because of the racial subordination and oppression of Black by White, Black women experienced their womanhood differently from White women.

During the eighteenth century, in the New World, generally speaking, the primary role for a White woman was that of mother. The Black mother's primary role was that of worker (the majority of Black women in the New World were enslaved workers). The dual ideologies of motherhood that existed for Black and White women served to reinforce the subordinate position of Black slave women and the exalted position of White women, whatever their social status. White women could claim their children; Black women like Angélique had no such luxury. White women had legal and patriarchal protection; Black women were vulnerable to and experienced all kinds of brutality.[31]

We will never know how Angélique reacted to the deaths of her children. Was she saddened? Or was she relieved that her children had escaped the harsh life that was slavery? If

Angélique harboured visions of escaping from slavery, her children would have been an impediment. Most runaway slaves in America and the Caribbean were men; only about sixteen percent were noted to be women. Women stayed put mainly because they had small children who would have made flight difficult.[32]

Slavery was violent, and enslaved women and men sometimes resisted violently. Killing her own children—through abortion or even infanticide—was one way for a woman to gain some control over her body, and to save her offspring from a life of permanent bondage. Yet the frequency of such behaviour in Canada is unknown. There is no way of knowing whether Angélique's children died of natural causes. Her first child, Eustache, was so sickly at birth that the midwife, fearing he would die right away, baptized him.

Angélique could have entertained the possibility of having a family of her own. Yet this would have been a shallow dream. As a slave, she would have little authority over her children. On the other hand, slave children were bonded to their mothers in a way they were not to their fathers. The slave system marginalized slave fathers by giving the children their mother's status and denying fathers paternal authority. Even though children could be sold away from their mothers, and mothers were denied ownership of them, their mothers were their primary caregivers, which often led to a close physical and emotional bond between mother and children.

If Francheville had indeed used Angélique as a "breeder" and had forced Jacques César on her, that situation quickly became untenable, if only because she had a mind of her own. By the beginning of 1733, the relationship between

César and Angélique had unravelled. Claude Thibault, a former soldier turned *engagé*, had entered the picture. Thibault, in the employ of Sieur Francheville as a three-year contract worker, claimed the attention of the slave woman. Thibault came from the Franche-Comté region of France, close to the Swiss border. Franche-Comté was an economically struggling area and a large majority of its young men joined the army as a way to stave off deprivation and starvation. The men of Franche-Comté found themselves all over the French overseas empire, fighting to enforce *pax gallica*. Franche-Comté was important to the Francheville household for another reason: it produced an abundance of miners, and it was from this region that Francheville and subsequently his associates recruited the bulk of the iron workers employed at the Saint-Maurice forges.

A great number of the written records pertaining to the regiments of the French army in Canada have been lost. It is not known to which regiment Thibault belonged. However, soldiers usually spent three to five years in the colonial army, after which they were discharged. On the other hand, their tenure could be lengthened if the colony was in a state of war. Demobilized soldiers, especially officers, had several options after their tour of duty was over. They could return to France, and many did; they could remain in the army; or they could remain in the colony and put down roots. The minister of marine encouraged them to pursue the last option, and sometimes gave them land grants to sweeten the pot. Some soldiers who chose to remain in the colony, if they came from the labouring class, hired themselves out as day workers or entered longer-term contracts, becoming *engagés*. These *engagés* were known as "thirty-six monthers" because the contract typically lasted for three years.

Thibault's entry into the Francheville household caused a stir. If Angélique had not already ceased her relations with César, she did so when Thibault arrived. They became lovers. Quite likely she knew Thibault from his days as a soldier. Montréal had a permanent military garrison, and Thibault could have been stationed there. He also might have spent time at the Hôtel-Dieu as a patient. The hospital was directly across the street from the Francheville home, and Angélique, it appears, struck up a friendly acquaintance with some of the convalescing soldiers. On the evening of the fateful fire, she had chatted with the soldier Latreille outside the gates of the hospital.

Thibault would prove to be an intractable worker who had no intention of being deferent to his employers. He chafed under the authority of the Franchevilles, all the while scheming to be rid of his indenture and flee to France. In Angélique, he met someone who shared his thirst for freedom. They began plotting their escape.

The bondswoman might have genuinely fallen in love with Thibault. But he also offered her a way out—something Jacques César could not do. Thibault was White, he was French, and he was male. If Angélique escaped with him, he could pose as her slave master. Thibualt, as a former soldier, knew the terrain of the frontier. Knowledge of the landscape would make their escape easier and would prevent them from getting lost in the woods. So, even if Angélique was in love with the Frenchman, she had other practical reasons for entering into an affair with him.

Thus, sometime in the first half of 1733, Angélique's mental and emotional universe underwent a revolution. She had given birth to three children and watched all three of them die. She left Jacques César, her slave lover, and entered into a liaison with the Frenchman Thibault. She was on the brink of a new beginning.

Meanwhile, Francheville continued the life he was used to. He sent men to gather fur, received a royal subsidy to invest in his iron mines, and planned his future. But in November 1733, he took ill and died.

Francheville's death marked a turning point in Angélique's life. Her master was hardly in the ground when she asked her mistress, Madame Francheville, for permission to leave. Did the slave woman ask for her freedom because her master had promised it to her before he died? In any event, Madame Francheville refused her bondswoman's request, and a rage began building up in Angélique. Unable to gain authority over her own life, Angélique lashed her mistress with her tongue. She cursed the widow, called her a bitch and a whore, disobeyed her, and subverted her authority at every turn.[33]

Slave managers and overseers in the New World frequently complained about slave women's tongues. Enslaved women were reputed to be saucy, insolent, and rude to their superiors. They were outspoken and talked back. This stereotype of the slave woman as the ultimate Jezebel must be placed in the context of their lives. Because enslaved women endured lives of physical hardship, violence, and psychological torture, talking back to their oppressors was one of the ways some defended themselves.[34]

A British commandant on the island of Trinidad expressed the opinion that slave women deserved punishment more often than men, for they used to great effect "that most powerful instrument of attack and defence, their tongue."[35] Some slave managers, unable to control the slave women under their charge because of their "long tongues," whipped them.

Angélique was a slave woman with a "long tongue." While Sieur Francheville was alive, his wife whipped Angélique on a regular basis. Francheville might have done the same. He might even have sexually abused her. Angélique fought back with her tongue. She cursed her mistress; she cursed the White workers in the household. She also turned her fury against the French in general: they were worthless people who were dogs, and they deserved to be burnt.

Angélique declared war on her mistress. She engaged Madame Francheville as if they were equals—yet they were not. Her mistress owned her life and body and could do with her what she wished. And it was this control of her destiny that Angélique was trying to break with her tongue—and her actions.

When she decided to take matters into her own hands, she became resourceful and, with the help of Thibault, planned her escape and eventually did run away. When she was caught, she was unrepentant. After she came back to the Francheville house, Angélique remained "hostile" to her mistress, threatening her with murder. On the morning of the fateful fire, she had a showdown with Madame Francheville, who left the house and went to mass in a state of frustration.

Angélique emerged as a rebellious slave after the death of Sieur Francheville. We don't know if she was "docile" before this time. There was tension in the household between mistress and slave, perhaps because of the use and abuse of Angélique's body. Thérèse Francheville may have been a jealous wife who beat Angélique because her husband frequented the bondswoman's bed. Angélique herself told the court that her mistress seldom beat her after the death of her husband. Was that because Sieur Francheville was no longer around to sleep with his slave woman and give his wife offence?

Though Angélique may have been saucy before the death of Sieur Francheville, the court transcripts suggest that it was on the passing of her master that she became "intolerable." But this source is limited. As a document that deals with the trial, it does nothing to put together the story of Angélique's life before 1734. How likely is it that Angélique was a "passive" woman before her master's death, and then suddenly transformed into an "uncontrollable" bondswoman? She was probably rebellious even before the death of her master, but got "worse" after his demise.

Angélique asked her mistress for her freedom, and when Madame Francheville dismissed her demands as preposterous, the bondswoman cursed her. In fighting back with her tongue, she was showing her owner that she was no longer afraid of her; she was telling the slaveholder in a clear voice that she was in control of her mind and spirit. By freeing herself from mental slavery, Angélique achieved the ultimate emancipation. Through her acts of rebellion, Angélique let Thérèse Francheville know in no uncertain terms that, although she was her master, she could not master her.

VI

First Fire, First Flight

IT WAS APPROACHING CHRISTMAS, just a few short weeks
after the death of Sieur Francheville, when Angélique asked
Madame Francheville for *congé*, or permission, to leave. By asking for *congé*, Angelique signalled her intention to leave
Montréal... and slavery. And that her mistress knew. What
prompted the bondswoman to ask for her freedom? It could
be that Sieur Francheville had promised the slave woman her
freedom "at some point in the future" and died before making
good on the promise. The assertive manner in which she asked
for her freedom suggests that she thought it was due to her.

But there are clues that Claude Thibault, the indentured
labourer in Madame Francheville's employ, was coming to
the end of his contract and had likewise declared his intention to leave Canada. Thibault and Angélique were lovers, and
Angélique wished to leave the colony—with Thibault. Yet to
argue that Angélique's sole motivation for flight was Claude
Thibault would be wrong. She desired her freedom for its
own sake, as her court case would reveal.

Madame Francheville refused her bondswoman's request. Infuriated, Angélique went on a small reign of terror in the household. She talked back to her owner, threatened her with death by "roasting," quarrelled with the other servants in the house, threatened them, too, with "burning," and made life so unbearable for her fellow servant Marie-Louise Poirier that she quit her job. Madame Francheville, seemingly unable to defend herself or the harassed servant, promised Poirier that she was going to sell Angélique in the spring and then Poirier could come back to work for her. Slave woman and slave mistress declared a psychological war on each other and bided their time. Madame Francheville had the upper hand, or so she believed.

Claude Thibault was also making life unbearable for his employer. Like Angélique, he was disobedient and insolent, and his mistress could not control him.

The new year came, and the tension between Angélique and her owner continued unabated. Madame Francheville made arrangements to have her bondswoman sold to François-Étienne Cugnet, a Québec government official and entrepreneur. She sold Angélique for six hundred pounds of gunpowder. Cugnet was also to pay for Angélique's transport to the capital.

The tensions escalated in the household when the slave woman learned that her mistress had sold her and protested the sale.

"Madame, please do not sell me. I will behave myself, I will do everything to please you. Just don't send me away."

"You are rude and quarrelsome. You disturb my household. You make trouble with the other servants. You are mean and malicious. I don't want you here anymore."

Thérèse Francheville also made plans for her own safety and protection. Afraid of being alone in the house with her "enemies," she had her niece Marguerite de Couagne come to live with her. In the early days of February, Madame Francheville's fears crescendoed, and she removed Angélique and Thibault from her house. Her stated reason: she was in fear of them, especially Angélique. She felt certain that, based on her threats, Angélique was going to burn down the house with her in it. She sent the pair to live with her brother-in-law and business associate Alexis Monière.

Monière, who had entered the fur trade as a voyageur, over time climbed the scale of the fur trade mercantile hierarchy and ended up as a middle-sized merchant outfitter. In this capacity, he partnered with large fur merchants to supply the interior posts with merchandise. He also ran a shop in Montréal and from it supplied the king's troops and the military establishment in general with needed goods. Monière was married to Madame Francheville's sister, Marie-Josephe de Couagne, who was Angélique's godmother.

Madame Francheville asked Monière to take Thibault into his employ and to keep Angélique until the ice broke on the river and the fishing fleet was ready to head to the Gulf of St. Lawrence. Then she would send Angélique on one of the boats to Cugnet in Québec.

Angélique, when she realized how her mistress was going to dispose of her, again raged at Madame Francheville and told her she was going to "make her burn."

What seems clear is that Madame Francheville, as a widow and a single woman, lost control of her slave woman and some of her servants. Though there is no evidence to back this up, it would appear that, when Sieur Francheville was alive, there was some kind of calm in the household, even if it was superficial. Francheville, who embodied "patriarchal authority" as master of the household, was able to enforce a kind of truce and keep intact the social convention of deference and obedience between slave/servant and master. When he died, the forced peace was broken, and his wife was unable to fix it.

Angélique, on moving to Sieur Monière's, knew exactly what was going to happen. She had been moved there as a safety precaution and would be sent to Québec as soon as nature allowed. Part of Madame Francheville's plan was to separate her from Claude Thibault. It would later come out at the trial that Angélique "threatened" Thibault, telling him in no uncertain terms that he could not commit to working for Monière, because that would tie him down and make him unable to leave with her when she did decide to escape.

The servants in Monière's household knew that the slave woman had been sold. One of them, Jacques Jalleteau, told her that she would be sent to the capital of the colony, and from there to the West Indies. Angélique, hearing the news of her sale from all sides, refused to be a sitting duck. Within twelve hours of taking up residence at Monière's, she and Thibault went into action. They arrived on a Saturday evening; in the early hours of Sunday morning, smoke spilled from the two rooms where they slept. The servants of the house discovered Angélique's bed on fire. Thibault's blanket was also in flames. Two house guests and the house servants successfully put out the blaze, and Angélique begged Catherine Custeau, one of Monière's servants, not to tell her employer of the fire. But Monière, who had smelled the smoke, rose from his bed and inspected the house. Finding everything in order, he went back to sleep. Custeau would later tell her employer how the "Negress almost roasted them" that night.

The following evening, Angélique and Thibault disappeared from the house. They probably intended to use the fire to cover their flight. Jalleteau would later testify that, before their flight from the house, Thibault told him he was leaving for Québec; Angélique, he said, told him she was going to Europe.

This was not a spur-of-the-moment flight. The couple had planned it even before Madame Francheville sent them to live with Monière. In fact (this seems to have been in January), when Madame Francheville had gone on a trip to nearby Longue-Pointe, Thibault and Angélique almost ran away after her departure. They chose to wait for her return, however, because she owed Thibault his wages and he wanted to be paid before he fled.

The couple had long made up their minds to run away together, and were just waiting for the ice on the river to harden. Some time earlier, before the pair went to live at Monière's, Thibault had hidden loaves of bread in a barn across the river in Longueuil in anticipation of their flight. When they were moved to Monière's, they felt the time had come.

Angélique and Thibault fled from Sieur Monière's house, determined to make it to a New England port. To make that a reality, they had to cross the St. Lawrence River and head south. It was mid-winter and the river was frozen solid. The fugitives crossed the river, perhaps in the vicinity of the present-day *Terre des hommes*, to Longueuil on the south shore, and from Longueuil made their way to Chambly on the Richelieu River, which flows into Lake Champlain. From Lake Champlain, the couple could reach a port in Maine,

New Hampshire, or Massachusetts, or more likely New York City. The Lake Champlain/Richelieu Valley corridor was very popular with traders and travellers, and was one of the principal fur trade and military routes from Montréal to Albany and New England. From a New England or New York port, Angélique hoped to board a ship for Portugal.

Longueuil was about twenty-five miles from Montréal, and Chambly was the same distance from Longueuil. So the couple travelled about sixty miles when they left Montréal. This was no mean feat, given the climatic conditions. Their arduous journey reveals their determination to escape confinement. One might ask why the pair did not head for Québec, the colony's capital and main outlet for Atlantic shipping. But the river was frozen and shipping suspended for the season. As well, Cugnet, the man to whom Angélique had been sold, lived in Québec; it would therefore be unwise to head there because the pair would likely be discovered as fugitives and arrested. It made sense for the escapees to trudge through the wintry forests to a southern port. In all likelihood, Angélique had some contacts in the English colonies, since she had lived there before she came to Montréal, and meant to use these contacts once she arrived in the vicinity.

The fugitives stayed in Chambly for two weeks. Their ability to make further progress was hampered by wintry conditions, lack of food, and their fugitive status. These stark realities must have made them realize they did not have some of the essentials to carry out a successful flight.

Meanwhile, back in Montréal, the authorities had broadcasted the flight of Angélique and Thibault and organized a manhunt for their capture. Officers of the constabulary combed the countryside and after two weeks caught the fugitives in Chambly. They arrested them and marched them back to Montréal.

Thibault was lodged in prison. Surprisingly, Angélique was returned to her mistress. When farm labourer Louis Langlois *dit* Traversy remarked to Angélique that she was "very bad" to run away and that she had better behave or her mistress would sell her, Angélique retorted, without remorse, "The snow will clear away, the earth will be uncovered and the tracks will no longer be visible." It is clear from her response that she was planning to escape again but would wait until winter passed, when there would be no conspiring snow. She would also wait until Thibault got out of prison.

When Angélique ran away, she was announcing boldly to Madame Francheville (and to White society at large) that she could not be mastered. Slave flight was disconcerting to Whites because it destabilized the "natural order" they had created by placing themselves at the top and Blacks at the bottom. Slave flight also belied the pervasive myth built up a by a White slaveholding class that slaves were happy with their lot and were treated well. When Angélique fled from slavery, she resisted and dismantled these lies that had come to define her existence as chattel. She was not a happy, well-treated slave; she was an enraged Black woman attempting to remove and smash the invisible iron collar placed around her neck, and the handcuffs and chains locked around her limbs.

When Angélique ran away, she took her struggles against slavery to another level. Before, she had talked back to her mistress and disobeyed her orders. After a while, that was not enough. By running away, she showed that she was serious about her emancipation and was determined to undermine the slave system.

Because of their marginalized and degraded status, enslaved people have often been seen as "enemies within the households" of their masters. They could not be trusted. Their owners lived in mortal fear of them. John Hope Franklin and Loren Schweninger, authorities on slave resistance, could have been writing about Angélique when they stated, "Slaves on occasion refused to work, demanded concessions, rejected orders, threatened whites, and sometimes reacted with violence. Verbal and physical confrontations occurred regularly, without regard to time and place."[1]

If, indeed, Sieur Francheville had promised Angélique her freedom and his wife had denied it to the slave woman, Angélique was determined to take it, and showed that she would do so at any cost. She demonstrated her contempt for her mistress's authority through her flight. She also hated her mistress with a passion. So strong was her hatred that she thought of murdering her; she also publicly expressed that thought.

If there was any doubt about the relationship between Thibault and Angélique, it was erased during Thibault's stay in prison. Angélique visited him and brought him food regularly until Madame Francheville discovered it and told her to stop. Angélique ignored her and continued visiting and taking meals to her lover. Angélique was out of control. Thibault's confinement did not prevent him and Angélique from meeting and plotting their next escape.

Montréal was a society conscious of rank and status. And Angélique was undermining her mistress's authority in the eyes of everyone, especially the labourers in the Francheville household. They were surprised that she had got off so lightly. She had run away, and likely had set fire to Sieur Monière's house, yet on her return to Montréal her mistress neither whipped her nor put her in jail. In fact, Madame Francheville seemed to have rewarded Angélique by bringing her home. The servants of the house remarked on this puzzling occurrence to Angélique, and warned her to "behave" or else her mistress would sell her. Angélique replied that her mistress was a "good woman," but if she sold her she would "make her pay." But Madame Francheville had already sold Angélique—the true reason for the slave woman's peaceful homecoming.

Thibault was released on April 8, after spending about five weeks in prison. He and Angélique began putting their new plan into action. On the day of his release, he went to Madame Francheville's to collect his wages and his belongings. Madame Francheville gave him an earful. She told him "not ever to set foot in her house again." To spite him further, in the heat of her anger, she added that she had sold Angélique. Free at last, Thibault received his wages and belongings and left.

Thibault ignored Madame Francheville's demand that he not "set foot in her house again" and visited Angélique several times at the house between April 8 and 10, when her owner was not at home. Undoubtedly, Thibault told Angélique that her sale was a fact. It was April, which meant that the ice on the river was thawing, and boats and canoes leaving for Québec would soon be on the river. Both realized that before long Angélique would be in one of those boats. They must have known that Angélique's sale meant their separation, and the smashing of Angélique's dream of returning to Portugal.

*

In 1734, Franche-Comté, the home of Claude Thibault, was still a young province of France. Historically, it had been part of the Holy Roman Empire, and when that entity dissolved, the province became part of Germany's hinterland. During the seventeenth century, it was annexed by Louis XIV in one of his many military campaigns and became part of France. The Franche-Comtois (the name of their state means "Free County"), a fiercely independent people, resented French rule and domination. One result of French annexation for the Franche-Comtois was that many of their young men were drafted into the French army. The French imperial army was heterogeneous. It included not only Frenchmen but also Germans, Flemings, Italians, Spaniards, and others—people who came under France's martial umbrella because of that kingdom's long reach in Europe and elsewhere. In fact, France under Louis XIV was the first country in Europe to have a standing army.

One of the rumours that circulated in France about soldiers overseas was that they never returned to France. There was some truth to this because, as in the case of Canada, the Crown encouraged the soldiers to settle in the New World. Claude Thibault was one soldier, however, who wanted to prove that belief a lie. As a Franche-Comtois, he might have been resentful about being drafted into France's overseas army; he might have been an even more resentful *engagé*. He hated Canada and his indentureship, and he planned on leaving the wretched place. If he had fallen in love with Marie-Joseph Angélique, and wanted to live a life in freedom with her, then it was imperative that he escape from Montréal.

As a former soldier, Claude Thibault would have been familiar with the interior trade and military routes. It was he who planned the logistics of the escape. He chose the Lake Champlain/Richelieu Valley corridor as their route. Along this corridor, the French maintained several forts, including two at Chambly and Saint-Jean. It is likely that Thibault had served at one of these forts and so knew the geography of the area.

Angélique and Claude Thibault's flight represented a collaboration between two sets of servile workers: the enslaved and the indentured. Flight from bondage by these two groups was a common feature of early colonial history. Bulletins and memos from such English colonies as the Carolinas, Maryland, and Barbados regularly announced the escape of slaves in the company of indentured servants. Likewise, in Canada, during the English regime, the *Québec Gazette* and the *Montréal Gazette* regularly broadcasted the joint flight of these two sets of servile labourers. Thibault and Angélique ran away during the French regime, and their collaboration suggests that others like them could also have escaped or attempted to escape. We know also that enslaved persons and contract labourers often worked in partnership to undermine their employers and the system. In 1735, for example, in Montréal, an enslaved African named Jean-Baptiste Thomas was arrested along with three indentured labourers. Thomas and his White friends were in the habit of stealing goods from Whites and fencing them. Thomas was brought in front of the courts, pronounced guilty, and hanged.[2]

Servants and slaves who joined forces saw themselves as oppressed workers against a common enemy—their owners or employers. They recognized a bond between them forged by servitude. At least to some degree, slaves and servants had more in common as bonded persons than a White indentured servant had with his employer. Whites in power feared this bond between Black slaves and White indentured workers and tried to break it by diverse means, including legislation. Powerful Whites felt that, if those most marginalized teamed up to resist, rebel, and revolt, then the elite class would lose its grip on society and its control over the lower classes. Committed partnerships between Black enslaved labourers and White contract servants spelt doom for the elite class. If these workers could put aside their "racial differences" and see clearly their common economic and social oppression, and move to overcome that oppression, a veritable revolution would occur.

Madame Francheville realized that Angélique by herself was weaker than when she partnered with Thibault; likewise, Thibault was probably weaker without Angélique. Madame Francheville must have determined, though, that Angélique was the more vulnerable of the two. And she was right. Her manservant was on contract, from which he would soon be released. He was White, male, and French, and thus would have opportunities to raise himself up when he was freed from his indenture. Angélique did not have those options. Madame Francheville wanted Angélique and Thibault to be separated because she felt that when they were together they influenced each other to undermine her authority and plan their flight.

For Angélique and Thibault, rank and status prevailed over considerations of race. They were also lovers and thus joined by bonds of passion. They supported each other's goal, which was to flee from Canada. Angélique wanted to get back to Portugal, and Thibault to France. One wonders how they were going to live together if their ultimate destinations were different. Angélique seemed to have thought about that, for during her trial Jacques Jalleteau told the court that

Angélique had told him while she was at Sieur Monière's that she would visit Franche-Comté on her way to Portugal.

✳

Madame Francheville had sold Angélique to François-Étienne Cugnet, her friend and business associate. Cugnet, as we have seen, was an original board member of the Saint-Maurice Forge Company that her husband had established. After Francheville died, the board was reorganized. Cugnet remained as its chair but also increased the number of shares he had in the company. It was renamed "Cugnet and Company." Cugnet was one of the most important men in the colony. He was a French-born lawyer who became a member of the Conseil Supérieur in 1730. Three years later, he was appointed its first senior councillor. Cugnet also directed the Domaine d'Occident. The Domaine was a royal resource primarily of fish, timber, fur, and seigneurial holdings. As the king's representative, Cugnet leased the land possessing these resources to entrepreneurs and received payments for the Crown.

Cugnet conducted trade for the Crown not only with the colony's merchants and traders in the *Pays de haut* but also with those in the West Indies. Like Sieur Francheville, Cugnet was connected to the upper mercantile and administrative circles in the French Atlantic world. The talk was that Cugnet would sell Angélique to the West Indies. That was certainly plausible, given his connections, and also because the West Indies was one of the sources from which Canada bought enslaved people. Mathieu Leveille, Canada's hangman at that time, for example, was a slave shipped from Martinique. Cugnet himself was an owner of enslaved Africans. The fact that the governor general of Canada, the Marquis de Beauharnois, owned two slave plantations in San Domingue also solidified the trade in enslaved people between Canada and the West Indies.

Transporting rebellious and unruly slaves from one place to another, especially to different points within the same empire, but sometimes across imperial frontiers, was one strategy used by slave owners to quash the spirit of the slaves and break their resistance. When a Panis slave led a mutiny at the Niagara garrison, instead of executing him, as was the usual punishment for such a deed, the authorities shipped him into West Indian slavery. Many of the accused in the New York slave conspiracy of 1741 were saved from the hangman's noose and transported to faraway places like Portugal and Newfoundland.[3]

Madame Francheville could not control Angélique, and she lived in fear of her. With her husband gone, she had no one to help her master the unruly slave. If she had felt she could call on kin and friends to help her control Angélique, that thought must have left her mind after the debacle at Monière's. The escape attempt no doubt confirmed in her mind that selling the slave woman was her only alternative. This she did—to Cugnet. And he planned to punish Angélique further by selling her out of the colony to a West Indian slave plantation. Angélique made up her mind to prevent this from happening.

Angélique's capture after her first flight only hardened her resolve to escape again. She would not back down. She locked herself in a struggle with Thérèse Francheville and White society. But it was a struggle whose outcome would only be known when the dust and ash settled.

VII

April's Fire

ON SATURDAY, APRIL 10, 1734, Thérèse Francheville returned from noon mass at Notre-Dame. A cold wind blew from the west, chilling the bones. Nonetheless, the thawing ice and accompanying mud were evidence that spring was on its way. It had not been a good winter for Madame Francheville. Her husband had died in November, leaving her a widow. Not only was she still facing the grief of losing her spouse, but throughout the winter she had been plagued by the machinations of her slave woman, Angélique, and her contract labourer Claude Thibault.

The church of Notre-Dame, on the street of the same name, was just a few blocks away from the Francheville house on rue Saint-Paul. As Thérèse walked home, she made her way slowly, her steps impeded by the slush and mud. No matter, she would be at home soon.

Madame Francheville, in all likelihood, reflected on Angélique, who was living in her household again. Angélique had not changed her ways—she was as rebellious

and rude as ever. She still quarrelled with Thérèse and continued "to speak against the French." Earlier that day, before
she left for mass, Madame Francheville had had bitter words
with her slave woman, who had again threatened to burn
down her house—with her in it. When she left for mass,
Madame Francheville left Angélique at the house with
three children: her niece Marguerite Couagne, and her
niece's two friends, ten-year-old Charlotte Desrivières and
five-year-old Amable Lemoine *dit* Monière. Marguerite had
been living with her of late. Madame Francheville had con-
fided to Ignace Gamelin that she was afraid of being alone
in the house with Angélique. Unbeknownst to Madame
Francheville, after she left for church, Thibault came to the
house and spoke with Angélique in the kitchen. He left
soon after.

After Madame Francheville returned from mass, she went
to make small talk with her neighbour, Madame Desrivières.
Angélique went on an errand to the de Bérey house, and
stopped to chat with their slave girl, Marie-Manon. The two
slave women watched as Mesdames Francheville and
Desrivières shared a joke and laughed out loud. Angélique
said to Marie-Manon that her mistress was "laughing now,
but soon she would not be laughing as she would not be
sleeping in her house that night."

Evening came. The church bells announced the hour of
vespers. The purple and indigo colours of twilight enveloped
the town. The guards were changed at the gates of the fortification. Inside their homes, some citizens dined and rested
after a day's work. Soon they would prepare for sleep. Others,
the faithful, completed their evening prayers at the church.
Madame Francheville was among them. At Hôtel-Dieu, the

nuns took a break from their duties, had supper, prayed, and relaxed for the evening. A calm settled over the town.

It was broken by the sound of someone screaming "Fire, fire!" Marguerite César, whose house was beside Hôtel-Dieu, heard the screams and ran to her window. She saw Angélique dash from the Francheville house, yelling "Fire, fire!" The children who had been in the Francheville house were also in the street, screaming "Fire!" Sieur Radisson, whose house was right beside the Francheville's, heard the screams and looked through his door. To his bewilderment, he saw Angélique running towards him shrieking "Fire!" He ran with her to the Francheville home, somehow got two buckets of water, realized that the smoke was coming from the granary, and headed in that direction with the buckets. Radisson noticed that the fire originated in the ceiling, under the roof. To get to it, he had to mount a ladder. He asked Angélique for a ladder, but she said there wasn't one in the house. The fire was spreading so rapidly on the Francheville's roof that Radisson feared for the safety of his own house. He quickly abandoned the Francheville house and ran home to save what he could.

The bell at the parish church began to toll the alarm. The news reached the garrison, and soon the soldiers beat out the alarm on drums. The local governor, Josué Dubois Berthelot de Beaucours, on hearing the news, organized the troops as fast as he could to fight the fire. Soon, soldiers and citizens were striving to put out the flames. By now the entire town had been alerted. Radisson had good reason to run home: the flames devoured Madame Francheville's house and spread immediately to Radisson's and the houses of other neighbours on rue Saint-Paul. The fire, now an inferno, moved across the street to Hôtel-Dieu and ate its way through the various buildings. The roof of the hospital wards collapsed. The nuns, who were in the convent taking their evening relaxation when the alarm sounded, collected what they could. The convent caught fire, but somehow the nuns were able to get out and make their way to the open garden, where many refugees had gathered. The fire continued its murderous run, devouring rue Saint-Paul, and the little streets that cut into it at right angles, then spreading to the houses on rue Notre-Dame.

It was the law that all able-bodied citizens, on hearing a fire alarm (the tolling of the bells, the beating of the drums), present themselves at the scene of the blaze and help fight the flames. They were to come prepared with ladders, axes, and buckets. Many of the citizens of Montréal, especially those from the western sector of the town, where the fire was least threatening, did just that. At first, they fought the fire. But as the flames spread so did their fears. They might have been brave, but they were not foolish. Self-interest prevailed. Many, like Radisson, abandoned their efforts and ran home to save their personal possessions.

Though at least half the houses in the lower town were made of stone, the other half were wooden. And almost every one of the buildings was roofed in wooden shingles, the most popular form of roofing. Wooden planks were also widely used. Only government buildings and some religious structures were roofed in the more fire-resistant stone tiles, tin, or slate. Shingles were a fire hazard: they allowed flames to spread rapidly from one house to another. In the previous decades, the government had issued ordinance after ordinance prohibiting the use of shingles, but the local inhabitants ignored them. Shingles were cheaper and easier to obtain than the more reliable slate and tin.

As late as 1775, government bureaucrat François-Joseph Cugnet (son of François-Étienne Cugnet), bent on enforcing government fire prevention regulations concerning shingles, noted that, during fires, "flaming shingles fly from area to area, spreading fires."[1] Elizabeth Simcoe witnessed a fire in Québec in 1796, and blamed shingles for its spread: "The church and houses, being covered with shingles, burnt rapidly, and the shingles, being light, were also easily blown by the wind, which had been high, and had it not changed probably the whole town would have been destroyed."[2]

In the 1734 Montréal fire, flying shingles wreaked havoc. The elements scoffed at the efforts of those brave souls, now mainly soldiers, who sought to put out the flames. As a strong wind from the west pushed the shingles and the flames into untouched buildings, the fire gained speed and momentum. It moved swiftly from house to house. The mud, slush, and thawing ice made the roads almost impassable and impeded the movements of the soldiers. Firefighting efforts were primitive. Buckets filled with water from the St. Lawrence River, or from wells in people's courtyards, and passed from hand to hand proved useless against the raging fire. Less than three hours after the smoke was first seen curling from Madame Francheville's roof, forty-six buildings, including Hôtel-Dieu, lay smouldering in ruins. Almost the entire merchant sector, mainly the houses along rue Saint-Paul, was destroyed.

The merchant quarter was the core of the town. As the economic and commercial heartbeat of the region, it was also the densest and busiest portion of Montréal. Space was at a premium, and buildings were crammed together. Along rue Saint-Paul, "houses were typically sited with their long walls parallel to the street, tight to the street line, allowing space for a rear courtyard for commercial, artisanal, or household use."[3] It is no wonder the fire was able to spread so rapidly. The fire spared the eastern part of the city, which held the "largest lots with the lowest building density." Here lived wealthy government and military officials in spacious mansions surrounded by stately gardens. The western portion of the town was also spared, and thankfully so: poor artisans and other members of the labouring classes lived in this sector, in houses made of wood.

Many of Montréal's leading merchants combined their business in fur with the wholesale trade. In Montréal, as in other colonial towns during that period, merchants constructed their homes with their families and businesses in mind. Work was not separate from home, and a typical merchant's house contained living quarters, merchandise storerooms, a granary, and a commercial shop. The second floor housed the kitchen, as well as dining, living, and sleeping quarters. The third floor, an attic, also contained bedrooms. Grains and other goods were stored in the attic. Basement vaults were used as storerooms, shops, and apartments. Thus, in the fire, the Montréal merchants lost most of their moveable possessions, their personal goods, and their merchandise, because home and store were located under one roof.

The fire also devastated Hôtel-Dieu, which stood directly opposite the Francheville house. The patients' wards and the nuns' residence were burnt to the ground. "Virtually nothing was saved except some mattresses, a very small bit of linen, and some medicine from the apothecary."[4] Though some of the hospital's buildings were constructed of stone, most of the outer buildings were made of wood. But all were covered in wooden shingles, and all succumbed to the flames.

The nuns became refugees on their own property. For a few nights after the fire, they camped out in the garden of the poor and in the courtyard, like many of the victims of the blaze. This was the second fire in thirteen years that had levelled Hôtel-Dieu. In fact, renovations following the fire in 1721 were not quite completed when the 1734 fire struck.

Fortunately, no one died because of the 1734 fire. It could have been more devastating had it not been for the colonial troops who were called out to fight the fire. While the frightened citizens scrambled to save their homes and possessions, the soldiers worked to contain the blaze.

Fire was the nightmare of colonial towns. People's lives, property, and possessions could be wiped out in an instant. Rebuilding was expensive, and colonial governments were always hard-pressed to find funds to rebuild towns. Given the hardships that fires engendered, authorities dealt harshly with suspected arsonists: arson was an offence punishable by death.

Some victims of the fire, including Thérèse Francheville, managed to save some personal effects. Though the hospital itself burned, the nuns' private courtyard, the garden of the poor, the small Chapel of the Virgin Mary, and some of the outer buildings remained fire-free, and these served as shelter for many of the victims. Ironically, Angélique and Thibault helped moved some of Thérèse Francheville's property to Hôtel-Dieu's garden of the poor. As they did, Madame Francheville confronted Angélique: "You set the fire, I know you did." Angélique replied, "Madame, however nasty I might be, I'm not wretched enough to commit an act of that sort." But Madame Francheville would not let up. She continued to harangue Angélique, accusing her of setting the fire, while the bondswoman pleaded her innocence.

With some of their possessions saved, many of those who had been burnt out of house and home gathered to spend the night in the hospital's courtyard, having nowhere else to go. The more fortunate ones found family members and friends to stay with until they could rebuild their homes. The de Béréys bunked with the family of Sieur de Gannes; Thérèse Francheville went to live with Sieur Tremon; Marguerite César stayed with the Baron de Longueuil. Some of the sisters of Hôtel-Dieu stayed on a farm owned by the Charon brothers in the northern suburbs.

Even before the soldiers had quenched the fire, the townspeople gathered in the hospital's courtyard began asking who had set it. There was no doubt in their minds that the fire was the work of an arsonist. They also felt they knew the answer to the question: the arsonist was none other than Marie-Joseph Angélique, the slave woman of Thérèse Francheville.

Angélique was among them and so heard their words. The hospital's gardener, Louis Bellefeuille *dit* La Ruine, told Angélique that "everyone was saying she set the fire." Angélique responded that she "would not be so stupid." If the slave woman thought the accusations would subside, she was wrong. No sooner had the courtyard refugees stopped pointing their fingers at her than they all heard the sound of drums. It was a soldier, announcing to the citizens through the beat of his drum that an announcement was forthcoming. François Roy, the town crier, accompanied the soldier, and he would broadcast urgent news. Roy's voice rang out loud and clear. He announced that Marie-Joseph Angélique, the "Negress of Madame Francheville," had set fire to the city. After Roy made his chilling broadcast, an army surgeon accosted Angélique, saying everyone knew she had set the fire. Angélique dismissed the accusations, confidently stating that she would not be such a fool as to set fire to her own house.

Someone passed around a bottle of syrup and brandy. Everyone, including Angélique, took sips. The Sulpician and Récollet fathers brought food for the refugees. They all, including the nuns, shared the food. Soon, in spite of the grief and shock, people grew weary and their eyelids became heavy. They prepared themselves for bed with the blankets the nuns had given out. Angélique found a spot in the Chapel of the Virgin Mary and wrapped herself in a green blanket she had secured from the nuns.

But what of Thibault? While the fire blazed, Thibault had helped Angélique move some of their mistress's belongings into the hospital's garden. But having done that, Thibault sat and watched the fire rage around him. When La Ruine asked him why he wasn't, like the others, throwing buckets of water on the blaze, Thibault calmly replied that he had had a long day and was very tired and hungry. Many of the townspeople had Angélique down as suspect number one; when Claude Thibault replied thus to La Ruine, he became suspect number two. By the time Roy made his announcement, Thibault had disappeared.

If Angélique was fearful, she did not show it. She mingled with the crowd, sharing their syrup and brandy. Yet when she bedded down for the night, all she could hear were the accusations and the voice of François Roy announcing her guilt and condemnation. She had reason to be fearful.

Night passed. Dawn came. The lower town, *la basse ville*, lay in ruins. The refugees slept in the courtyard of the burnt-out hospital, their vulnerable bodies covered by smoke-infused blankets. Those who managed to sleep, upon waking at dawn, may have hoped that what had passed the night before was nothing more than a horrible dream. But as their eyes opened and they saw the buildings smouldering, they knew the fire was a nasty reality. They had lost their homes, and for a while their lives would be turned upside down.

They also knew it was Marie-Joseph Angélique who had started the fire. Hadn't François Roy, the town crier, broadcast that news the night before? The arsonist had slept with them in the courtyard. She had shared their food and drink, all the while denying her involvement in setting the blaze.

For Angélique, dawn brought with it an intensification of her fear. She knew that soon officers of the Maréchaussée, the city constabulary, would come looking for her. She knew, but she could not run. What was the point? When she ran in February, had they not tracked and found her? Then, her only offence was flight; now, it was arson. If she ran, the authorities would have the combined forces of police, army, and militia hunting for her. And they would find her, she was sure of that. A Black person trying to hide in a hostile White environment? An almost impossible task. Immobilized by fear, and perhaps by resignation, she stayed put in the Chapel of the Virgin Mary.

Even before dawn dissolved, the police began their investigations. They knew the fire had started on the roof of Madame Francheville's house, in the attic. The granaries were housed in the attic and, incidentally, so was Angélique's bedroom. They went to Sieur Tremon's, where Madame Francheville had taken refuge, and questioned her. She told them she suspected that Angélique had set the fire. She made a deposition and signed it. The police questioned other residents, who pointed the finger at Angélique. That same morning, members of the constabulary marched to the hospital courtyard, searched for Angélique, found her in the chapel, arrested her, and escorted her to the town jail. The officers searched for Thibault too, but did not find him. They issued a warrant for his capture and arrest.

Why did Angélique remain in the garden of the poor? She stayed because the gates of the city were closed and closely guarded by the police and militia, and she could not escape even if she tried. She stayed because she knew Thibault had betrayed her by running away without her. Some time after moving Madame Francheville's furniture to the hospital and eating his supper, Claude Thibault had vanished into the smoke-filled air.

✳

The Montréal fire of 1734 has been described as "the most spectacular crime that a slave ever committed in Canada."[5] The historian who said this assumed that the fire was caused by arson, and that Angélique was the culprit. Pierre Raimbault and the court tribunal in Montréal certainly thought so. However, they felt that Thibault was also criminally responsible. But with Thibault nowhere to be found, Raimbault had to use what he had. Angélique was the main suspect; Thibault was cast as an accomplice. Angélique was taken into custody. She languished in jail for all of April 11, and on the following day, the authorities, led by Pierre Raimbault, judge for the jurisdiction of Montréal, and François Foucher, the king's procurator (chief attorney or prosecutor), began criminal proceedings against her.

VIII

The Aftermath

THE MORNING AFTER the fire, the lower town was a scene of charred ruins. Smoke hung thickly in the air. People sifted through the debris, trying to assess the extent of the damage to their lives and livelihood. Houses, furniture, papers, goods, and stocks amounting to hundreds of thousands of livres were gone. However, in the midst of the ruin, there was one bright spot: no lives had been lost.

Along with the ordinary citizens, government and Church officials did their own review of the wreckage. The governor of Montréal, Josué Dubois Berthelot de Beaucours, sent news of the fire and the attendant destruction to his superiors in the colony's capital. Later on, the colony's two top officials, Governor Charles de Beauharnois and Intendant Gilles Hocquart, would meet with the Conseil Supérieur to discuss the urgent matter. They would then dispatch the king's engineer, Gaspard-Joseph Chaussegros de Léry, to review and report on the fire and make recommendations.

Meanwhile, governor and intendant would give leave to

their representatives in Montréal to command the resources of the treasury to assist the victims of the fire and pay for the damages. The king's storehouse was usually stocked with supplies to provide for the needs of the military. But in times of emergency, these provisions were used to meet the needs of ordinary citizens. Immediately after the fire, officials distributed blankets, flour, corn flour, wheat, dried meats, trousers, overcoats, textiles, pots, pans, and other kitchen utensils. Items amounting to over 3,000 livres were dispensed at the king's pleasure, though even this outpouring could not adequately meet the needs of the people.

Because it was spring and ships bound for France would soon be leaving the Québec port, Beauharnois and Hocquart put pen to paper and wrote to Maurepas, the minister of marine in France, informing him of the tragic incident. The letter, written in May, has disappeared from Beauharnois's and Hocquart's papers in the colonial archives, but the two men sent a more detailed letter in October, on what was probably one of the last ships to leave Québec for France that year. In this letter, the governor and intendant detailed the destruction wrought by the fire and pointed out that the mercantile community and Hôtel-Dieu were hit the hardest.

> ...the fire which happened in Montréal the 10th April before, at seven o'clock in the evening; the fire having spread to the roof of the house of the widow Francheville, located on the shore of the river, consumed the neighbouring houses so quickly that, in spite of our efforts, in less than three hours forty-six houses were destroyed, of which the Hotel-Dieu was one of them. The majority of these houses belonged to the best

wholesale merchants; in general they have lost almost
all their moveable possessions, personal effects, and
merchandise. The sieur Lestage, who was the wealthiest wholesale merchant in the colony, is said to have
lost 200,000 livres, and other wholesale merchants or
property owners of the said houses have lost possessions in similar proportions to that amount (namely
the widow Francheville, the Sieur Béréy, Radisson,
Deschaillons, Joncaire, Périgny, Gamelin, Guillory
and others...[1]

With these bigger merchants, and others, losing so much in
the fire, Montréal's commerce—the lifeblood of the society—had been dealt a severe blow.

But perhaps the greatest blow to the town and its inhabitants,
and to the citizenry of the surrounding countryside, was the
destruction of Hôtel-Dieu. The history of Hôtel-Dieu is inter-
woven with that of Montréal. The town, as already noted, was
founded in 1642 by members of the Société de Notre-Dame.
Among the members of this society was the indomitable Jeanne
Mance. Today, Mance is celebrated as one of the founders and
pioneers of Montréal, and for good reason. She helped the
fledgling settlement get off the ground by founding its first hospital, Hôtel-Dieu, in 1644. After spending some time in
Montréal, Mance returned to France, raised funds for the hospital from Jérôme Le Royer de La Dauversière, an early sup-
porter of the Montréal colony, and came back to Montréal with
three nursing sisters to staff the hospital.

As the town grew, so did the hospital. By the time of the
1734 fire, the nursing staff had grown to forty, with six assistants. There was also at least one physician-surgeon, a male, of

course, on staff. Hôtel-Dieu was both hospital and cloistered convent. The nursing sisters called themselves the Religieuses Hopitalières de Saint-Joseph à la Flèche, as their initial support came from a French institution of that name. From the time of Mance onwards, the hospital expanded tremendously, not only in physical size but also in influence. The Montréal sisters came under the religious authority of the Sulpician fathers, and Hôtel-Dieu itself, situated on rue Saint-Paul, was less than a stone's throw from the Sulpician seminary on rue Notre-Dame.

Hôtel-Dieu was a social and military hospital and provided indispensable services to the region. Given that Montréal was the largest military garrison in the colony and the colony was always in a state of war or readiness for war, Hôtel-Dieu's importance cannot be overestimated. Sick and wounded soldiers had to be cared for. But the hospital cared for everyone—soldiers, habitants, aristocrats, and slaves. It was at the heart of Montréal, and was perhaps more important to Montréal than even the Church.

Yet, in spite of all the good work that the nursing sisters dispensed to the community, the hospital had a "tragic history of destruction."[2] It was first destroyed by fire in 1695, and was rebuilt. Fire once again claimed the hospital in 1721, and it was again rebuilt. Thirteen years later, in 1734, the flaming enemy ravaged Hôtel-Dieu once more, and the nuns found themselves for a third time without shelter, and the town without a hospital. In 1805, fire would once again destroy the hospital.

Hôtel-Dieu was a self-contained and self-sufficient institution. Walls enclosed it, and at the centre was a garden and courtyard created for the exclusive use of the cloistered nuns. The garden served for recreation and contemplation, and for growing herbs, which the sisters used as medicines. The hospital had wards for men, women, and the poor, and the complex also contained a bakery, a drug dispensary, a laundry, a shoemaker's shop, a small chapel dedicated to the Virgin Mary, a garden and courtyard for the poor, and several outer buildings.

Bonds of blood, marriage, and business connected the nuns to the rest of Montréal society. Many of the nursing sisters came from the upper echelons of society and were linked to the leading military, judicial, and commercial families. For example, at the time of the fire, Suzanne de Couagne, sister of Madame Francheville, was a Hôtel-Dieu nun. The mother superior, Mother Françoise Gaudé, was related to the de Couagne family. Sieur Francheville, when he was alive, had loaned the sisters money. Sieur Montigny, who gave shelter to the nuns in his spacious house after the fire, had two daughters who were nursing sisters at Hôtel-Dieu. At the time of the Conquest in 1760, Sister de Ramezay, daughter and heiress of the famous administrative Ramezay family, was the Mother Superior of the Québec branch of Hôtel-Dieu. And Thérèse Francheville herself would spend her last days at the hospital.

For many girls from wealthy and aristocratic families, entering the convent was a viable alternative to marriage. When these young women took their vows to become nuns, they also took their dowries to the Church. This act symbolized that they had become brides of Christ. Yet they were working nuns. They ran the hospital, trained themselves in the art and science of medicine and pharmacy, initiated and invested in real estate and business ventures, rented out their rural properties, and made articles to sell to local people and visitors.

When, on April 10, 1734, the nuns heard the cry of fire, they were as alarmed as everyone else and tried to save themselves and their property. However, the hospital was situated directly across from the Francheville home and was soon engulfed in flames. Sister Marie-Anne-Véronique Cuillerier, the eighteenth-century historian of Hôtel-Dieu, in her book *Relation de Soeur Cuillerier*, gives us an intimate account of the impact of the 1734 fire. She tells us that, early in the blaze, the roof of the hospital and convent fell in. When the nuns got out of the burning buildings, they took refuge in the garden of the poor, with the rest of the victims. Most of the hospital buildings were destroyed. Sister Cuillerier wrote, "The losses were enormous: the furniture, the vestry linen, the articles for sale (the money from which was used to provide for the needs of the sick and the nuns) and the supplies on hand, the register of minutes of persons taking the veil or making a profession, all were destroyed in the fire. The consecrated vessels of the church were saved, however."[3] Sister Cuillerier notes that the destruction of the pharmacy was a tremendous loss.

But there was some good news. As the chronicler notes, the nuns managed to pull the sacred vases from the fire, and by some miracle the small Chapel of the Virgin Mary escaped the flames. Some nuns took refuge inside the chapel. Among the group were some who were witnessing for the third time the destruction of their beloved hospital. Seeing the havoc around them, remembering past events, and foreseeing a bleak future, the nuns broke down and wept. The nuns were filled with such desolation that, even though they were hungry and thirsty, they were unable to touch the food the Sulpician fathers brought them.

The nuns and their patients spent the next two nights among the ruins. Mother Gaudé did what she could for the relief of the victims—both nuns and refugees. "But what could she do, having nothing to give?" laments Cuillerier.[4] The *Relation de Soeur Cuillerier* tells us that the nights were cold (it was the beginning of spring) and the thawing mud "came up to our knees."[5] The nuns planned a course of action. A group of nuns took the sickest patients to the Saint-Joseph farm, a property owned by the nuns and located in the northern suburbs. A second group of sisters took another batch of patients to a farm owned by the Charon brothers (a lay religious order). The remaining members of the religious community stayed among the ruins of the hospital and their convent.

At this stage, the Sulpicians stepped in. Acting on behalf of the government, the vicar, Monseigneur Louis Normant, rented a large house (the largest house in Montréal, in fact) from Sieur Jacques de Montigny. The house was large enough to lodge the three scattered bands of sisters. For Montigny, helping the Hôtel-Dieu community was personal. Two of his daughters, Marie-Marguerite and Marie-Josephe, were members of the community. The Sulpicians also rented a house across the street from Montigny to lodge the patients. The nuns were reunited at Montigny's house on May 20, more than five weeks after the fire.

Montigny's property was located in the spacious eastern sector of the city, near the chapel of Notre-Dame-de-Bon-secours. The proximity to the chapel was a great boon to the usually cloistered nuns, because they could walk to mass without mingling with those from outside the community. They constructed a covered walkway connecting the house to the chapel, which allowed them to walk to church in private and shielded them from the inquisitive eyes of the public.

The letters of Beauharnois and Hocquart provide more

details on the impact of the fire on Hôtel-Dieu. These two officials were aware of the value of the hospital to the community. They knew that the hospital was indispensable to the city, and especially to the military establishment. They wrote to Maurepas:

> L'Hôtel-Dieu has occupied all our attention, considering the state in which the fire has left it. M. Hocquart has had the honour of informing you...that all the buildings, be they those belonging to the nuns or those of the poor, were destroyed by the fire. Virtually nothing was saved except several mattresses, a very small bit of linen, and some medicine from the apothecary. The destitution in which these nuns find themselves, in all things, and the poverty of a hospital in Montréal where can be found the greatest number of troops, have compelled us under your good pleasure to place the nuns in the house of Sieur de Montigny near the chapel of Notre-Dame de Bon Secours, and the sick in the neighbouring house where they are being tended to as they had been before at the Hôtel-Dieu. We have taken the liberty to act in your name for the rest of these two houses, which have settled at 750 livres for both of them, until the hospital can be re-established.[6]

The officials also informed Maurepas of the poverty of the nursing sisters and of their inability to rebuild the hospital.

> We have examined the diverse means by which the re-establishment of Hôtel-Dieu can be achieved, and after having reviewed the state of temporal affairs of this community [meaning the community of nursing sisters] and

the expenses that it must pay, we have the honour,
Monseigneur, of addressing to you a summary document
to which are attached different statements either of the
revenues of the community of the hospital, of the out-
standing debts that are owed to them and the debts that
the community must pay, and that which was burned or
lost in the fire. You will see, Monseigneur, by these statements that the revenues of this house do not permit the
nuns to even to attempt their re-establishment; we have
thus appealed to the charity of the people of this colony
and particularly those of the government of Montréal
who maintain a deep affection for this community
[Hôtel-Dieu].[7]

The officials pressed their point. It was absolutely necessary
to rebuild the hospital, and the only viable way to do so was
with the king's money.

To speak truthfully, the majority have contributed already
to this undertaking. The inhabitants of the countryside.
through our gentle appeals and our letters circulated by
the parish priests and militia officers, have supplied them
[the nuns] with a part of the wood necessary for the roof
of the buildings. They have acquired a bit of monetary
help from the wealthiest inhabitants, and a bit of wheat,
and from the labourers of Montréal some days of work
given free of charge. At the present time, all of this
amounts to about 3,000 livres, a very modest sum with
which to commence the work if we have not taken the
liberty to procure for them from the Treasurer of Marine
the sum of 5,000 livres, which was used to pay for the

floor boards, the timber beams for the roof, the payment of the workers, and other work necessary for the hospital; and, confident in the hope that they have in your kindness, during this summer they have started to reconstruct a part of the walls, and to set the beams, and to cover part of the building in order to protect it from the harsh winter weather. And that is all they could do this year. They will not be in a state to undertake anything more, if you do not have the kindness, Monseigneur, to procure for them some appropriate assistance from the king.[8]

The officials then appealed to Maurepas for further financial assistance and reminded him that, in the last Montréal fire, he had given a generous contribution to the rebuilding efforts: "You were kind enough to procure for them a sum of 18,000 livres after the fire of 1721, a fire which did not do nearly as much damage to them as this past one."[9]

Then there was the issue of the fortifications. The wall around Montréal was still being constructed at the time of the fire. The Crown had harnessed the resources of the land—human power, corvée labour, and excessive taxation— to continue and complete the fortifications. If the citizens wanted a wall for their protection, they had to reach deep into their pockets and pay for it. Prior to the fire, Sieur Raimbault, lieutenant general for civil and criminal matters, had prepared the tax rolls. The inhabitants owed 5,000 livres in taxes for the fortifications. However, the fire turned the town upside down, and the administration had to reconsider how to go about the business of taxation. For one thing, the fire halted work on the wall. Further, it became obvious that the homeowners and building owners victimized by the fire would be unable to pay their portion. Their share of the taxes came to 1,000 livres, but the administrators, knowing their distress, discharged these sufferers from their obligations. Whatever material resources the victims now possessed had to be invested in rebuilding their homes and businesses. The intendant and governor had no choice but to resign themselves to the status quo and hope that the remaining sum of 4,000 livres would "be paid by the other inhabitants and communities of the town."[10]

Responding to the appeal from Beauharnois and Hocquart, Maurepas gave the Hôtel-Dieu community a grant of 10,000 livres and approved an annual grant of 1,500 livres "to be made until the work of rebuilding was complete." The reconstruction of Hôtel-Dieu continued bit by bit, and eighteen months after the fire the nuns and the sick returned to the newly reconstructed hospital. Rebuilding was finally completed in 1743.

The fire affected people in other crucial ways. The papers of Sieur Francheville and Madame Francheville went up in flames. Some of these documents would have served as important sources for generations of historians. Sister Cuillerier tells us that important papers of Hôtel-Dieu also went up in smoke.

Attached to Beauharnois and Hocquart's missive to Maurepas were some letters of appeal from at least three worthy sufferers. Sieur Deschaillons, a retired military officer, owned two of the houses that burned. He lived in Québec, so he had been renting out these houses to supplement his pension. Intendant and governor appealed to Maurepas to provide some financial assistance to Deschaillons, as he was in need and had a family to provide for.

Likewise, Madame de Ramezay, widow of former Montréal governor Claude de Ramezay, had her house on rue Notre-

Dame destroyed by the fire. Madame de Ramezay has become a legend in Canadian history because she ran several business ventures and did not remarry upon the death of her husband but charted a business career as an "indomitable widow." However, as a victim of the blaze, she too appealed to Maurepas for help. "She has lost everything," wrote Beauharnois and Hocquart. They reminded the minister that Madame de Ramezay's husband had served the king for many years as a dutiful and loyal servant in his capacity as governor of Montréal.

The other letter was from the notary Charles-René Guadron de Chevremont. He had lost all his furniture and other personal effects in the fire and wrote to the minister appealing for assistance. Gaudron de Chevremont was to act as one of the legal assessors and assistant judge in Angélique's trial.

The fire had other long-term consequences. It led to new and more effective fire-prevention regulations. No sooner had the blaze cooled in Montréal than the king's engineer, de Léry, began an investigation of the situation. De Léry was responsible for the defence of the town, in that he had to discover its vulnerabilities and make recommendations. It was he who had designed the stone wall that surrounded the city. For de Léry, investigating the 1734 fire seemed like déjà vu. In 1721, when a fire burned out of control in Montréal, de Léry had investigated it and made recommendations for fire prevention. The intendant at that time, Michel Bégon, made de Léry's recommendations into law to better prepare the town if fire should strike again:

> At the sound of the bell, everyone, rich or poor alike, was to run to the fire with a bucket and axe. Every home was to have a ladder in good condition and to have its chimney

swept once a month. Any new home built was not to extend out into the street. Only stone houses shall be built in the future, and all newly built houses whose roofs are being redone shall not be covered in shingles.[11]

By 1734, when the next blaze occurred, at least half of the houses in the town's core were made of stone. However, many people ignored the regulations and roofed their houses with wooden materials. The clause in the 1721 ordinance about covering the roof with stone tiles was repeatedly disregarded, mainly because of the high cost.

Upon his investigation of the 1734 fire, the engineer saw once again how easy it was for the town to burn. Shingles, as usual, posed a problem. The houses, especially in the core of the town, were too tightly packed together. De Léry's representations to the intendant resulted in a new fire-prevention ordinance that provided for every aspect of fire prevention, from chimney care to Montréal's first firefighting brigade:

> The ordinance provided for the manufacture of 280 buckets, eighty to be made of leather and the rest of wood; 100 axes and the same number of shovels; twenty-four iron hooks or joined poles with chains and cords that could be used to pop off the rafters; twelve long ladders, and twelve hand battering rams....All these instruments were marked with a fleur-de-lys.
>
> The equipment was to be stored in four places: at the guardhouse and with the Sulpicians, the Récollets and the Jesuits....Chimney sweeping was made mandatory, and every chimney was to have a ladder that could easily reach the chimney through an appropriate opening. The attic of

every house was to be provided with two battering rams long enough to reach the ridgepole. The lieutenant general of the city was to draw up a list of carpenters, masons and roofers who were to be divided into two squads, each under the direction of a master worker. The members of these squads were to be the first on the scene of a fire, on penalty of a six-livre fine.[12]

In spite of the thoroughness of the ordinance, the authorities felt it necessary to mandate that citizens provide themselves with their own axe and bucket, which they were to take to the scene of a fire. Failure to bring one's own equipment to a fire "would be punished with a fifty-livre fine and the stocks."[13] Beauharnois and Hocquart told Maurepas that the new ordinance contained provisions not included in previous regulations. They also assured the minister that they meant for this new ordinance to be "carried out to the letter."[14] The precautions must have worked because, with the exception of a fire twenty years later that destroyed the Bonsecours Chapel, Montréal had no more serious fires until the time of the English regime.

But these changes would be some time in coming. In the first days after the 1734 fire, the shocked and angry people of Montréal demanded retribution for their misery and tribulations. The April fire had devastated the city and "plunged into misery"[15] almost every shopkeeper, merchant, nun, widow, worker, and soldier, many of whom had to start again from scratch. Their demands would be satisfied. The king's hand of justice had a long reach, and it would ensure that whoever was responsible for the crime would be made to pay.[16]

IX

The Trial

IN THEIR LONG EPISTLE to Maurepas, Beauharnois and
Hocquart expressed what came to be the most popular opinion about the perpetrator of the blaze. "This incident took
place because of the wickedness of a Negress slave belonging
to the Widow Francheville, who, as a result of some displeasure expressed by her mistress, deliberately set fire to the granaries located in the said house..."[1] It became a historical
"fact" that it was Marie-Joseph Angélique who set fire to
Montréal in 1734. And for the next two and a half centuries,
historians, creative writers, journalists, and other commentators would echo the governor and intendant by declaring
Angélique guilty of arson. The officials responsible for criminal justice in the jurisdiction of Montréal shared
Beauharnois's and Hocquart's belief. But it would be a mock-
ery of the king's justice for any accused person to be convicted and condemned without a trial.

When the officers of the constabulary dragged Angélique
from the garden of Hôtel-Dieu, they took her to the city's

prison. In the years leading up to Angélique's arrest, the prison had undergone significant changes. In 1708, it had only two cells, but in 1720 a courtroom was built, as were chambers to lodge the jailer. In 1730, the intendant ordered a wall built around the prison as a protective measure. Despite these additions, the prison was not intended to be a place where long-term sentences were served. No one languished there for months or years; punishments were carried out almost immediately after judgment was pronounced. Hangings, whippings, being placed in the stocks, and other forms of public punishment took place at the market (today's Place Royale). If a long-term sentence was imposed, the unfortunate offender spent it not in prison but in the king's galley as a royal slave.

Eighteenth-century prisons were not places of repose. They were meant to put terror in the hearts of evildoers. The cells were cramped, damp, dark, and dirty. They swarmed with vermin. Hunger was the order of the day, food being a crust of stale bread and a jug of rancid water. The Montréal prison in which Angélique was lodged was no different. Her cell was small but long enough to hold the body of a grown person lying down. There were no windows, and a strong wooden door locked her in. Her bedding was straw, and she was fed the customary jug of water and piece of bread. Angélique spent April 11 locked in jail while the authorities prepared their case against her.

François Foucher, Montréal's *procureur du roi* (the king's procurator or attorney general), would present the case against Angélique. Foucher had come to Canada in 1722 as Intendant Bégon's secretary and in 1727 received the appointment as the *procureur du roi* for Montréal. As the king's attorney, he was responsible for overseeing the investigations into criminal cases and initiating the proceedings. He wasted no time in Angélique's case; on the morning of April 11, he asked Pierre Raimbault, the lieutenant general for criminal and civil matters and judge for Montréal, to allow him to begin his investigations. It is instructive to note that, in Foucher's request to Raimbault to begin the investigations, he was already suggesting that Angélique was guilty. In the missive to Raimbault, Foucher commented that according to "common opinion" it was Angélique who had set the fire, and that she had previously tried to escape from Montréal with Claude Thibault. He also declared that Angélique had often threatened Madame Francheville and Montréal itself with fire; that on the day of the fire, the slave woman had said her mistress and her neighbours would not sleep in their homes that night; and that Angélique set the fire in the attic of the Francheville home.

Foucher continued:

> With this taken into consideration, Monsieur, we beseech you to permit the said King's procurator to obtain information about this affair, and, however, to arrest and conduct to the royal prisons of this town the said negress and even the said Thibault (considering, according to a common rumour, he had been seen with the said negress last night) in order to be questioned by you, Monsieur, and the interrogations and information acquired to be communicated to whomever will be in need of them.[2]

Foucher's statements reveal that he had done some prior investigations and received intelligence about Angélique's recent doings. Even before the trial began, Foucher was already building up a case against Angélique.

Raimbault wrote back to Foucher authorizing him to imprison Angélique and to summon the witnesses. Foucher issued subpoenas and, with Raimbault, took down witness depositions. He also directed the police to begin a manhunt for Claude Thibault.

The proceedings surrounding Angélique lasted from April 11, when she was arrested, to June 21, when she was hanged. The investigations and interrogations stretched from April 12 to June 4, when the judge handed down the death sentence. The second phase of the proceedings then commenced, with Foucher launching the appeal and sending the case to the Conseil Supérieur in Québec. The appeal process ended on June 12, when the Superior Court upheld the conviction and Angélique was returned to Montréal. From June 15 to June 21, there were more interrogations, tortures, and then, finally, execution.

The French legal system was inquisitorial and therefore hostile. The accused was presumed to be guilty, and it was incumbent on her to prove her innocence. Louis XIV had banned lawyers from practising in New France, so accused prisoners had to defend themselves. They had no right to due process or a trial by jury. Cases were heard by a tribunal, which consisted of the judge, the *procureur du roi*, and the *greffier*, or king's scribe, whose job it was to write down the witnesses' testimonies, the words of the accused, and all the questions posed by the judge. Royal notaries were also part of the tribunal. They helped prepare cases and gave legal advice. In Montréal, a trial took place either at the courthouse or at the prison, which had a small courtroom attached to it. Sometimes trials alternated between both places.

Criminal trials in New France followed the prosecutor's intense and elaborate investigation. Witnesses were called to give testimony before the *procureur du roi* and the judge, and the accused was then questioned. This interrogation consisted of a series of questions being fired at the offender, who had to answer quickly or be presumed guilty. It was said of the French judges that they overwhelmed "prisoners with hostile questioning so severe that it could be called the first stage of torture."[3] If the prosecutor believed more investigation was needed, he called more witnesses and recalled the accused. This latter aspect of the trial was hostile: questions would rain down on the accused with the intent of "breaking" her.

If necessary, the prosecutor would also recall of some of the major witnesses for further questioning, to make sure they stood by their original stories. The next step, the confrontation, had the prisoner and each witness face off against each other. The witness repeated to the prisoner's face what he had earlier told the judge. During the confrontations, the prisoner attempted to discredit the witness by denying or challenging the testimony in order to, she hoped, establish her innocence.[4] The tribunal sat and watched, with the scribe recording the exchange. Afterwards, the witness and the accused could change their stories. Further cross-examination of the accused followed if the prosecutor still had doubts.

Torture was standard in criminal cases in New France, especially if the prosecution suspected that the accused was withholding crucial information. The system of torture was two-tiered. First there was *la question ordinaire*, a single round of torture that the prosecutor hoped would induce the accused to confess. If that did not work, then the prosecutor moved to *la question extraordinaire*, a more intense and excruciating round of torment usually applied by the hangman. The accused generally confessed under *la question extraordinaire*.

Angélique's trial involved all these aspects of criminal procedure. The key players included not only Foucher and Raimbault but also Claude-Cyprien-Jacques Porlier, the scribe, and four notaries—Jean-Baptiste Adhémar, Nicolas-Auguste Guillet de Chaumont, Charles-René Gaudron de Chevremont, and François Lepailleur—who were called in as legal advisers. Gaudron de Chevremont, who was a judge for his seigneury of Île Jésus (a Montréal suburb), would also act as assistant judge in Angélique's trial. There were at least two dozen witnesses, including Thérèse Couagne de Francheville, Angélique's mistress; her neighbours Marguerite César, Alexis Monière, Étienne Radisson, and Jeanne de Béréy; the domestics Catherine Custeau and Marie-Françoise Thomellete; the slave girl Marie-Manon; and three children, Marguerite de Couagne, Charlotte Desrivières, and Amable Lemoine *dit* Monière.

Others rounding out the dramatis personae included the town crier, who on the night of the fire went through the streets announcing that it had been set by the "Negress of Madame Francheville" (several weeks later, he would also announce the guilty verdict); members of the colonial police who arrested Angélique and sought out the witnesses; the bailiff and the jailer; the governor, the intendant, and the members of the Conseil Supérieur; and, last but not least, the torturer and royal executioner, Mathieu Leveille. But, of course, Marie-Joseph Angélique was the main character. Moreover, she was the only voice in her own defence. She was the slave woman who had "awkward visions of freedom"[5] and had taken steps to liberate herself. She had failed.

On the morning of April 12, the prison keeper transported

Angélique a few blocks from the jail to the courthouse. And so began one of the most spectacular trials to come out of eighteenth-century Canada. The Montréal court was responsible for civil and criminal matters for the city proper and the outlying districts. At the time of Angélique's trial, Pierre Raimbault had been working as the king's judge for seven years. He was an important figure in the judicial and political world of Montréal and New France. As judge, one of his duties was to help the prosecutor gather evidence and prepare the case.

Raimbault was born in Montréal in 1671 and by the time he was twenty had established himself as a cabinetmaker. He began his legal career as a notary in 1697 and was made royal notary two years later, launching a remarkable legal career that saw him appointed as king's attorney, then a subdelegate of the intendant, or local governor. In 1720, he became lieutenant of police, and seven years later he was appointed lieutenant general for the court of Montréal.[6]

Angélique's was the most remarkable trial that Raimbault or the notaries had ever presided over. Arson in the eighteenth century was a capital crime; this meant it was punishable by death. If death was not recommended, the defendant could expect severe physical punishment, long-term imprisonment, or banishment. In Angélique's case, the authorities had no intention of banishing her.

The first step in the trial was to examine and interrogate the prisoner, and this Raimbault commenced on the afternoon of April 12. In order to establish guilt, the court required only the testimony of two supposedly impartial witnesses and the confession of the accused. Raimbault called more than two witnesses, however; in fact, close to two dozen made depositions, and he examined each three times. All but one spoke against Angélique.

Let us go back to the afternoon of April 12, 1734, and look at the scribe's first entry in the court ledger. "The year one thousand seven hundred and thirty four, the afternoon of the twelfth of April," he wrote, "we, Pierre Raimbault, official of the king, lieutenant general, for civil and criminal matters, for the royal jurisdiction of Montréal, went to the chamber of the royal prison of this city, and brought before us the Negress of demoiselle Francheville, named Angélique, the latter, in virtue of our order of yesterday, at the request of the king's procurator." The entry then continued: "The aforementioned, after pronouncing an oath to tell the truth, was interrogated by us as follows: asked about her age, her qualities, and her residence. She stated that her name was Marie-Joseph, her age twenty-nine, that she had been born in Portugal and that she had been sold to a Flamand [a man from Flanders or one who lives there] who sold her to the late Sieur Francheville about nine years ago, where she remained ever since."

During his questioning, Raimbault established that Angélique had previously tried to run away from slavery, and that she had attempted to do so with Claude Thibault, her lover and fellow worker in the Francheville household. She "said it was only about six weeks ago that she went with Thibault, whose first name is Claude, with the intent of going to New England," recorded the scribe, "and that they only got as far as thirty leagues [from Montréal] in order to proceed to New England and from there to her country of Portugal."

Pierre Raimbault had done his homework. By the time the blaze cooled, he knew that Angélique had threatened to burn her mistress if Madame Francheville did not give her *congé*, or permission to leave. The court transcripts provide a record of the first exchange between Raimbault and Angélique:

RAIMBAULT: Did you threaten to burn your mistress if she did not give you leave to depart?

ANGÉLIQUE: No.

RAIMBAULT: On the day of the fire did you not tell the Panise [enslaved woman of Aboriginal ancestry] of Sieur de Béréy that her mistress would not be sleeping at home that night?

ANGÉLIQUE: No, I would have been possessed by the devil to have done so.

RAIMBAULT: Did you not say to someone who accused you of having caused so much loss, and the present fire, that she would see more, for the rest of the city would burn?

ANGÉLIQUE: No. On the contrary, the Widow Francheville blamed me for setting the fire to the house. I told her that however nasty I might be, I am not wretched enough to commit an act of that sort.

RAIMBAULT: When the fire began to appear on the roof of the Widow Francheville, you stopped the young girl, Desrivières, from yelling and warning of the fire, pulling her back by the apron when she tried to warn Widow Francheville.

ANGÉLIQUE: The girl you mentioned and Miss [Marguerite] de Couagne were playing, and I wanted to prevent them from running in the mud. I wanted them to play on the doorstep.

RAIMBAULT: Before the fire appeared on the roof, did you not take water and food to the pigeons up on the roof, where the fire began?

ANGÉLIQUE: Yes, it is true that I took food and water to the pigeons, but I did not go alone. The Widow Francheville went up with me.

RAIMBAULT: Did you not go up to the attic, where the pigeons were, after dinner?

ANGÉLIQUE: I did not go up there at all.

Raimbault: On the night of the fire, did you have a green blanket?

ANGÉLIQUE: Yes.

Raimbault introduced in this initial interrogation what for him were some of the most crucial elements in the case against Angélique: Marie-Manon, the Aboriginal slave girl of Sieur de Béréy, had heard Angélique say that her mistress would not sleep in her house on the night of April 10; someone else had heard her say that she would "burn" her mistress; and she had even tried to prevent Desrivières from warning people of the fire.

Raimbault clearly thought that Angélique had set the fire. She was a recalcitrant slave who had threatened her mistress with burning and even bragged to a fellow slave about what she planned to do. She had gone to the roof to feed the pigeons and could easily have set the fire at that time. She had even prevented an eyewitness from warning others of the blaze. There were a lot of holes in the picture Raimbault was trying to paint, but there was something ominous in several of Angélique's responses.

When her answers were read to her, Angélique declared that they were truthful and that she was sticking to them. When asked to sign the document, she declared that she could not write. Judge Raimbault, Foucher, and Porlier signed the document. Porlier also wrote: "In light of the interrogation and conclusion above noted that it be ordered that the Negress will be questioned once again."

In the following days, Raimbault issued subpoenas to a number of residents, asking them to appear before the tribunal as witnesses in his case against Angélique. On April 14, Étienne Volant de Radisson, a colonel in the city's militia and first cousin of François Poulin de Francheville, was the first witness to appear.

Radisson, who lived next door to the Franchevilles, had lost his home to the fire and was boarding with a neighbour. He related that around 7:00 p.m. on April 10, the evening of the fire, Angélique came and told him there was a fire at her house. "Immediately, he took two buckets full of water and carried them and climbed the stairs with her to the attic. He saw the fire had caught the floorboard of the pigeon-house. The Negress cried out 'my God, fire is everywhere,' and went back downstairs. He did not see a ladder; he asked Angélique for one, but she said there was none. He went back down to save his house, which was adjoined to that of the late Sieur Francheville."

Radisson went on to say that he had "since heard it said by Madame de Béréy that her servant had told her that the said Negress had said several hours beforehand that her mistress, who was with Madame Desrivières, 'that *chienne*, will not be laughing soon, because she will not sleep in her house.'"

Radisson's testimony placed Angélique at the scene of the fire and proved that she was the first one to know about it. He also repeated Marie-Manon's assertion that Angélique had said her mistress "would not sleep in the house tonight." Almost every witness after him repeated this statement, which was quickly becoming a "fact."

Thérèse de Couagne de Francheville was the next to bear witness. Raimbault recorded that she was thirty-six years old and the widow of the late Sieur François Poulin de Francheville. He also noted that since the fire she had been staying in the home of Sieur Alexis Monière, a friend, relative, and business associate. It seems that by this time the widow had left Sieur Tremon's house to stay with Monière. Widow Francheville confirmed that Angélique was her slave. She first testified "that she doesn't know at all who set the fire in her house and she does not know the circumstances under which the aforesaid Negress went up to the roof."

Madame Francheville said that on the morning of April 10 she went up to the attic with Angélique, but there was no fire there at that time. She left the house at noon to go to the midday mass, and Angélique stayed at home. Madame Francheville also told the tribunal that the day before the fire Claude Thibault had been at her house, asking for money he had earned for work he did for her before he fled with Angélique in February.

She testified that she told Thibault, perhaps unwisely, that she had sold Angélique, that she no longer wanted to keep her, and that he was not to set foot in her house again. She reported seeing Thibault again on the night of the fire, when he appeared in the garden of the hospital and was helping to carry items that had been saved from her house. Madame Francheville concluded that it was "the Negress who set the fire because there was no fire in the chimneys."

Madame Francheville introduced a new line to the story. She cast Thibault in the role of informer and gave Angélique a motive for setting the fire. When Thibault appeared at the Francheville house on the morning of April 9, he had just come from prison. He had been lodged there since early

March, when he and Angélique had been captured on their escape attempt. Madame Francheville's belief was that Thibault had told Angélique that she had sold her, and that Angélique, out of revenge, had set the fire in the evening.

The next person to bear witness before the court was Madame Francheville's ten-year-old niece, Marguerite de Couagne, the daughter of Sieur de Couagne, a captain in the military and a royal engineer. Marguerite, who was currently attending school with the nuns of the Congregation of Notre-Dame, repeated what the others had said before her. She had heard it said that Angélique had told Marie-Manon that Madame Francheville would not sleep in her house that night. She added that two or three times prior to the fire she had seen Thibault with Angélique in her aunt's kitchen.

The next witness was Marie-Manon, the slave girl of Sieur de Béréy. She was an important witness, for Angélique's threatening remarks about her mistress had been made to her. "Shortly before the fire appeared in Madame Francheville's house," wrote Porlier, recording Marie-Manon's deposition, "the one testifying was sitting at the front of the de Béréy house, next to that of the late Sieur Francheville, when the Negress came to her and tickled her to make her laugh. She told her she was not in the mood to laugh. Angélique returned to Madame Francheville's and then came back out at once, laughing and saying excitedly, 'Madame Francheville is laughing well with Madame Desrivières but she will not be in her house much longer and will not sleep there.'" Marie-Manon went on to say that Angélique left, and shortly thereafter she saw Angélique come into the street and look three or four times up and down, then in the direction of the roof of the Francheville house. Angélique then made the Couagne girl and the Desrivières girl go into the house, and a quarter of an hour later somebody screamed out that there was fire. Having come out of the kitchen of the de Béréy house, Marie-Manon saw the pigeonhole of the Francheville house on fire, and Angélique, who was outside, turned pale and screamed "Fire!" Marie-Manon said she then turned to Sieur de Béréy and told him what Angélique had told her about Madame Francheville not sleeping in her house, and that "now she knows why the Negress had made such a statement."

Charlotte Desrivières, the ten-year-old playmate of Marguerite de Couagne, was the next to give a statement. She said she was playing in the Francheville courtyard with Marguerite when she heard someone going up the stairs; Angélique then appeared in the kitchen. Their friend and neighbour, five-year-old Amable Lemoine *dit* Monière, was also present and told her it was Angélique who had gone up the stairs. When the fire appeared, Charlotte and her playmate went into the street, but Angélique came out of the house and insisted that they return.

Charlotte Desrivières was the last witness for the day. The following day, April 15, the first witness was Hyppolyte de Senneville, a fifteen year old. His father, Sieur de Senneville, was a lieutenant and assistant regimental adjutant in the military. Hyppolyte added nothing new, but the testimony of the next witness, Marguerite César, was pivotal.

Madame César, whose home was also destroyed by the fire, testified that

> about a half an hour before the fire appeared on the roof of Madame Francheville's house, she was leaning on her window overlooking the street and saw the aforesaid Negress in

front of the house of her mistress. The Negress looked uneasy. She was looking from one side to the other and stopped for a long time, her face turned toward [Madame César]. She then saw Angélique return to the house, and leave shortly after. Angélique continued her strange behaviour, looking up and down the street and then in the direction of the square, where the hospital was. She was annoyed at seeing Angélique acting so unusual and wanted to try and find out why. She went out into the street to see what the said Negress appeared to want to discover, and she became tired, not seeing anything from one end of the street to the other to give rise to the Negress looking for such a long time. She returned to her house to rest, feeling unwell, and scarcely was sitting down when somebody cried out that there was a fire. Madame César also reported that she "knows the said Negress to be nasty."

The investigations continued with Jeanne de La Baume, another neighbour. She testified that she could not say anything positive, not having seen Angélique set the fire. But the moment she saw the fire, she believed it was Angélique who had set it and told Sieur Radisson what she thought. She had heard two or three times from the children that Angélique had threatened her mistress, saying she would burn her and cut her throat. The former servant of Madame Francheville, Marie-Louise Poirier, had told her, since leaving Madame Francheville's service, that Angélique had said "if she could one day return to her country and there were any French people there, she would make them all perish."

The next person to testifiy was Marie-Louise Poirier, Madame Francheville's former servant. Poirier said she did not know who had set the fire, but she suspected it was Angélique. She stated that, about eight days before the fire, she left the home of Thérèse Francheville because Angélique had threatened her after Poirier had prevented Angélique from drinking brandy and going out without permission. Poirier added that, when she was leaving the household, Madame Francheville told her she would be able to come back soon, because when spring arrived she would be selling Angélique. She said Angélique had told her several times that "if she ever found herself in her country and there were any White people there, she would burn them all like dogs, that they weren't worth anything." Poirier also reported that, when Angélique fled in the winter with Thibault, she stole three deerskins from the Widow Francheville.

From the accounts of La Baume and Poirier, one gets the distinct impression that Angélique had a fascination with burning and fire. She had threatened to burn her mistress and likewise to burn all the French if she ever found them in Portugal. Both women implied that Angélique had carried out her threat to burn the French by setting fire to her mistress's house, a fire that got out of control and destroyed the lower portion of the town.

A few other witnesses, such as domestic Marie-Josephe Bizet, made depositions but added nothing new. However, Jean-Joseph La Flamandière, a surgeon in the army, brought new insights. He had heard the town crier shouting the news of the fire and telling the public that it was Angélique, the slave of Madame Francheville, who was the culprit. He testified that, on the night in question, he took refuge in the garden of the hospital, helping to save and gather together furniture and other effects. There he saw Angélique drinking with two men unknown to him. He reproached her, and she told him it was not alcohol they were drinking but syrup. He went and told the nuns, and they ordered him to return and fetch Angélique. On returning, he found her, but not the two men. He led Angélique into the sleeping area where the nuns were, but she left about fifteen minutes later and went to sit on a straw mattress in the courtyard.

The last witness to appear before Raimbault that day was Françoise Geoffrion, a widow who worked as a domestic for one Sieur Barbel on rue Notre-Dame. She testified that at about one in the afternoon on the day of the fire, while going up the street to the hospital, she met Angélique. She asked Angélique if she was going for a walk and if she was still living with Madame Francheville. Angélique replied that she did not have time to go for a walk and that, while she was still living with Madame Francheville, she would not be for long.

And what of Claude Thibault, Angélique's alleged co-conspirator and lover? He was under suspicion for aiding her, but since the morning after the fire he was nowhere to be found. The king's court wanted him, so on April 19, the governor's office issued a warrant empowering officers of the police and the military to capture and arrest Thibault.

On May 1, new witnesses were brought before the tribunal. The first was Louis Langlois *dit* Traversy, a labourer on the farm owned by Madame Francheville in the Saint-Michel district. Traversy said that, eight or nine days after Angélique was captured (following her escape attempt), he was in the kitchen of Madame Francheville's house. He said to Angélique that she was very bad, that she should not have left as she did, and that she had better watch out or her mistress would sell her. Angélique replied, "The devil of whores, if she sells me she will repent." He asked, "What will you do?" She responded, "We are not saying what we would trouble to do. The snow will clear away, the earth will be uncovered and the tracks will no longer be visible." Traversy stated that Angélique spoke with "rage and fury."

Angélique's comments were a reference to her flight. It was the footprints she and Thibault had made in the snow that gave them away and led to their capture. She was hinting that the next time she made her move there would be no snow to reveal telltale signs. If Traversy's words were true, then Angélique had begun planning her next escape as soon as she was returned following her first attempt.

Marie-Françoise Thomellete, the wife of Traversy, also testified. She stated that she encouraged Angélique "to be a good Christian," and told her that if she did not please her mistress, Madame Francheville would sell her. Angélique replied that if Madame Francheville sold her, she "would repent, she would make her burn." When Thomellete told Angélique that they would hang her if she did that, Angélique laughed and replied that that would not bother her in the least. A few days after Angélique was returned to the Francheville household following her flight with Thibault, Thomellete asked her if her mistress had beaten her for what she did. Angélique said "No, she is not bad at all. I will pay her back well."

By the time Traversy and Thomellete were through, Raimbault and the tribunal must have believed that Angélique was *une méchante*, a very bad person. It's clear that they did not seek out any other suspects, with the exception of Thibault. In their minds, Angélique was the only one who had a sound motive. They suspected that she was in league with Thibault, and that they had set the fire together. But Thibault was missing, and Angélique was in their custody. It did not cross their minds that anyone else could have been responsible.

The tribunal adjourned for a day and reconvened on May 3. On that afternoon, at the city jail, Raimbault began the proceedings by interrogating the accused. Porlier recorded Raimbault's questions and Angélique's responses for posterity.

RAIMBAULT: Why were you so determined, with Thibault, to set fire to your mistress's house?

ANGÉLIQUE: I never spoke to Thibault or anyone else about committing such an act.

RAIMBAULT: Is it not true that the said Thibault, in order to avenge the fact of being imprisoned for setting out with you for New England, prompted you to set the fire in the attic of the said Madame Francheville?

ANGÉLIQUE: No.

RAIMBAULT: What time did you go up to the attic with the fire, and in which spot did you set it?

ANGÉLIQUE: I never carried the fire up to the attic. I only went up to the attic once, the morning of the day it caught fire, and Madame was with me. I don't know where in the attic the fire started.

RAIMBAULT: Was it not true that you were shocked when you went up to the said attic with Sieur Radisson?

ANGÉLIQUE: Yes, I was shocked to see the fire in the attic, because the only fire was in the chimneys of the house.

RAIMBAULT: Explain why you told Sieur Radisson that there was no ladder when he attempted to go up to the attic to throw water on the fire.

ANGÉLIQUE: I never spoke to him about it. There was a stairway, and ladders in the attic to go up to the pigeons' nest. When he asked for a ladder, this was to climb up to a window to save whoever was in the room, because he said that you could no longer climb up the stairs.

Raimbault tried to make Angélique confess that she had indeed gone up to the attic on the evening of the fire, and that she had said to Marie-Manon that Madame Francheville would not sleep in her house that evening. But Angélique denied these allegations.

RAIMBAULT: Tell us if Thibault did not warn you that your mistress had sold you.
ANGÉLIQUE: No. But I had heard from the valet of Monsieur the Commissioner that they were going to send me to the Islands [the West Indies] for what I had done by escaping with Thibault for New England. Madame had told me ten to twelve days before the fire that she wrote to the Quartermaster about selling me. She said that I was too mischievous, and that she did not want to deal with me anymore, that I was always quarrelling with her servant, that I was always creating a commotion in the house. I told Madame that I never wanted to leave her service, that all she had to do was to dismiss her servant [Marie-Louise Poirier] and that I would do just fine by myself, that she would be happy with me. That is what made Madame Francheville tell Poirier to go to work somewhere, and that when I was no longer there she [Poirier] could return to serve her.

Angélique's poignant and heartfelt answer is revealing. She did not want to be sold again. She had learned that she was going to be sold to the West Indies and must have known or heard about the horrors of West Indian slavery. Further, the bondswoman did not want to share her domestic duties with other servants. She told her mistress that she could "do just fine" by herself. Her answer indicates that, even though she did want to leave Canada, it was definitely not for the West Indies. She wanted to return to Portugal, and to do so on her own terms.

Raimbault continued with his questions.

RAIMBAULT: Did your mistress not scold you on the day of the fire, and did you not go into the kitchen to brood?
ANGÉLIQUE: No, Madame was scarcely in the house.
RAIMBAULT: Isn't it true that, before the fire started, you went to the Panise of Sieur de Béréy and told her that "Madame Francheville is laughing right now, but she will not be in her house for very long and she will not sleep there"? And did you not tell Marguerite de Couagne and Charlotte Desrivières, who were playing outside, to enter the house?
ANGÉLIQUE: I wanted to make them go inside because they were playing in the street, where there was mud, and that Marguerite had her feet covered in it.
RAIMBAULT: Why did you go three or four times into the street to look in the direction of the roof, having no reason to do so?
ANGÉLIQUE: I was on the street several times but I never looked in the direction of the roof, having no reason to do so.

Raimbault tried another tack.

RAIMBAULT: Wasn't it because your mistress reprimanded you harshly that you threatened to burn her or cut her throat several times?

ANGÉLIQUE: I never threatened her with any such thing.

RAIMBAULT: Didn't you say, that once you are in your country, if you found any French people there you would make them all perish and burn like dogs? And didn't you say this because you were angry about the terrible treatment you received from your mistress?

ANGÉLIQUE: Whenever my mistress sometimes mistreated me—which was not very often—I would become angry and leave the house. But I never said anything close to what you are asking me.

RAIMBAULT: Tell us how long before the fire your mistress had mistreated you.

ANGÉLIQUE: She hadn't mistreated me since the death of her husband.

RAIMBAULT: Isn't it true that you carried the coals up to the attic, and that caused the entire conflagration?

ANGÉLIQUE: No, I did not set the fire at all.

RAIMBAULT: Did you not get into a quarrel with Marie-Louise Poirier, the servant at Madame Francheville's, because she prevented you from drinking brandy, and wasn't it for this reason that she left her mistress?

ANGÉLIQUE: No, I only drank when the shop assistant sometimes gave me some in the morning, as he did Poirier.

RAIMBAULT: Didn't you steal three deerskins and several other things from your mistress when you set out with Thibault to New England?

ANGÉLIQUE: No, I stole nothing; neither did Thibault.

RAIMBAULT: A few days before the fire, didn't you see and

talk several times with Thibault, even during the night and the next day of the fire, and didn't you also speak to him on the day you were arrested and put in prison?

ANGÉLIQUE: I spoke to him only two times before the fire, when he came to get his pay from Madame Francheville and the day of the fire, when he was helping. I saw him in the space of about half an hour when he entered [the courtyard of Hôtel-Dieu], and he left before I was captured.

RAIMBAULT: Isn't it true that on the day of the fire you told Françoise Geoffrion that you wouldn't be living at the Widow Francheville's for very long?

ANGÉLIQUE: I did not say any such thing.

RAIMBAULT: Didn't a man [Traversy] tell you that you had better watch out or Madame Francheville would sell you, and didn't you say, "That devil of whores, if she sells me she will repent"? And when he asked you what you would do, you said, "We do not say what we will do"?

ANGÉLIQUE: I never said anything like that or had the intention.

RAIMBAULT: Didn't you tell someone that if your mistress sold you you would burn her?

ANGÉLIQUE: I never said it or had the desire to do so.

The scribe read Angélique's testimony back to her. She declared that her answers were truthful and she was sticking to her testimony. The interrogation being done, "she was placed in the hands of the jailer and sent back to prison."

Angélique languished in prison for five more days. Pierre Raimbault, not satisfied with the testimonies he had, sought additional information. On May 6, he brought Alexis Lemoine *dit* Monière before the tribunal.

He testified that, the day before Angélique fled with Thibault, Madame Francheville asked him to take the slave woman into his house until spring because "she was ill-natured." He consented. Madame Francheville also asked him to lodge Thibault and take him into his employ. During the night, he was awakened by smoke and inspected the house with a lantern but did not see anything. His servant told him the next morning that the fire had been in the straw bed of Angélique, who had put a number of unusual splinters on the floor around where she slept. She lit the splinters, and when some noise erupted, she turned the straw bed onto the fire, attempting to put it out. That same night, the bed where Thibault was sleeping also caught fire. The following day, he and Angélique ran away.

Catherine Custeau, a domestic in Monière's household, clarified the situation regarding the fire in her master's house. Custeau said that, on that night, she was passing the room where Angélique was sleeping and saw her blanket on fire. She threw water on it, and Angélique told her not to say anything. Half an hour later, Monière arose because he smelled smoke, but he found nothing when he searched the house, and Custeau did not let on what had happened. The following morning, she told the other domestics that they had run the risk of being "roasted by the Negress."

Jacques Jalleteau, a house servant in Monière's employ, also made a deposition. He reported that he was asleep when the fire broke out. He awoke and found Thibault near the kiln, putting out the fire. That same evening, Thibault left and told him he was going to Québec.

Ignace Gamelin, a friend and business associate of the Franchevilles, was the next to testify before the tribunal.

Gamelin confirmed that Madame Francheville had made arrangements to sell Angélique to François-Étienne Cugnet. She told him she was "planning to send [Angélique] to Québec on the first fishing vessel on the proposition of Monsieur Cugnet, who would give her 600 pounds of powder for the price of the Negress." Gamelin further stated that Madame Francheville had said she didn't dare sleep alone in her house because she was afraid of what Angélique might do. Madame Francheville had also told him she wasn't out of the house on the day of the fire except to go to church, that Angélique had never served her well, and that Poirier had left her on account of Angélique.

The last witness for the day was Jeanne Nafrechoux de Béréy, the owner of Marie-Manon. She repeated the now well-known story of Angélique saying that Madame Francheville wouldn't laugh for long because she would not be sleeping in her house. Marie-Manon had also told her that Angélique had tried to prevent the little girls from raising the alarm about the fire, and that Angélique had crossed the street, looked up and down, and fixed her gaze on the roof of the Francheville house.

The testimonies were stacking up against Angélique. Monière, Custeau, and Jalleteau had all related that the night she and Thibault came to their house, a fire was started. Though they did not say the pair did it, the fact that the fire started in the rooms where they slept cast immediate suspicion on them. Also, Madame Francheville had stated that she was in fear for her life with Angélique in the house. Was she convinced that Angélique would indeed burn her? Raimbault was building a case against Angélique and

Thibault. It was not airtight, but in the minds of everyone in Montréal, they were guilty of arson.

Having heard testimony from nineteen witnesses, Raimbault cross-examined Angélique on May 6, this time at the city jail.

RAIMBAULT: Didn't the flames that caused the fire on April 10 begin on the roof inside the attic of Madame Francheville's?

ANGÉLIQUE: I don't know if the house caught fire from the inside, but when people were yelling that there was a fire I went outside and saw the roof on fire. [Angélique noted that the fire began on the side of the roof in the direction of Sieur Radisson's chimney.]

RAIMBAULT: Where were you when Sieur Radisson came to throw water on the fire?

ANGÉLIQUE: I don't know who went up first. All I know is that someone went up there and asked for water, and by that time I was in the street.

RAIMBAULT: Before you fled Madame Francheville's home last winter, did you not say, as you have said since, that you would burn Madame Francheville and Sieur Monière because of the reprimands and bad treatment they were giving you?

ANGÉLIQUE: No, I did not say that before or after.

RAIMBAULT: Is it not true that the day before the Sunday you fled with Thibault, intent on going to New England, you started a fire in your blanket that night in the room where you slept at Sieur Monière's, and that Thibault had also started a fire in the bed where he slept, also in Sieur Monière's house?

ANGÉLIQUE: My blanket caught fire because it touched the

furnace. A servant awakened me. Thibault's blanket also caught on fire because he was sleeping close to the fireplace. RAIMBAULT: You are not telling the truth in denying that you and Thibault had purposely set fire to your beds that Saturday night. Because the following Sunday you took off together and were found after fifteen days in the depth of the woods behind Chateauguay.

ANGÉLIQUE: The fire took place on Friday night, and we didn't leave until Sunday evening at seven thirty.

RAIMBAULT: Tell me which house you went to after your flight from Sieur Monière, and how long did you remain there before setting out for New England?

ANGÉLIQUE: We did not enter any house. We crossed the river immediately and went as far as Longueuil. Then we went to a farmhouse. Thibault had hidden there five to six loaves of bread. From there we went on the road to Chambly, then we entered into the woods, where we spent the night and part of the next day. We spent a week in the woods; the other time we were running. We entered no house.

RAIMBAULT: For how long before your flight from this city had you been planning to go to New England?

ANGÉLIQUE: We made our plans when Madame Francheville was away in Longue-Pointe. We were waiting until the river was frozen over in front of the city to cross over on the ice. We waited eight days to settle Thibault's account with Madame. Thibault gathered some bread for the journey. He decided to leave Montréal without settling his account with Madame. We left on the Sunday evening.

Angélique was changing her story. In her first testimony, she had said it was Radisson who first came to help fight the fire.

In this cross-examination, she claimed she did not know who first came to the house. It was certainly obvious to the tribunal by this point that Angélique's story was not holding water. She also revealed that she and Thibault had been plotting their escape well before the fire at Sieur Monière's.

The couple stole away in the middle of February. But they had planned to leave even before Madame Francheville sent them to stay at Monière's. Montréal was an island, and escaping from it meant crossing water, in this case the St. Lawrence River. The couple's plan was to wait until the river was frozen solid, then to cross to the south shore.

It seems that Angélique was propelled to escape because she was afraid of being sold. When her mistress told her at one point that she was thinking of selling her because she was an incorrigible servant, Angélique begged her not to and promised to behave. But she did not trust her mistress and started to make plans. When Jallateau made his deposition, he stated that both Thibault and Angélique had told him they planned on going back to Europe. And this Angélique admitted at the trial. They escaped to New England so they could get on a boat to Europe. This, too, she never denied.

On the afternoon of May 12, Raimbault began the confrontations. In these sessions, the accused was given the opportunity to challenge the stories of the witnesses. The confrontations also allowed both parties to change their stories. This was one of the few chances the prisoner had to establish her innocence. Raimbault brought Marie-Manon to the jail to confront Angélique. Raimbault read Marie-Manon's testimony to the prisoner, who denied all that was alleged. When Marie-Manon insisted that her story was true, Angélique retorted, "You are a miserable liar and a vile person."

On the morning of May 14, Raimbault confronted Angélique with Marguerite César, the woman who claimed to have watched Angélique look up and down rue Saint-Paul and gaze at her mistress's roof. Angélique did not deny César's allegations but responded that it was her business to look from one side of the street to the other.

In the evening, Raimbault brought Françoise Geoffrion, who had said she saw Angélique walking on the banks of the river and was told by her that she would not be living at her mistress's much longer. "There's nothing bad in Geoffrion's statement," Angélique countered. "My mistress had told me that she had sold me, that she had written to the intendant for that purpose. So I could easily have said what I said to Geoffrion."

The following day, Raimbault called a new witness: Louis Bellefeuille *dit* La Ruine, a gardener in the service of the poor at Hôtel-Dieu. La Ruine's testimony was incriminating to Thibault. As Porlier recorded it:

> At the start of the fire at Hôtel-Dieu, [La Ruine] went down into the vault of the church and, seeing Thibault eating dinner, told him his surprise at finding him quietly eating while the fire was everywhere. Thibault responded that he was tired and exhausted, not having eaten all day. He then left Thibault to help save the hospital's effects. He added that, after the hospital had burned and he had withdrawn into the garden, a man who was in the service of Sieur D'Auteil came with a bottle of liquor, which was shared around. Another man, one Pierre, brought a flask of liquor. They drank among themselves and gave some to the Negress, who gave them some syrup from a flask.

La Ruine said he then told Angélique that "people were saying it was she who set the fire," and that she responded, "So you would think that I am so stupid as to go and set fire to our house." La Ruine added that he saw Thibault and Angélique moving furniture and other effects that belonged to Madame Francheville, who was also present in the hospital's garden.

Later, Raimbault brought Marie-Louise Poirier, the former Francheville domestic, to confront Angélique. He read Poirier's testimony to the prisoner, and again she challenged it. Angélique said she knew that Madame Francheville had told Poirier she would take her back when Angélique had been sold. Poirier had also accused Angélique of having stolen deerskins from Madame Francheville when she fled with Thibault in the winter. This Angélique refuted, saying she had bought the furs from Monière's servant for six francs in silver. She said she had brought the money with her from New England when she was first sent by Nichus Block, her Flemish master, to the late Sieur Francheville. She also denied Poirier's assertion that she had said if she ever returned to her country she would burn all White people like dogs. However, she did admit that she had said to Poirier that the French "weren't worth anything."

Raimbault continued the confrontations with Louis Langlois *dit* Traversy. Angélique claimed that all she had said to Traversy was that she should have waited to run away until there was no more snow so she wouldn't have left tracks. She denied calling her mistress a "whore." Traversy persisted with his story, however, until finally Angélique said, "My poor Traversy, you could be mistaken."

Raimbault staged more confrontations. Marie-Françoise

Thomellete was brought in. She repeated that, when Angélique was captured after her escape attempt and brought home, she told Angélique to behave or her mistress would sell her, and that Angélique then said if that happened she would "burn or grill" Madame Francheville. According to Thomellete, when she reminded Angélique that "they will hang you" for that, "the Negress began to laugh and jump up and down and then lie down."

Angélique denied these accusations and said, "Thomellete is wicked to say this, it is not true."

In the days that followed, Raimbault recalled more witnesses for further questioning, but they said they had nothing "to add or to subtract" from their stories.

If Raimbault was hoping that Angélique would confess to her crime, he was disappointed. And because she wouldn't confess, he had to extend the trial by examining new witnesses and re-examining old ones until he could sufficiently prove that she was the culprit.

Meanwhile, Claude Thibault was still missing. The tribunal felt he was crucial to their case. So on May 25, Raimbault went to the marketplace, accompanied by François Roy, the town crier, and announced that Thibault was to appear before the tribunal in eight days and that there was a warrant out for his capture and arrest.

More confrontations followed. At 6:00 a.m. on May 27, Angélique was faced with Charlotte Desrivières and then Étienne Radisson. She denied Desrivières's accusation and changed her story when Radisson's was read to her. Porlier wrote, "After hearing his deposition, the accused said that it was not she who went to warn Sieur Radisson of the fire, and that she neither went upstairs nor to the attic with him or with anyone else."

At 7:00 a.m. five-year-old Amable Monière was brought to the town hall to confront Angélique. When Amable repeated her story, Angélique replied, "My little Amable, come here next to me and tell me who told you to say that. I will give you a piece of sugar [candy]."

Later in the morning, Raimbault once again cross-examined Angélique.

RAIMBAULT: When you were taken to prison, you asked where Thibault was. Why?

ANGÉLIQUE: That was without design. I asked because I believed that he was still in jail. I knew from a soldier who was in the dungeon that Thibault had come to get his belongings the day after I was arrested.

RAIMBAULT: What conversations did you have with Thibault when he came to get his belongings, and what did he bring you to eat?

ANGÉLIQUE: He neither spoke to me nor brought me anything to eat. I ate some bread that the daughter of the caretaker gave me.

RAIMBAULT: Previously you said the fire started in the attic, and that there was no fire in the fireplace; later, you said you did not know if the fire started inside or outside.

ANGÉLIQUE: I cannot say if the fire started outside or inside. I can only say that there was no fire in the fireplace, since there were only three small half-burned logs in one and a few embers in the other.

RAIMBAULT: Did you not go to warn Sieur Radisson that

there was a fire, and did you not go upstairs with Sieur Radisson, who was carrying two buckets?

ANGÉLIQUE: I did not go to Sieur Radisson and did not go upstairs with him or into the attic.

Either Angélique was confused or she did not remember her previous statements to the tribunal. On May 3, she had admitted that indeed she did run over to tell Radisson there was a fire at the Francheville home. Raimbault had caught her in a lie, or in a very confused state of mind, and he pounced.

RAIMBAULT: You are disguising the truth. On May 3, you admitted that Sieur Radisson had climbed the stairs with you to the attic carrying two pails.

ANGÉLIQUE: I don't know if Sieur Radisson climbed up the stairs, and I did not see anyone else climb the stairs. I only heard the call for water.

There's no question that Angélique was confused and disoriented. She was being questioned almost daily and was in a state of perpetual anxiety. She was confined to a cold and damp cell, was living on bread and water, and had no moral or other support. Thibault, her lover and confidante, had disappeared. She spent her days and nights in a hostile environment with people bound on proving that she was an arsonist. Perhaps it is not surprising that her responses to Raimbault's questions had become contradictory. Even if she was consciously lying, that is understandable; she was trying to save her life. However, her misrepresentations had become obvious to the tribunal.

RAIMBAULT: Where were you when the house caught fire?

ANGÉLIQUE: I was on the steps of the house, speaking across the street to one named Latreille, who was standing at the door of the Hôtel-Dieu. I did not cross the street until Latreille screamed "Fire."

RAIMBAULT: Did you not beg Monière's servant not to say anything to him when the fire broke out at his house?

ANGÉLIQUE: That is true. I asked the servant not to say anything for fear that Monière would be in a rage because he got up from his bed smelling smoke and went upstairs with his son with a lantern.

RAIMBAULT: Wasn't it the same night that fire broke out downstairs in the room where Thibault slept?

ANGÉLIQUE: The fire did not start downstairs until Sieur Monière had made his inspection and had gone back to bed.

RAIMBAULT: Why did you prevent Thibault from going to work for the commissioner by threatening him?

ANGÉLIQUE: Thibault and I had agreed to go away together. If he committed himself to work for someone else, I would still have gone, but all alone. I wanted to leave because several people had told me that Madame wanted to sell me in the Islands.

RAIMBAULT: Why did you tell us previously that the little girls had not played in the courtyard of the Widow Francheville, yet today you admitted it?

ANGÉLIQUE: I did not see them there, but since the girls said it, I believe it. It must have been during the time that I was playing with Marie, the Panise.

RAIMBAULT: Do you know where Thibault is now?

ANGÉLIQUE: I don't know. I always believed he was in town until now. I don't know where he is.

RAIMBAULT: Why did Thibault run away, and did he tell you he was going to Chateauguay?

ANGÉLIQUE: I don't know anything. Thibault did not tell me if he was going to Chateauguay or anyplace else.

RAIMBAULT: How many times did Thibault go to the Widow Francheville's on the day of the fire?

ANGÉLIQUE: He did not do that at all.

RAIMBAULT: Did Thibault not tell you that the widow had told him she had sold you, and that she did not wish Thibault to set foot in her house anymore?

ANGÉLIQUE: Thibault did not speak to me at all. It was Madame herself who told me.

RAIMBAULT: Why did you go into the street, look from one side to the other, then towards the roof, while the little girls were playing in the courtyard?

ANGÉLIQUE: I was only doing what I was accustomed to, and the girls were playing in the street.

With that, Raimbault ended his interrogations. There is no doubt that Angélique was a determined and feisty woman, even manipulative. And Raimbault tried to show that she had manipulated Thibault. When he asked her why she "prevented" Thibault from working for Monière by "threatening" him, she did not deny this but calmly gave an explanation. If Thibault had committed to working for Monière, he would not have been in a position to escape. She would still have fled. But she did not want to leave by herself.

A week later, on June 4, Raimbault brought Madame Francheville to the jail to confront Angélique. Porlier wrote:

The accused said that she takes great exception to this witness, and will bear ill will against her for her whole life because the entire evening of the fire she was conversing about her, accusing her of having set the fire. After hearing the witness's full testimony, the accused said she did not go up to the attic on the day of the fire, except in the morning with her mistress, that she did not see Thibault the day before, and that it was more than eight days before when Widow Francheville went to Longue-Pointe.

The widow said her statements were true, that the Negress took food to Thibault in prison seven or eight days before he got out, and that was after the Negress had driven Poirier from the house. When she became aware that Angélique was taking food to Thibault, she reproached her, and forbade her to take anything to him.

Later in the morning, Angélique was once again cross-examined. Raimbault pressed the point about Thibault's presence at the house on the day of the fire. He told Angélique she was lying when she said Thibault had not come to the Francheville residence either the day of the fire or the day before. Angélique insisted that he was last at the house at least eight days before the fire. Raimbault told her that was impossible, because Thibault had got out of prison only on the evening of April 8 and that he could have gone to the Francheville house on that evening or on the morning or evening of April 9 or 10.

Raimbault then produced the prison ledger to back up his point. Thibault had indeed entered prison on March 5 and left on April 8. There was no way he could have come to the house eight days before the fire, as Angélique was proposing. Raimbault felt he had caught her in yet another lie.

By noon, Pierre Raimbault was ready to hand down judgment in the case. He had called twenty-four witnesses in an inquiry that had lasted close to two months. He had several times in his writings called this case "unusual," "extraordinary," "remarkable." Everyone called to testify knew each other, and Angélique. Masters, servants, slaves, soldiers, wives, widows, husbands, children, and merchants had testified. And after a gruelling two months, the court was ready to give its verdict. Raimbault must have been exhausted; Angélique, likewise. She had remained amazingly cool during the interrogations. She had challenged some of the witnesses, spoken frankly, changed her story at times, and even been manipulative. While she was certainly trying to protect Thibault, it had become clear that they were partners in crime. They were both unruly servants who had plotted and planned their escape. Though all of Montréal had seen them together on the night of the blaze, moving Madame Francheville's furniture to the courtyard of the hospital, Angélique denied seeing Thibault. She was protecting him even as she tried to save her own life. Did she believe she could beat the charges, then flee forever with Thibault from Montréal?

On June 4, Angélique sat in her jail cell and waited for the verdict. Her attempts to free herself from slavery had ended ignominiously. Whatever Raimbault's decision, she already had the reputation of being an arsonist. It did not help her case to have confessed that she would bear ill will towards her mistress "for her whole life."

Raimbault had built a case based on innuendo, insinuation, hearsay, and Angélique's bad reputation. Yet he was following established and recognized legal practices. The fact that Angélique was a slave did not help her in any way. She occupied the lowest rung in New France's society. She was Black, a stranger, and thus the ultimate outsider. Montréal was looking for a scapegoat, and she fitted the description.

June 4 was the day of decision. On that day, Angélique would learn if she would live or die. While the king's judge, the prosecutor, and the notaries returned to their chamber to deliberate, Angélique sat in her cell and called on her God and all the saints, especially the ones after whom she was named—Mary and Joseph.

X

The Verdict

THE TRIAL ENDED. The lieutenant general decided he had more than enough evidence to reach a sound conclusion. The interrogations on the morning of June 4 were to be the last.

The court had called at least twenty-four witnesses. Though no one had actually *seen* Angélique set the fire, most stated that they suspected she was the one who had done it. A ten-year-old child had "heard" her going up to the attic. A neighbour had seen her looking up and down the street and fixing her eyes on the roof shortly before the roof went up in flames. The slave girl of Sieur de Béréy claimed that on the evening of the fire Angélique had said Madame Francheville would not "sleep in her house that night." Three servants declared that Angélique had, in their presence, threatened to "burn" her mistress and "cut her throat." Sieur Monière and his domestics related that they suspected Angélique and Thibault of attempting to burn down their house in February. Madame Francheville testified that Angélique had indeed threatened to burn her if she did not give her *congé*.

Another domestic stated that Angélique had told him she wanted to go to France and planned on doing so. Sieur Radisson testified that Angélique had refused to help him find a ladder when he had attempted to put out the fire in the Francheville house. But perhaps the most incriminating evidence against Angélique came from five-year-old Amable Lemoine *dit* Monière, who said that on the day of the fire Angélique had placed some coals onto a shovel and gone up into the attic.

Pierre Raimbault, king's councillor and judge, felt he had conducted his inquiry well and had heard enough. A fire had started on the roof of Thérèse de Francheville's house. Prior to the fire, neighbours had seen and heard Angélique behaving strangely. She was the one who had announced the fire to the neighbours. Her mistress said there had been no fire in the chimneys of the house that day, though Angélique insisted that there had been a few half-burned logs and some embers in one of the chimneys.

Raimbault was convinced that Angélique was the arsonist, and had been motivated by revenge towards and hatred of her mistress because she had sold her. The king's judge felt he had an airtight case against Angélique.

Late in the morning of June 4, the tribunal was ready to hand down the verdict and sentence. The officers of the court met in the *salle d'audience* at the prison. Raimbault asked the notaries for their decision. Charles-René Gaudron de Chevremont, as the lead notary and assistant judge, went first:

> After having carefully examined the case made against the accused, I find that the said accused is sufficiently guilty and convicted of having started the fire in the house of the

widow Francheville, which caused the conflagration of part of the town. For punishment, I judged that she be condemned to make honourable amends, and to have her hand cut off, and that she be thrown alive into the fire in a place in this town deemed most appropriate, after having been subjected to the *question ordinaire et extraordinaire* in order that she name her accomplices and that the judgement of the one named Thibault be delayed until the said accused has suffered such interrogation.

Chevremont had a personal stake in the Angélique case. The house he had been renting was burned in the fire, and though he managed to save his papers, he lost all his furniture. Clearly, he was not the most objective of assessors. In his heart must have lurked revenge.

Jean-Baptiste Adhémar advised "that the said Negress be condemned to make honourable amends with a torch in her hand, and then her hand be cut off, and then she be burned alive, having first been subjected to *la question ordinaire et extraordinaire* in order to determine the names of her accomplices." Adhémar added that, in making honourable amends, Angélique should hold in her hands a burning torch.

François Lepailleur wrote, "I find the accused to be duly guilty of the crime of which she is accused; for her punishment, I recommend that she be condemned to make honourable amends at the doors of the church, that her hand be cut off, and that she be then burned alive after having been subjected to *la question* in order to determine the names of her accomplices."

Nicolas-Auguste Guillet de Chaumont concurred: "I find the accused to be clearly and duly guilty and convicted of having started the fire in the house of [Madame]

Francheville, and for the punishment of this crime, I recommend that she make honourable amends with a torch in her hand, that the hand be cut off in front of the cathedral of this town, and that she be then thrown alive into the fire, after have been subjected to *la question ordinaire et extraordinaire*, in order that she declare the names of her accomplices."

The court found Angélique guilty of setting fire to her mistress's house and the subsequent burning of the city. The punishment the tribunal named for Angélique, it believed, was commensurate to the crime she committed.

Being burnt alive, boiled, quartered (the body divided into four parts), dragged behind a running horse, flung upon spikes, poured over with hot oil or tar, or hung in a gibbet—all these were common forms of capital punishment and torture in Europe and European-dominated societies, meted out to the poor and the enslaved.

The punishment the justices came up with showed that they felt the offence to be despicable and the offender and the memory of her should be erased from the land. In Catholicism, being burnt alive meant that one's soul did not have a chance to be redeemed and enter paradise. One was condemned perpetually to hell. It was the ultimate punishment. In life, Angélique had been marginalized from society. Likewise, in death, she would be banished from the garden of paradise.

The jailer brought Angélique from her cell to the *salle d'audience*. Raimbault told her to sit on the "stool of repentance" and remove her shoes and her head scarf. As judge, it was his duty to read formally to her the verdict and the punishment. He concurred with his notaries. In ponderous tones, Raimbault condemned Angélique to death.

All evidence considered, we have found the said accused sufficiently guilty and convicted of having started the fire in the house of demoiselle Francheville, which caused the conflagration of part of the town. For the punishment of this crime, we have condemned the accused to make honourable amends, nude except for a shirt, with a cord tied around her neck, holding in her hand a burning torch two pounds in weight, before the principal door and entry of the parish church of this town, where she will be led by the executioner of high justice, in a rubbish cart, with a small placard in the front and at the back with the words "arsonist," and there, with her head bare, and while kneeling, to declare that she wickedly set the fire and caused the said conflagration, of which she repents and asks pardon in the name of the king and of justice. After this, her hand will be cut off, on a post that will be raised in front of the said church. Then she will be led by the said executioner in the rubbish cart to the public square, to be then tied to a post with an iron chain and then burned alive, her body to be reduced to ashes, and those same ashes to be thrown to the winds. Her worldly goods to be seized and confiscated and put in the king's possession. She will be subjected to *la question ordinaire et extraordinaire* in order to obtain the names of her accomplices.

With regards to the said Thibault, we have ordered that, upon consideration of the testimonies offered by the witnesses, the said Thibault will be subjected to questioning, in order that after *la question* has been applied to the said Negress and her interrogation communicated to the king's attorney with the description of contempt of court, all the proceedings reported so that judgment can be passed because of the said contempt of court as we will see fit.

> Passed and delivered in Montréal court by us, [Pierre Raimbault] lieutenant general, assisted by J.B. Adhémar, Auguste Guillet de Chaumont, Gaudron de Chevremont and François Lepailleur, royal notaries and practitioners, 4 June 1734.

Raimbault and the four notaries signed the documents, as did Claude-Cyprien-Jacques Porlier, the court scribe.

Porlier does not record Angélique's disposition or emotional state. But we can imagine that she must have been visibly shaken on hearing her judgment. Did her screams echo throughout the walls of the courtroom? Or did she slump in stunned silence?

The punishment handed down by the court came straight out of medieval European discourse on crime and punishment. Angélique's punishment was that reserved for arsonists and witches: the removal of the right hand, death at the stake, and the casting of a person's ashes to the four winds. The casting of the ashes was the final insult. It meant not only that the condemned was denied a funeral and burial, but also that her spirit would roam the earth forever—in agony and despair.

Joan of Arc, declared to be a witch by her enemies, was burnt at the stake. Millions of Europeans accused of one capital crime or another, especially witchcraft and heresy, ended their lives at the stake; some had their hands severed before being roasted. The laws of France, no matter how severe, were implemented in New France.

Execution of judgment was usually carried out on the same day. But this was not to be in this case. François Foucher, the *procurer du roi*, stopped the judges in their tracks when he said he was going to appeal the case. Porlier wrote, "At that moment, the king's prosecutor having entered the room and having read the sentence written by the others, said that he would appeal the sentence before our lords of the Sovereign Council of this land, and signed it."

E.-R. Massicote, a historian of early Montréal, notes that Foucher's action was strange. After all, it was he, as king's prosecutor, who had diligently and determinedly amassed the evidence against Angélique.

What of Claude Thibault? Louis Bellefeuille *dit* La Ruine said that while the fire raged Thibault calmly sat and ate his meal. He refused to fight the fire because, he said, he'd had a long day and was tired. Judge Raimbault believed it was Thibault who encouraged the bondswoman to set the fire. That made him guilty as instigator and accomplice. The court insisted that Angélique name her accomplice, and that she name Thibault, because in New France there was a "legal assumption that women were irresponsible by nature and could be dominated by men..."[1] This assumption held that "women who participated in crimes were considered to be less culpable than their male partners, who were suspected of leading [them] astray."[2] Angélique, in addition to being a woman, was also enslaved, and slaves, likewise, were assumed to be irresponsible, childlike, depraved, and irrational. Moreover, she was Black, and according to the racist discourse popular in Western societies, Black people (most of whom were enslaved) had the same "nature" as slaves: they were incapable of planning and executing big projects. The court felt that Angélique, as a Black enslaved woman, could not have acted alone—there was a mastermind behind the fire, and that mastermind was the White male, Claude Thibault. Race, gender, and status made Thibault the villain. But, as mentioned earlier, Foucher was simply carrying out his duty as a conscientious official. The Coutume de Paris gave the condemned the right to appeal.

The court also felt that Thibault was guilty because of his amorous association with the bondswoman. During the trial, an order was broadcasted telling Thibault to present himself before the court. But he failed to do so. Later, a warrant was issued for his arrest and capture. But he was never found, so he was charged with contempt of court and in his absence found guilty. Thibualt had found his liberty, but Angélique was not so lucky.

The judgment and sentence that the Montréal court pronounced over Angélique was to be expected. The slave woman had no defence other than "I did not do it." And no one believed her. Many families had been burnt out of house and home and had lost all their furniture and other personal effects. The government had to find tens of thousands of livres to pay for the damages done by the fire. This was perhaps the most important criminal case that Judge Raimbault had presided over, and he could not allow it to be said that he was soft on the accused. Everyone—from governor to judge to soldier to citizen—was calling for blood. Someone had to pay. There was no way out for Angélique.

Moreover, she had not endeared herself to anyone. She had quarrelled with her mistress, demanded that Madame Francheville release her from bondage, chased a servant away from the house, left the house whenever she wanted without permission, had a liaison with Claude Thibault, made plans to go with him to New England and Europe, and partially executed the plan. She was a slave woman who did not act like a slave. Though her status was servile, she did not have a servile mind.[3]

Marie-Joseph Angélique had acted as though she was free from authority. And no one, not even a free person or an aristocrat, was free from authority. In a paternalistic and hierarchical society such as New France's, there was always a higher authority to which one must bow. Slaves and servants obeyed masters; children obeyed parents, especially fathers; wives obeyed husbands; and everyone obeyed the laws of the government and the Church. "Everyone, except the king, had a natural superior on earth and anyone who claimed to be free from authority was a threat to public order."[4]

In Judge Raimbault's mind, Angélique had challenged and showed utter disregard for the authority of her mistress and of society. In fact, she had mocked authority. As a result, she became out of control and a menace to society. Now she had to be brought into line, had to be disciplined. The preamble to the 1670 criminal ordinance of Louis XIV's Coutume de Paris, the legal code of France, which was also enacted in New France, began by stating that "criminal justice restrains by fear of punishment those who are not restrained by a consideration of their duty."[5] Angélique would now be restrained by punishment because consideration of her duty had failed to restrain her.

But there was another step to be taken before justice could be done. The law demanded it. The accused must be taken to Québec to present her appeal. Raimbault honoured Foucher's request and immediately sent Angélique and her file, under guard, to Québec to face the judges of the Conseil Supérieur.

XI

The Appeal and Final Judgment

THE CONSEIL SUPÉRIEUR handed down judgment on June 12. It therefore took a week or less for Angélique's party to get from Montréal to Québec. The weather was warm, the St. Lawrence was flowing freely, and travel downstream to the capital was swift.

Québec, in addition to being the colonial capital, and thus the seat of government, was also the largest and most populous town in New France. The town grew above and below a steep cliff that rose from the shore of the St. Lawrence River. At the top of the cliff, which rose to about three hundred feet, lay the Upper Town. There, the land broadened into a wide plain. Upper Town was the centre of the colony's administration. The governor lived in his château here, as did most members of the Conseil Supérieur, bureaucrats, and other employees of the Crown. The religious communities (which owned a good portion of the unused land in Upper Town) could also be found in this part of the city. Here, too, were the bishopric, the seminary, the Récollets, the Jesuits, the Ursulines, and the sisters of

Saint-Augustine. The latter had established the city's hospital, Hôtel-Dieu, and they still ran it. The principal and the richest merchants of the city lived in Upper Town, as did the king's engineer, de Léry. This segment of the capital had its own share of blue-collar workers, domestics, and poor.

At the base of the cliff, fronting the St. Lawrence River, lay the Lower Town. This was the economic heart of the colony. The harbour and the king's shipyards were in Lower Town, and all ocean-going vessels began and ended their journey here. Naturally, the wharves, shops, warehouses, bakeries, butcheries, and workshops of all kinds were to be found in this area. Lower Town was the principal abode of merchants, who dominated life in this sector. Peter Kalm, the Swedish botanist, who visited Québec in 1749, related that the merchants of Lower Town built sturdy, handsome three-storey stone houses.[1] Lower Town was well populated and bustled with activity. It was also the main residential area for labourers, artisans, domestics, and such "temporary" residents as ship captains and sailors. Lower Town and Upper Town were joined by steep roads, giving the residents of the city easy access to either sector.

The intendant, the second most important person in the colony, did not live in either Lower or Upper Town but in the *quartier de palais*. The Palace Quarter was an intermediary area between the west side of Lower and Upper Town. It bordered the Saint-Roch neighbourhood and lay close to the banks of the St. Charles River, a tributary of the St. Lawrence. The Palace Quarter was also the site of several shipyards, warehouses, and small docks. Notaries and other public servants and some artisans and domestic workers made the Palace Quarter their home. In this neighbourhood was the intendant's palace (the district was named after the palace), a formidable self-contained complex that included not only the intendant's residence but also council chambers of the Conseil Supérieur, the *palais de justice* (courthouse), the prison, a chapel, the king's storehouses, and the armoury. Today, the ruins of the palace complex lie in the area bounded by rue Vallière, côte de la Potasse, and rue Saint-Vallière West.

Like the two other seats of government, Trois-Rivières and Montréal, Québec had its own lower court, called the *prévôté*. The town also held the admiralty court (responsible for all marine matters and maritime trade) and the ecclesiastical court. In 1734, Québec had a population of six thousand and, like Montréal, its population was divided by class, race, and rank.

Sometime before June 12, a canoe from Montréal bearing the prisoner Angélique ended its journey on the bank of the St. Charles River. The prisoner, with chains manacling her hands and feet, was helped from the boat by her guards, who promptly marched her to the prison in the intendant's palace.

On the morning of June 12, Angélique was escorted to the chamber of the Conseil Supérieur to face the judges. The highest court in the land, the Conseil Supérieur was established in 1663, when Canada became a royal colony. The Conseil had three main functions: it made, interpreted, and published laws and ordinances; it functioned as a court of first instance; and it heard appeals from all the lower courts for civil and criminal cases. It was best known for this last function. The decisions of the Conseil overruled those of all other courts. Citizens could bypass the *prévôté* and take their cases to the Conseil.

Prior to 1703 (when it was known as the Conseil

Souverain), the high court had only seven ordinary councillors, but it added five more to its number in that year. Of the twelve councillors, there was a first councillor, who functioned as the dean of the body. The governor, the intendant, the bishop, the attorney general, the chief scribe or clerk, the provost of the Maréchaussée (constabulary), several bailiffs, and the commissioner of marine (who gained a seat in 1733) also had obligatory seats on the Conseil. Excluding the bishop, the bailiffs, and the clerk, these men all had a deliberate voice and voting rights.

The king appointed the councillors on the recommendation of the minister of marine. Councillors were generally men with "long service in the king's business, some knowledge of jurisprudence, and orthodoxy in religious matters."[2] Those with backgrounds in the military, administration, or the judiciary were most favoured. There were exceptions, of course, such as Michel Sarrazin. Sarrazin was a physician and surgeon, appointed because of his ability as a doctor. But even Sarrazin had some military background. He had served in the Canadian army as a surgeon and had seen many battles.

However, some members of the Conseil had to have a thorough knowledge of law, especially that of the Coutume de Paris. The attorney general was one such person. Several of these officials were career lawyers who had served in the *parlement* of Paris, or other French *parlements*, and had come to Canada in service to the king. Some first councillors were also trained lawyers. Further, the intendant, usually from the old French nobility, had some legal training.

Membership in the Conseil depended on one's religious orthodoxy. A councillor not only had to be a member of the Roman Catholic Church, but also had to attend church regularly and conduct himself (publicly) in a decent manner while he served on the Conseil. For his appointment to be confirmed, an investigation into his religious character was conducted, and if he passed (as he usually did) he was issued a religious certificate. The councillor also had to be twenty-two years or older.

By the beginning of the eighteenth century, membership was for life, though the king could terminate an appointment if he thought it necessary. The overwhelming majority of the councillors came from noble or distinguished families. Most were French-born. The king's bureaucracy was reserved for the sons of the French elite. It served as a place where they could find work and fulfill their ambitions. Talented Canadian-born men were excluded from the Conseil Supérieur and other upper echelons of power until close to the end of French rule in Canada.

The high court judges, like many other government officials, were not well paid. For example, the first councillor and attorney general received 500 livres per annum for their services, and an ordinary councillor got 350 livres. (Salaries were raised during the 1750s.) Because of the low salary, councillors had to engage in other income-yielding ventures. Some, like the controller of the marine, held important posts and received good salaries. Not a few were merchants, leaders of the militia, shopkeepers, seigneurs, or notaries.

However, what the councillors lost in money, they gained in power, privilege, honour, status, and dignity. To hold a seat on the Conseil was to be exalted. The councillors were the principal lawmakers and law interpreters in the colony, and thus the ultimate judges. When they heard appeals or suits, their judgments altered the life course of the colonists who stood in front of them. As great dignitaries, they marched in church ceremonies directly behind the governor and intendant, occupied the pew behind these two officials, and took communion after them.

It was the intendant, as president of the Conseil, who decided when meetings would be called. He summoned the councillors and determined quorum (it had to be five in a criminal case). At any given session of the Conseil, it was unlikely that all twelve councillors would be present; usually, the presence of at least seven judges made it possible to conduct business. All councillors had voting rights, as did the other members of the Conseil (the intendant, governor, attorney general, commissioner of marine, and provost judge). The Conseil met forty to fifty times a year, always on a Saturday.

It was an "extraordinary assembly" of councillors who took their seats in the council chamber to hear Angélique's appeal. The Montréal fire had rocked the colony, and Angélique had gained notoriety as a result. The importance of the case is emphasized by the number of judges who were present. Excluding the bishop, governor, intendant, and two scribes, eleven councillors, all but one, were in attendance. These included the judge of the provost court, Pierre André de Leigne, and the judge of the Maréchaussée, Charles-Paul Denys de Saint-Simon. Though the record is silent on this, Pierre Raimbault and François Foucher from Montréal might also have been in attendance.

The most important member of this most august body was the governor, the Marquis Charles de Beauharnois. Born in 1671, he came from one of the great administrative clans of France. The Beauharnois family's ascent up the ladder of great success was helped tremendously by intermarriage with the famous and distinguished Colbert and Phélypeaux families, who gave France no less than four great ministers of marine, the king's most powerful servants. Even before their well-thought-out marriages to ministerial families, the Beauharnois family had dominated the upper echelons of the king's service. They secured themselves positions in the magistracy and the army. But after the Marquis de Beauharnois's cousin, Jérôme Phélypeaux, Comte de Pontchartrain, was appointed minister of marine in 1699, the Beauharnois men began entering the admiralty as top administrators. With their connections, they carved out impressive careers in the colonial service. The Beauharnois family gave New France no less than three intendants and two governors general.

The Marquis de Beauharnois's father, François, was a lawyer in the *parlement* of Orléans. As a young man, the marquis entered the marine and fought in many of Louis XIV's continental and overseas wars. On one of his war ventures, Beauharnois stopped in Canada in 1703 to visit an older brother, François, who was intendant of the colony.

In 1716, the marquis increased his wealth with his marriage to a rich widow, Renée Pays. Through the marriage, he gained her estate, worth 600,000 livres; included in the estate were three slave plantations in Saint Domingue, the future Haiti. Beauharnois managed his slave plantations long-distance and earned a generous income from them.

It was Maurepas, the minister of marine, who appointed Beauharnois (his cousin) to the governor general's position in Canada in 1726. The marquis would serve for the next twenty-one years.

As a former professional soldier, one of Beauharnois's main

concerns was Canada's defence against the English and the various Native groups. He strengthened the forts in the west and on the Great Lakes, started a fortification around Québec, and completed the wall around Montréal. He waged war against the Fox Indians, scattering them and reducing them to slavery. He also drew his sword against the Sioux and the English. As an administrator, he promulgated many laws and decrees.

Beauharnois's function on the Conseil was quiet but purposeful. As governor, he was the most powerful official in the colony, and hence on the Conseil. As commander of the army, he could use his soldiers to enforce his wishes on the Conseil, if he so chose. The governor's opinion was forceful, and he also had the ear of the king. Councillors and potential councillors did well to side with the governor as he could make or unmake them in his recommendations to the Crown.

The intendant, Gilles Hocquart, was also a member of the noblesse. Born in 1665, he came from a background in financial bureaucracy and the magistracy. Like Beauharnois, he was related to people in royal service who wielded great power and had influence over the king. His father, Jean-Hyacinthe, was a lawyer and intendant of Touloun and Le Havre. Hocquart's family began grooming him for a career in the financial service when he was only eight years old. At that age, he began working in the marine in Rochefort, and there gained vital experience. Between 1721 and 1729, he was the chief financial administrator for that city.

Because of his experience and skill in finance, as well as his connections, Hocquart was appointed supreme controller and acting intendant of Canada in 1729. Two years later, he became full intendant. He and Beauharnois had a very amicable relationship, and together were able to administer the colony with little friction between them.

By the time of Angélique's appeal, Hocquart had served as intendant for three years and would serve for another fourteen more. Historians of New France consider him one of the ablest of intendants. Hocquart was interested in the industrial, agricultural, and commercial development of Canada. He sponsored the Saint-Maurice ironworks, supported the early tile industry, and introduced new strains of grain to the colony. He renovated the shipyards at Québec and built several ocean-going vessels. He also supported a policy of trade with the West Indies. Among his more lasting achievements were the roads he built between Québec and Montréal, and Lake Champlain and Montréal.

Hocquart helped the citizens of Montréal get back on their feet after the 1734 fire by dipping generously into the colonial treasury for subsidies. We know that he had little sympathy for Angélique. In one letter to Maurepas, after the fire, he called her "wicked and wretched."[3]

Though the governor was the ultimate repository of power on the Conseil, the intendant functioned as president of the body. As mentioned, the intendant called council meetings and determined quorum. When a case came up for deliberation, it was the intendant who called upon the councillors for their opinions.

The intendant, perhaps, had greater influence over the councillors than either the bishop or the governor. He was closer to the councillors, and they wanted to impress him and win his favour. The intendant also made and promulgated decrees. Raymond Cahall, an authority on the Conseil, commenting on the close relationship between intendant and councillors, notes, "In administrative business, [the] intendant and councillors were intimately associated, for the great fundamental ordinances that governed New France were for the most part made by them jointly."[4]

The bishop played an ambivalent role on the Conseil. He was once a very powerful person on this body—almost as powerful as the governor. But the Church lost the struggle with the state for supremacy, and by 1688 the bishop was appointed only as an honorary member of the Conseil. Having lost direct power, the bishop exercised his influence through the clerical councillor and other friends on the Conseil. However, the bishop still enjoyed the privilege of sitting at the head of the council table.

The bishop of Québec, Pierre-Herman Dosquet, was not present at Angélique's appeal; he was away in France on business. Eustache Chartier de Lotbinière, vicar-general of Québec, quite likely represented the bishop and sat in his seat. The court dossier that contains the documents for Angélique's appeal lists Chartier as one of the assembly.

Another important official was the first councillor. He tended to be the longest serving member of the Conseil. The first councillor's primary role was to conduct the investigations of the cases, thereby serving as the reporter to the Conseil.

François-Étienne Cugnet was the first councillor. If Cugnet thought there was a conflict of interest in sitting on the slave woman's appeal, he did not say so. But Cugnet was the man to whom Madame Francheville had sold Angélique for six hundred pounds of gunpowder. Because of the fire, the sale did not go through and Cugnet lost a slave. Was he bent on vengeance?

Appointed to the Conseil in 1730, Cugnet had risen rapidly

through the ranks. Within three years he was appointed first councillor. This was highly unusual, as Cugnet was the most junior of the councillors and that post was usually reserved for the most senior. However, Cugnet had been trained as a lawyer in France and had practised law in the *parlement* of Paris before coming to Canada. His metropolitan legal training must have stood him in good stead. Cugnet exercised great power as director of the king's domains. He was well connected to the colony's elite and had enormous influence over them. He was favoured not only by Governor Beauharnois and Intendant Hocquart, but also by their superior, the minister of marine, the Comte de Maurepas. It was during this period that both Hocquart and Beauharnois had recommended François Poulin de Francheville and his board, which included Cugnet, to Maurepas for a loan of 10,000 livres to get the Saint-Maurice forges going. Now, as first councillor, Cugnet would have a deciding hand in Angélique's fate.

In our time, Cugnet would be removed temporarily from the bench. It would be pointed out that, as Angélique's buyer and one who was still doing business with her mistress, he had a conflict of interest. The Conseil did make provisions for such eventualities. An accused could refuse judgment by the Conseil if he or she pointed out that one of the judges was hostile. But the accused had to be free and White, not a nonentity like Angélique.

The attorney general who sat at Angélique's appeal was Louis-Guillaume Verrier. This official came from a long line of lawyers and had himself studied law. Before coming to Canada to take up official duties, Verrier had practised law in the *parlement* of Paris. When the office of attorney general was made vacant, Maurepas sent Verrier to Canada to take up the post. He arrived in September 1728 and served as the king's chief attorney for the next thirty years. Verrier had the distinction of giving the first law lectures in North America. These he began in 1736 in Québec and continued until his death in 1758.

As the attorney general, Verrier had to be trained in the laws of France. He also had to have knowledge of past decrees of the Canadian high court. When a case was brought before the Conseil, the first councillor presented it to the attorney general and conferred with him on each aspect of the case. The attorney general led the Conseil through the processes and procedures of law and, in the case of appeals, instructed the Conseil on how it should proceed according to the Coutume de Paris. It was the attorney general who reviewed the documents and tried the case. He interpreted the law, reached a conclusion, and proposed the legal remedy. He also "steered the Council toward his conclusion and proposal."[5]

Another important councillor was Jean-Victor Varin de La Marre, the colony's controller. Varin had come to Canada in 1729 with Hocquart, on the same ship, and had taken up the position of *greffier*, or scribe, in the marine. He rose rapidly through the ranks. Recommended by Hocquart, Varin later became controller or commissioner of marine. In that post, he had the colony's finances under his control. In February 1733, he was appointed to the Conseil Supérieur and remained in that post for the next sixteen years.

With his appointment as Supreme Court judge and controller, Varin joined the colony's economic, political, and judicial elite. He had a dazzling career as controller, and at the time of Angélique's appeal he was at the height of his fame and power. But he had one weak spot: he loved money. Varin was implicated in the *Affaire du Canada*, the speculation and fraud that characterized the Canadian government in the last days of the *ancien régime* in the colony. Fearing that he might be found out, Varin skipped to France. But that did not save him. "In December 1761 Varin was arrested in connection with the *Affaire du Canada* and imprisoned in the Bastille on a charge of having 'during part of the time that he served as financial commissary…tolerated, encouraged, and committed abuses, embezzlements, acts of betrayal of office, and breaches of trust in the furnishing of the king's warehouses.'"[6] Varin was found guilty and banished from France. He also had to pay 800,000 livres to the king. After seventeen years in exile, Varin was allowed to return to France, where he died in the 1780s.

Michel Sarrazin became a member of the Conseil in 1707 and remained a councillor until his death in September 1734. Born in France in 1659, he did not follow the typical path to the Conseil. He was not a jurist, nor did he have a background in colonial administration. He was, as we have seen, a medical doctor. In 1685, he came to Canada as a surgeon in the colonial regiments. Campaigning with the troops against the Iroquois in the Upper Country, he was fascinated by Canadian flora and fauna. He became an avid naturalist, botanist, and zoologist and devoted all of his spare time to these interests.

Sarrazin regularly sent specimens of Canadian plant and animal life back to France. He became a corresponding member of the Academie des Sciences de Paris, and wrote and published articles on Canadian flora and fauna. He also immersed himself in his medical practice, inventing diverse medicines, and battled several epidemics in the colony, without succumbing to any. His superiors had nothing but the highest praise for his medical work. Sarrazin was an experienced member of the Conseil and, at the time of his death, held the post of keeper of seals.

Charles Guillimin came from a noble family in Britanny. When he arrived in Canada as a young man, he had enough money to invest in the St. Lawrence fisheries and the French wholesale trade. Luck smiled on Guillimin and he prospered, becoming one of the wealthiest merchants in the colony. Guillimin was also a shipbuilder (he constructed at least seven ocean-going vessels at Québec), a realtor, an outfitter, and a militia commander. When the colonial government found itself short of cash, Guillimin loaned it 40,000 livres. For his efforts on behalf of the colony, he was installed as a councillor in the Conseil in 1721, serving until his death in 1739. However, towards the end of his life, Guillimin found himself greatly in debt, with creditors beating down his door.

Another key member of the Conseil Supérieur was the clerk of the court, or secretary. He was usually a notary and thus had knowledge of the law. Like many other colonial officials, François Daine acquired and "held several offices at the same time to increase his revenues."[7] Each office held its own remuneration. Daine's career was typical of those who climbed their way through the colonial bureaucracy. In 1715, Daine was working as the king's writer in the registry at Trois-Rivières. In 1721, he was in Québec, newly married, and a year later he was appointed chief clerk of the Conseil Supérieur, overseeing several deputy clerks. During his career in New France, he held the roles of lieutenant general for civil and criminal affairs (judge) for the provost court of Quebec, controller of the Compagnie des Indes Occidentales, director of the king's domain, and subdelegate of the intendant. Daine was still serving as chief scribe of the Conseil Supérieur at the time of Angélique's appeal.

In the days following the French defeat in 1760, Daine acted as spokesperson to the English on behalf of the inhabitants of Québec. He also settled disputes among the citizens "by French laws."[8] Daine was not implicated in the *Affaire du Canada*, and he was praised for his honesty by the French government. He returned to France in 1764, when it became clear that the English would be the new masters of Canada.

Jean-Claude Louet was the royal notary of the admiralty court of Québec. As clerk for that court, he was present at the Angélique case, given its prominence. We know that Louet acted as co-writer with Daine as his signature is also on Angélique's trial documents.

Several bailiffs, guards, and police officers also served the Conseil. And, of course, there was the royal torturer and executioner. What would the dispensation of justice be without one to carry out judicial executions and punishments? The executioner was indispensable to the Conseil, yet the government always found it difficult to procure a hangman because the office was despised by the general public and no one wanted to apply for the job. Convicted murderers were usually pressed into service as the colony's executioner. They had two options: either take the job or be executed. They usually chose the first option.

In 1733, with the office of executioner vacant, Governor Beauharnois obtained, from the Caribbean island of Martinique, a slave-murderer by the name of Mathieu

Leveille for the post of hangman and torturer. Leveille had murdered a fellow slave in Martinique and would himself have been executed had it not been for the vacant post in Canada. He sailed north to the colony.

Leveille was a royal slave in service to the king, appointed by the Conseil Supérieur. He lived in Québec, and suffered from the cold and loneliness in his new home. The Canadian government then bought a female slave named Angélique-Denise, also from Martinique, to comfort Leveille "and warm his bed." Severely dislocated, physically and psychically, Leveille never reconciled himself to Canada. He died of pneumonia in 1736, at Québec's Hôtel-Dieu. After his death, the government sold Angélique-Denise to a local merchant.

Leveille, the Black slave hangman, would be the one to place the noose around the neck of Angélique, the Black slave.

When Marie-Joseph Angélique was marched into the council chamber, she saw a seating arrangement of the councillors that very much reflected the hierarchy, rank, and status that was so much a part of life in Canada. The judges sat around a long, rectangular table. At the head sat the governor, with the bishop (or his representative) to his right and the intendant to his left. The councillors, beginning with the most senior, sat on either side of the intendant and bishop. The attorney general and the clerk sat at the foot of the table. The prisoner stood facing the three most distinguished officials and some of the judges.

We do not know if Leveille was present. There is no mention of him sitting at the table. He was not a councillor, just a necessary tool in the dispensing of justice.

The Conseil was the supreme judicial authority in the land, and as such could exercise mercy in cases of appeal that involved the death penalty. The Conseil, at times, modified harsh sentences imposed by the lower courts. Perhaps Angélique was hoping for this.

There she stood, a lone, marginalized Black woman, facing the most powerful men in the colony. They were separated from her by race, gender, status, and occupation. Some, like Cugnet and Hocquart, had already made up their minds against her. As White men, settlers, rulers, imperialists, slave-holders, and colonizers, these men all had internalized perceptions about Black people and enslaved Africans. Beauharnois, Cugnet, and Varin were implicated in the Atlantic trade of goods and slaves. The governor ran three slave plantations in the West Indies, had brought Leveille from Martinique, and owned twenty-seven slaves in Québec. Cugnet and Varin, in their posts as merchants and businessmen, traded with the French West Indies. They had intimate knowledge of planta-tion slavery and the slave trade.

The judges on the Conseil were men who held the lower orders in disdain, who drubbed their inferiors, who held slaves in the own households, who reduced nations to slav-ery, and who bartered in the flesh of humans. These men could hardly be expected to show mercy to a Black slave woman accused of burning down property.

The distance between Angélique and the judges was vast. Each of these men had long and distinguished biographies. Their lineage was known—some, like Hocquart, from the twelfth century. Angélique, on the other hand, was *une esclave*, a person with no family connection, no great lineage, no distinguished blood. It was only because of the spectacular fire she was accused of setting that her name made it into the official documents.

Québec was a small town; the government bureaucracy

was also small. Everyone knew each other, and the members of the elite—including the judges of the Conseil—were closely joined in marriage and business. Councillor Nicolas Lanoullier had married the daughter of Judge Pierre André de Leigne. Intendant Gilles Hocquart, president of the Conseil, had created, mentored, and supported a small group of councillors who were responsible for the finances of the colony. Among this group were Thomas-Jacques Taschereau (agent of the treasurers general of the marine), Jean-Victor Varin (controller), François Foucault (king's storekeeper at Québec), and François-Étienne Cugnet (director of the Domaine d'Occident). "These men formed the core of Hocquart's judicial clientele in the Conseil Supérieur." Councillors like Taschereau invested in Cugnet's ironworks, and Foucault and Varin went into business together.

Connected to each other by ties of blood, business, and values, these judges formed a formidable wall in front of Angélique. The judgment that emanated from the Conseil, likewise, could not be anything but formidable.

✳

It was Saturday, June 12. At 10:00 a.m., the Lower Town bustled with activity. Ships docked, sailors and crew disembarked, labourers carried stock to warehouses and stores, people shopped for the upcoming week's supplies, and street urchins played and tried to rob unsuspecting visitors. And on everyone's tongue was the name "Angélique," the "notorious Negress" who had burnt Montréal and now faced justice at the courthouse.

Some spoke with drunken breath about the "damn

Negress." The enslaved, and there were many, may have spoken in hushed tones and secretly wished that Angélique might be set free. Their masters eyed them suspiciously, afraid that they carried vengeance in their hearts and could be spiteful enough, like the "wretched Negress," to roast them in their beds.

What was Mathieu Leveille thinking? He had a most odious task. Did he have a tortured conscience, knowing that in all likelihood he would kill one of his own? Or did he believe he was only doing his job, that it was the Conseil and the government who would really be doing the killing?

It was Verrier who told Angélique to sit on the "stool of questioning." He and the other judges interrogated her. She told them what she had told Raimbault, Foucher, and the notaries every day for almost two months. No, she had not set the fire, and she did not have an accomplice. Unconvinced, Verrier dismissed her to an outer chamber. He started the deliberations. He took the councillors through the points of law. He made his proposal. Angélique was guilty and should be condemned to death. Hocquart took the votes. All agreed. Daine and Louet wrote down the proceedings, the judges' decision, and the court's verdict.

The condemned would

> make reparations for the fire set by her, and other cases mentioned in the proceedings, by making honourable amends naked underneath a shirt, a rope around her neck, holding a glowing torch weighing not more than two pounds before the principal door and entrance of the parish church in the city of Montréal, where she will be led and driven by the executioner of the highest justice,

there on her knees to say and declare in a loud and intel-
ligible voice to have wickedly and ill-advisedly committed the aforesaid fire, of which she repents and begs for-
giveness of God, the king, and justice; that done, to be led
to the public square...of Montréal and hanged and strangled there until limp at the gallows, which will be placed
there for this reason, and then her limp body placed on a
lit pyre to be burned and consumed, the ashes thrown to
the wind, her belongings obtained and confiscated by the
king; the aforesaid Marie-Joseph Angélique beforehand
tortured to obtain from her mouth revelations of her
accomplices; ordained that preliminary investigation of
the refusal to submit to a court of law begun against
Claude Thibault will begin again.[9]

Like the Montréal court, the Conseil Supérieur marked
Thibault as a suspect and wanted him caught and arrested to
stand trial. The Conseil ordered a new search for Thibault. In
concluding, Daine wrote that Angélique would be sent back
to Montréal for execution, and that the decree of the condemnation would "be read, published and posted in...the
three cities of Québec, Montréal, and Trois-Rivières at the
diligence of the Attorney General."[10]

The Conseil upheld the Montréal court death penalty, but
modified it. Perhaps it was Verrier who recommended that
the harsher aspects of the punishment be removed. There
would be no cutting off the right hand, and Angélique would
not be burned alive, as recommended by the Montréal court.
Perhaps that was why Foucher had launched the appeal. As a
lawyer, he was well aware that the high court often modified
grisly punishments given by the lower court.

After passing judgment, Cugnet and Daine went immediately to read the sentence to Angélique, who sat under guard in an outer chamber. This was the end of the road for Angélique. Her case had been heard by both the lower and upper court, and she had lost. The state had brought out its full judicial arsenal against her; she did not stand a chance.

Perhaps Angélique crumbled to the ground when the men read the sentence to her. Perhaps she was unmoving. We do not know. Neither Daine nor Louet recorded her emotions for posterity.

Because she was from Montréal, the sentence was not carried out on the same day that judgment was passed, as was usual. Angélique was marched back to the docks in chains, and under guard. She boarded a canoe bound for Montréal. Mathieu Leveille was a member of her party. He had a job to do in Montréal.

XII

The Execution

NOW WE RETURN to where we started.

Angélique lost her appeal and returned to Montréal to die. Judge Pierre Raimbault set the date of the execution for June 21. In the days that followed Angélique's return from Québec, the judge and his assistants prepared themselves for the final interrogation of the condemned, to take place on the morning of the hanging.

In that final interrogation, Angélique continued to deny that she had set the fire, and so the judge called in Mathieu Leveille, the "master of the means of torture," and he applied the boots to Angélique's legs and began to pound and shatter them with his hammer. Angélique broke under the relentless application of the torturer's instrument of punishment, and she screamed that it was she who had set the fire, but that she did it all by herself. The judge was satisfied—but not completely, because Angélique still refused to name Claude Thibault as her accomplice.

She did confess her guilt, not that confession would save

her. With or without it, she would still be hanged. The Sulpician, Father Navetier, gave her the last rites, and Leveille took her in the rubbish cart to the main door of Notre-Dame, where she made her honourable amends. The royal carpenter, attached to the Maréchaussée, built for Angélique a hanging post in the middle of the burnt-out area, quite likely in front of her mistress's house. The usual place of execution was at the marketplace, at the corner of rue Saint-Paul and Place Royale. But the authorities wanted to punish Angélique to the maximum by having her see the work of her hands as she died. The carpenter also took bundles of faggots and made a huge pyre.

It may have been that the slave woman's heart twisted within her as she thought of her life and her last day on earth, this day when the sun was highest in the sky. As Angélique mounted the steps of the scaffold to her doom, her life since Portugal may have flashed before her eyes. The uprooting from all that was familiar. The trip across the vast and turbulent body of water known as the Atlantic. Her servitude to Nichus Block and the tumultuous nine years in Montréal in bondage to François Poulin de Francheville and his wife. Her relationship with Jacques César, the birth and death of her children, the death of Francheville, the affair with Claude Thibault, the fire in Monière's house, the fire in her mistress's house that burnt the city, the disappearance of Thibault, her arrest, imprisonment, and trial. The verdict. The sentence. Leveille lacing the *brodequins* around her legs. The approaching death.

She may also have thought of the irony of it all. A slave killing another slave. One condemned to be royal executioner, the other condemned to death.

It was a Monday, a day when the townspeople did not work, so everyone turned out to see the spectacle of the hanging, to gaze upon the Black woman who had burnt their town. She passed in the rubbish cart, her head bare, her legs a bloody mass, her body covered with the garment of the condemned.

As Angélique looked at the crowd that had come out to view her execution, and as she heard the rumbling among them, perhaps her mind went back to Portugal. Perhaps she heard the traditional songs of loss and longing, of death and grief, the voices of those who would be later known as Fado singers, said to be inspired by the singing of enslaved Africans and Black Moors in Portugal lamenting their exile and bondage. Perhaps Angélique heard their throaty voices echoing as they travelled with the foamy waves to the eastern shore of Canada, through the gulf of the St. Lawrence, flying with the wind upstream on that great river, past the bounteous fisheries of Tadoussac, past the cliffs of Québec, past the town of Trois-Rivières, and finally to Montréal. These voices, borne on the wings of urgent breezes, flew swiftly to the *escravo* (the Portuguese word for slave), and she must have wept.

The Virgin Mary is the patron saint of Montréal, and Angélique received her name at her baptism. Joseph was the husband of Mary, and the bondswoman also received his name. These two saints were known as rescuers of children, helpers of the poor, and comforters to those in need. In the hour of her death, perhaps she called upon these saints to help and comfort her. And it could be that these two saints, in their guise as healers of tortured souls and menders of broken hearts, walked with Angélique as she climbed those dreadful steps to the gallows and Leveille wrapped the rope around her throat. Perhaps these saints enfolded Angélique with their numen as her neck broke and her spirit flew from her body. In death, Marie-Joseph Angélique found the liberty she had long sought.

Porlier, the king's scribe who dutifully recorded Angélique's trial, also wrote about the end of her life:

> In the year seventeen hundred and thirty-four, on the 21st of June, at three o'clock in the afternoon, the present *arrêt* [judgment] was by me, the undersigned *greffier*, read in the prison of the accused, and after the sacrament of confession was administered to her by Monsieur Navetier, priest of the Seminary of Saint Sulpice, she was handed over to the *executeur de la haute justice*, who led her to the door of the parish church of this town, where she made *amende honorable* with the torch in her hand, after which she was taken by the said executioner to the unoccupied space before the burned house, where she was hanged and strangled and then thrown into the fire, and her ashes were then thrown to the winds. In fulfillment of the *arrêt* carried out on this said day and year as indicated above.[1]

Angélique, the Arsonist

EVERYONE WHO COMMENTED on the fire, from Beauharnois and Hocquart in 1734 to playwright Lorena Gale in 1997 and historian Allan Greer in 1997, maintained that Angélique set fire to her mistress's house. Indeed, most of the witnesses who gave depositions affirmed their belief in the bondswoman's guilt. To her credit, Madame Francheville did say, "I cannot say for certain that Angélique set the fire, but I believe she did." However, Angélique was found guilty and condemned on hearsay and suspicion. She has come down in history as "the slave woman who set fire to Montréal." Was she wrongfully convicted?

I believe not. Angélique had good reason to set the fire. And her motive was revenge. Her mistress had not only refused to set her free, but had also sold her. Added to that, Angélique was an abused slave who was bent on fighting back. She detested the French in general, her mistress in particular, and wished them all dead.

Angélique had made her intentions clear when she ran away in February and tried to burn down Sieur Monière's house. She was a slave, but she had no respect for and fear of her mistress in particular and White society in general. Mentally, she was beyond the control of those who exercised authority over her.

Here is what I believed happened. Angélique planned to escape after learning she had been sold and decided to use fire to cover her tracks. The first scheme at Sieur Monière's house did not work out, but she still held fast to her idea of escape and arson. While Thibault was in prison, Angélique continued to visit him, and the two conspired. Thibault got out of prison on April 8, came to the Francheville house, collected his wages and belongings, and left. However, he continued to visit Angélique when Madame Francheville was out.

On the evening of April 10, the slave woman put live coals under the crossbeams just below the roof and fanned the flames. Then she ran into the street and began walking up and down, fixing her gaze on the very spot from which she believed the flames would burst. That was when Marguerite César observed her strange behaviour.

As Angélique gazed at the roof, smoke erupted from it, and the bondswoman knew she had been successful. Yet she yelled "fire" because, after all, she had to display the right behaviour. The children ran from the house, and one of them, Marguerite de Couagne, wanted to run and warn her aunt, who had gone off to mass. Angélique prevented her from doing so. The fire soon consumed the roof and began its disastrous spread.

Thibault appeared out of the dusk, and he and Angélique began moving some of Madame Francheville's possessions into the garden of the poor at the hospital, across the street from the burning house. And there they remained. By this time, the fire had spread to neighbouring houses and build-ings, including those of the hospital. The hospital's garden was soon packed with refugees. The Récollets and Sulpicians came with food. And Thibault, like the rest of the gathering, ate. He finished his meal and refused to help with the fire-fighting efforts.

At this point, Thibault and Angélique should have fled together. But they did not. Why? Because the town crier walked through the town, shouting that it was Angélique who had set the fire. Everyone was now pointing the finger at Angélique. As a precaution, the gates of the town were sealed and under guard. For Thibault, Angélique was now a liability. If they were seen together, they surely would be arrested. Perhaps they quarrelled as they remained together in that brief period in the hospital's courtyard. What is certain is that Thibault fled without Angélique. His fear got the better of him. He likely knew the soldiers who guarded the gates and perhaps talked his way out. If he had worked on the fortifica-tions, he would have known the wall was not yet completed, and there were openings through which he could make his escape. Once he got beyond the confines of the town, it was easy to make a clean break. And that was what he did.

Thibault was never caught. For two years, the colonial authorities searched for him, and in his absence found him guilty. But it was all in vain: he had disappeared into thin air. This was not how he and Angélique had planned it, but he betrayed her. Angélique set the fire to cover her tracks; Thibault grew apprehensive at the consequences and aban-doned her.

While most contemporary and modern commentators agree that Angélique did set the fire, they disagree as to her motive. However, the accepted wisdom is that the enslaved woman set the fire because she wanted to run away with her White lover, Claude Thibault. The "in love with Thibault" thesis has gained some currency because of Marcel Trudel, the acknowledged authority on slavery in New France. In his 1960 publication on slavery, Trudel played up Angélique's amorous intent, and this was echoed by Raymond Boyer in 1966.[1] Over thirty years later, Robert Prévost would write that Angélique "set fire to her mistress's house, hoping to distract her mistress's attention so that she could flee with her lover."[2]

By emphasizing love as Angélique's primary motive, these writers not only rob her of the agency that she exhibited in her quest for liberty, they also diminish the violence inherent in slavery. For them, Angélique did not flee because she found her enslavement humiliating, awful, and suffocating; she fled because she was "in love." If we take this reasoning one step further, it is easy to conclude that slavery could not have been so bad. I believe that the "in love" thesis advanced by these authors speaks to their unease with the race, gender, and power relations intrinsic to slavery. Whites exercised almost unlimited power over the lives of enslaved Black people. This unequal power relationship between Whites and Blacks was an everyday and institutionalized feature of slavery. And it has shaped modern-day race relations in Canada. Trudel and his cohorts are all modern Québec historians, and they may have been influenced by the fact that today one does not examine (publicly) the race question in Québec unless one is talking about the French and English. These historians refuse to see that Angélique was an enraged woman who wished to run away from enslavement not because of Thibault, but because of slavery itself.

Yet those closest to the event did not give an amorous intent to Angélique's action. For example, Beauharnois and Hocquart, in their letter to Maurepas, while noting that Angélique had had an affair with Claude Thibault, did not ascribe that as even a secondary motive. They stated clearly that the bondswoman was bent on revenge: "the accident took place because of the wickedness of a Negress slave belonging to Widow Francheville, who, as a result of some displeasure expressed by her mistress, deliberately set fire..."[3] Pierre Raimbault and the other judges felt likewise.

And even as the centuries rolled by, historians of Montréal and slavery continued to place the revenge motive in the foreground. One commentator, who called himself "R.E.," surmised in 1917 that Angélique ran away because she wanted to return to Portugal.[4] Around the same time, O.M.H. Lapalice, writing on the subject of Black enslaved people in Montréal, ascribed Angélique's actions to revenge.[5] Likewise, in a 1925 issue of *La Patrie*, Angélique was the "vengeful" slave.[6]

And I concur with this view. Perhaps she was in love with Thibault, but that was not her primary consideration in setting the fire. Thibault's entry into her life coincided with her desires and plans. She saw clearly that if she teamed up with him her chance of succeeding was greater than if she tried to escape by herself. During their first flight, it was Thibault who hid loaves of bread in a Longueuil barn. Thibault was the one familiar with the geography. It was important that they follow the *right* track to New England and not end up confused and lost in the woods. And Angélique did have a hold over Thibault. When Madame Francheville sent them to live with Monière, she contracted Thibault to work for him. Angélique told Thibault in no uncertain terms that he could not commit himself to working for Monière because that would tie him down. Angélique said she could leave by herself—her desire was strong enough—but she did not want to. She was less familiar with the surrounding geography than her lover. And she knew very well that a Black woman travelling alone would arouse suspicion.

But in the end, Thibault, motivated by self-preservation, left Angélique to face her destiny alone. Whatever love he might have felt for her was banished by the sickening fear he experienced when he considered the hangman's rope around his neck. Thibault may have found his way to New England or New York, and from there to Europe. Or he may have remained in an English colony, beyond the ken of French authorities.

So, on June 21, when Angélique broke under torture and confessed that she had indeed set the fire and that she had done it with a small stove, she was telling the truth. She was also being truthful when she said that she had done it by herself. She did indeed place the burning coals beneath the ceiling of her owner's house, her heart filled with a glorious and fearsome pounding. She had decided that she was going to take fate into her own hands by burning down her house of bondage. The Black slave woman from Portugal, whose body was an item of commerce in the hands of Whites, passed from master to master, from port to port, for the sake of Mammon, she whose name changed so many times over the course of her short life, whose body was whipped by Madame Francheville and perhaps used by Sieur Francheville, would have her revenge.

She would roast, burn, and grill them, and so do to them what they had been doing to her all her days. With determination, she blew hard on the coals on the cross beams, and they burst into flames.

EPILOGUE:

A Silenced Voice Heard Again

HOW DO WE UNEARTH the Black past—one rooted in slavery? How do we recover the story of Angélique that lies buried in obscurity? The transcripts of her trial present themselves as the surest means to do so. The trial itself took place in the lower court at Montréal, while the appeal happened at the high or supreme court in Québec. In addition to delineating the trial, the transcripts also narrate the story of her life, mainly the Canadian portion of it. Given the early date of the trial, 1734, I make the bold claim that Angélique's trial transcript constitutes the first slave narrative in North America.

A slave narrative is the personal account of the life and adventures of an ex-slave, often written while the author is living in freedom, as either a manumitted person or a fugitive. According to scholars, the first recognized and extant slave narrative was published in 1760. Angélique's story was recorded in 1734, fully twenty-six years before the publication of that work.

Beginning in the eighteenth century and continuing into the nineteenth, Blacks in the United States, Europe, and Canada, the majority of whom were former slaves, wrote their autobiographical narratives. These authors penned hundreds of such accounts between 1760 and 1860.

Slave narratives functioned as part autobiography and part antislavery polemic. They almost always began with the phrase "I was born a slave" and then launched into a detailed description of the protagonist's enslavement—the horror and misery, the trials and tribulations—the escape and flight to freedom, and the life lived (usually dedicated to the abolitionist cause) in freedom. But such narratives also had a decidedly political aim: antislavery. The Black authors eagerly used their writing to attack and condemn the institution of slavery and call for its end. Many of the narratives were sponsored by abolitionist societies and used as part of the antislavery propaganda arsenal.

The narratives were at once tales of enslavement and redemption and of ignorance and enlightenment. Ignorance was associated with enslavement because slaves were not allowed to read or write or acquire any form of formal learning. Freedom was coupled with enlightenment because, when freed, the former slaves acquired literacy, which then enabled them to compile, write, or relate their stories. The narratives were frequently an extension of the authors' speech: prior to writing down their stories, they had told them to audiences on numerous occasions.

The slave narrative as genre reached its apex in the middle of the nineteenth century with the publication of the life stories of such authors as William Wells Brown, Frederick Douglass, Henry Bibb, Harriet Jacobs, James Pennington, and

Mary Prince. These autobiographies became national and international best-sellers, being published in numerous editions and several European languages.

But the slave narratives of the nineteenth century had eighteenth-century antecedents. In 1760, Briton Hammon launched the written Black autobiographical tradition with the publication of *The Narrative of the Uncommon Sufferings and Surprising Deliverance of Briton Hammon, A Negro Manservant to General Winslow*.[1] Hammon's work is a rousing tale of shipwreck off the coast of Florida, capture by Florida Indians, and sojourns in Martinique, Santo Domingo, and Jamaica until the author's eventual redemption and subsequent return to his master. Though *Uncommon Sufferings* was no antislavery polemic, it was a signal text in the nascent Black literary tradition. It is considered by scholars to be the first published slave narrative. Within a few years, other Black autobiographers on both sides of the Atlantic would put pen to paper and tell their stories.

In 1770, James Albert Ukawsaw Gronniosaw, a Nigerian, published the history of his life—from his capture in Africa, his journey across the Middle Passage, and his enslavement in the West Indies and England to his gaining his freedom in England and his conversion to Christianity.[2] In 1785, John Marrant, a Black Loyalist, followed up with his *Narrative of the Lord's Wonderful Dealings with John Marrant*. Marrant, an evangelical Christian, was captured by Cherokee Indians of the Carolinas, but he converted the chief and his daughter and many members of the tribe to Christianity. Marrant's Christian influence among the Cherokees led to his release. Afterwards, he was pressed into service in the British Navy as a musician, saw action in the Revolutionary War, continued his preaching in Britain and later headed to Nova Scotia, where he established churches. Finally, he returned to Britain, where he published his autobiography.

Two years later, another Black Atlantic resident, Ottobah Cugoano, published his narrative, *Thoughts and Sentiments on the Evil and Wicked Traffic of the Slavery and Commerce of the Human Species.* Cugoano, a Fanti from what is now called Ghana, meant to use his text to influence British officials about the evils of the slave trade and slavery so that both practices would be abolished. Cugoano himself was a survivor of the Middle Passage, and so spoke first-hand about the misery Africans endured in their journey to the New World.

Olaudah Equiano was Cugoano's friend, and like him, an abolitionist. Equiano, who led a life full of adventure and wonder, published his narrative in 1789. He wrote of his capture as a young boy from Igboland in Nigeria, his enslavement in the West Indies, and his purchase by an English naval officer, who took him around the world. Equiano went on expeditions to the South Pole, saw military action in Turkey, and was in General Wolfe's camp at the fall of Canada in 1760. Having gained his freedom, Equiano married an English woman and became a fervent abolitionist and leader in the Black community. His book, *The Interesting Narrative of the Life of Olaudah Equiano or Gustavus Vassa, the African, Written by Himself,* influenced the structure of the nineteenth-century slave narratives.

Another autobiographer from this period was John Jea, also a Nigerian. Jea was enslaved in New England, saw action during the Revolutionary War, and became a preacher in France, England, and the United States until his retirement in England. Jea has the distinction of being an early "war resister." While

Jea was in France, the American Revolutionary War broke out, and the American consul there ordered Jea to enter naval service on the side of the Americans. Jea refused, saying he would not fight against Great Britain and that, furthermore, he was not an American but an African. For his refusal, Jea was imprisoned by the American consul.

In 1796, the Canadian Loyalist Boston King penned his *Memoirs of the Life of Boston King, A Black Preacher* while studying at a Methodist College in England.[3] It was published in 1798. King was a witness to the great historical dramas of his day. Around him the Revolutionary War raged. He escaped from his South Carolina plantation and joined the British Loyalist forces. However, the Crown lost the war and in its aftermath transported thousands of White and Black defeated Loyalists to Nova Scotia and other Canadian territories. King and his fellow Black Loyalists found life difficult in Nova Scotia. They faced racial discrimination and were ignored by the Crown, despite their loyal service to it during the war. Disheartened, King decided to leave Canada and the entire North American continent and go to Sierra Leone, where the British were founding a new colony.

Religious conversion is a main theme in these narratives. Most of the narrators saw their conversion to Christianity as a turning point in their lives and discussed it at length. However, these narrators, in addition to being "pious pilgrims," were also fervent antislavery activists. Equiano, Jea, and Cugoano, in particular, condemned slavery and the slave trade. Equiano, for example, wrote that Europe would have to account to God for the misery it heaped on Africans. In fact, Cugoano wrote his narrative as a tool in the battle against the enslavement of his fellow Africans.

Other Africans in Europe and America wrote non-autobiographical literary texts: graduate dissertations, treatises, letters, books of poetry, and sermons. In 1773, Phillis Wheatley, Boston's slave poet, published a collection of poetry that became a hit on both sides of the Atlantic. Wheatley was reviewed by some of the leading intellectuals of Europe and America. Other Black writers of the period include Jacobus Capitein, a free Dutch African who completed a dissertation; Anton Wilhelm Amo, a Ghanian who earned a doctorate in philosophy from the University of Halle in Germany; Francis Williams, a mixed-race Jamaican who studied at Cambridge University and wrote books; and Ignatius Sancho, an African Briton who in 1782 published a volume of correspondence written by and to him.

These acts challenged all Western ideological and philosophical assumptions regarding Black people. It was no accident that the Black literary tradition began during the period of European Enlightenment. We associate the Enlightenment with the concepts of liberalism and progress, which were articulated in notions of equal rights, autonomy, and freedom of men. It was during the Enlightenment that Europe came of age, became "modern." Yet, as American scholar Cornel West declares, Black slavery and the slave trade "were the ignoble origins of Western modernity and the criminal foundations of American democracy. They constituted the night side of the Age of Enlightenment, the reality left unlit by the torch of natural reason."[4] West further argues that Europe's modernity, success, and wealth were "predicated initially on the terrors and horrors visited on enslaved Africans on the way to, or in, the New World."[5]

Enlightenment thinkers, from the Scottish David Hume and the American Thomas Jefferson to the Germans Georg

Hegel and Immanuel Kant, all justified the enslavement of Africans on the premise that (following René Descartes's propositions) Africans lacked reason. One proof of this was the absence of writing or the creation of a literature by them. The argument ran that Africans lacked reason because they were "inferior," and thus were fit for slavery. This argument would be elaborated in the nineteenth century, especially between 1830 and 1860 in the United States, under the theory of slavery as a "positive good" for Africans.

Black authors understood the implications of the racist pronouncements that White intellectuals and writers were making. In taking up the pen to write their stories, they challenged the prevailing racial constructions and stereotypes and sought both to shape public discourse on the Black and slave question and to fashion a new identity for themselves, collectively and individually. By engaging in the act of thinking, recording, and organizing, the ex-slave became a full human, a thinking person, a "man," a "man of letters." That is why it was so important for authors to append to the title of their books "Written by Himself/Herself." This device was intended to prove to the world, especially the traducers of Black people, that Blacks/slaves were thinking beings who could express their own thoughts and write them down themselves. All kinds of Black writing, even writings deemed "apolitical," were highly charged political acts.

Ex-slave authors, through the act of writing, were also claiming their own voice to tell their stories. In so doing, they became the authority in that telling. Yet not all the narratives were "*written* by themselves." Several were related by the narrators to an amanuensis or scribe. The stories of Briton Hammon, Mary Prince, and John Anderson, as well as

Benjamin Drew's *Narratives*, were all told to amanuenses.[6] This method of recording a slave narrative was used not because the narrator was illiterate, though this was sometimes the case, but because reading and writing at that time were two separate skills. Mary Prince could read, but we are not sure she could write. John Anderson could both read and write. Likewise, many of the narrators of Drew's *Narratives* were well-educated, literate persons. However, the nature of the production of the narrative depended on the aims and financial stability of the sponsoring organizations, and several of these organizations had the narrators tell their stories to a scribe.

At the time of the production of her narrative, Mary Prince was living in the home of London abolitionist Thomas Pringle. She had been badly abused by her owners, who had abandoned her in the streets of London. Pringle rescued her. Living in the Pringle home at the same time was antislavery writer Susanna Strickland. Pringle asked Strickland to record Prince's narrative, so Prince related her life story to an amanuensis. Prince's narrative became a bestseller, and Strickland married Major John Moodie. Soon after the marriage, the Moodies moved to Canada, and Susanna Moodie became a foundational writer in Canadian literary history.

The narratives that former slaves told to scribes served the same function as the chronicles written by the ex-slaves themselves. They were *printing* their voices, and through this medium they hoped to reach a wider audience. Whenever Black writers produced literature or took the stage to lecture, they were creating new and alternative knowledge that stood in opposition to the discourses on Black people produced by

Whites. The fact that Black/ex-slave abolitionists came from the context of an oppressive environment and had experienced racism, whether individual or systemic, infused the writings and lecturing of Black writers with a powerful authority. For over two centuries, others had spoken for them and about them, and had constructed dubious and damning discourses about them, which not only denied them their humanity but also made them invisible. Ex-slave authors, by writing, relating, and publishing their autobiographies, were laying claim to their own voices, their humanity, and a fully embodied self.

✳

There is a little-known and thus under-studied tradition of the slave narrative in Canada. Mention is often made of Boston King and John Marrant, two "Black Enlightenment" writers who published their life stories. But they were not the only Canadian slave narrators. In the early 1850s a Boston Quaker abolitionist named Benjamin Drew travelled to Canada West and wrote down the narratives of over three hundred Blacks, some of whom, like Harriet Tubman, had escaped from slavery. Drew also interviewed free-born Black people. One of the oldest narrators was Sophia Pooley, who had lived in Canada since the Revolutionary War era. To give an idea of her age, Pooley said, "I guess I was the first colored girl brought into Canada."

During the "period of crisis" in the United States, between 1830 and 1860, when slaveholding was challenged by abolitionists, runaway slaves, and revolutionists, a plethora of slave narratives were written by escaped slaves. Many of these authors had escaped to Canada, where they started a new life and raised families, and they include Henry Bibb, Jermain Loguen, Josiah Henson, and Samuel Ringgold Ward. Henson, for example, escaped to Canada in 1830 from slavery in Maryland, and lived here for the rest of his life. He died in 1883. Henson published his narrative, *The Life of Josiah Henson, Formerly a Slave, Now an Inhabitant of Canada*, in 1849.[7] He became world-famous as Uncle Tom, the proto-type "old male slave" that Harriet Beecher Stowe used in her groundbreaking novel *Uncle Tom's Cabin*. Henry Bibb, who escaped from slavery in Kentucky and moved to Canada in 1850, published the country's first Black newspaper, *The Voice of the Fugitive*, in which he recorded the narratives of numerous escaped slaves. Previously, in 1849, Bibb had published his autobiography, entitled *The Life and Adventures of Henry Bibb: An American Slave*. Henson, Ward, and Bibb became famous fugitives and prominent Canadian Black leaders. Another Canadian writer was Jim Henson, who had also fled Maryland. Henson made it all the way to Grey County, Ontario, where he put down roots. In 1889, he published his life story, *Broken Shackles*.

These works are documents of Black life, history, and culture. And they are of primary importance given that, until recently, people of African descent have been invisible at worst and marginalized at best in the telling of the history of North America. This is even more true of Canada than of the United States. One historian, Maureen Elgersman, asks that newspaper advertisements, bills of sale, bills of hire, and contracts made between slaveholders be considered as authentic evidence of the Black presence in Canada, and even as forms of slave narrative.[8] Since one of the current projects of the present generation of chroniclers of Black history is to rescue marginalized people from historical obscurity, Elgersman's appeal makes sense. Like the archaeologist, we must dig and unearth these sources that tell the unknown stories of African Canadians. I would add wills and court records and transcripts as sources that narrate the stories of enslaved Black people, even if these stories are incomplete.

In 1760, when England took Canada from France, after seven years of war, one of the consequences was the introduction of newspapers to the colony. Slaveholders, both English and French, used newspaper advertisements to tell stories about their slave property.

In July 1779, the *Quebec Gazette* advertised the following:

> Run-away from the subscriber, a Negro slave named Ishmael, about 35 years old, 5 feet 8 inches high, pretty much marked with the small-pox, wears his own hair which is black, long and curly; has black eyes, broad shoulders, and tone of voice peculiar to New England, where he was born; reads English tolerably well, and can speak a little French. He has on an old hat bedawbed with white paint, an ozenbrig frock and trowsers, a check shirt, a short white flannel jacket, and a pair of mochissons.

Brief though it is, this ad relates Ishmael's flight from slavery, some of his vital statistics, and his linguistic skills, and hints at his odyssey from New England to Québec. It is quite likely that Ishmael came with his owner to Canada during the Loyalist migration. It is not known whether he was recaptured.

In July 1795, the *Upper Canada Gazette* advertised:

> For sale…a Negro wench named Chloe, 23 years old,
> understands washing, cooking, etc. Any gentleman willing
> to purchase or employ her by the year or month is
> requested to apply to Robert Franklin, at the receiver
> general's.

This gives us a glimpse into Chloe's life. We know her age
and that she could cook and clean. We also know that she was
owned by a member of the Upper Canadian elite.

Through these brief notices, we see threads of the story of
Black people, marginalized and held and disposed of as chattel. Much the same picture sometimes comes to us from third
parties. For example, in 1793, when William Vrooman bound
Chloe Cooley with ropes, threw her in a boat, and sold her
across the river, eyewitness Peter Martin related the incident
to some Upper Canadian politicians. The legislators recorded Martin's testimony, and their record becomes a stand-in
narrative about a crucial moment in the life of a terrorized
and degraded Black woman.[9]

Another source of narrative is court records and transcripts
of trial. Under the *ancien régime*, both in Europe and the
colonies, court proceedings were elaborate and intense.
Because trials were, in fact, hostile interrogations, and confessions were often brought on by torture, a large body of writing about the accused was amassed by scribes. Within these
chronicles were "biographies" of the accused. This was the
case for Marie-Joseph Angélique.

Her trial was first heard in the lower court in Montréal.
The judge was Pierre Raimbault, the king's prosecutor was

François Foucher, and Claude-Cyprien-Jacques Porlier was the scribe. Foucher prepared the witnesses and brought forward the case on behalf of the Crown; Raimbault interrogated; Angélique answered; Porlier wrote. At the end of the trial, the court condemned the accused to death. The case was appealed and heard before the Conseil Supérieur in Québec. Given the importance of the case, two scribes, François Daine and Jean-Claude Louet, recorded the event. It is from the transcripts written by the scribes of the lower and upper courts that a life history of Angélique unfolds. What were Porlier, Daine, and Louet if not her amanuenses?

Angélique's trial record opens like a classic slave narrative: "Said her name was Marie-Joseph Angélique, she was 29 years old. She was born in Portugal. She is the slave of Widow Francheville..." As in the slave narratives, Angélique's says in the opening sentence her name, place of birth, and social status. Porlier then records the interrogations, which reveal Angélique's life story as a slave in Montréal, her unhappiness with her lot, her attempts to escape it, her quarrels with her mistress, her insubordination, and her hatred of the French and Whites in general. The story climaxes with the events leading up to the fire, the fire itself, Angélique's arrest and condemnation, and her execution at the gallows.

Though the trial transcripts were not "written by herself," they nonetheless were "related by herself." They are her story. When the scribes wrote down Angélique's history, they were preserving for posterity the first known Black slave narrative in North America. The trial documents must be read as the first piece of Black literature—written and oral—that we have in Canada.[10]

Not only does Angélique's story hold an important place in

literary history, it is also the first story we have of a Black slave woman during this early colonial period.[11] Almost all of the "Black Enlightenment" authors of the eighteenth century, whether scholars or authors of narratives, were men. Though they did present a Black voice in defence of their humanity and open up a space for Black literature, a female Black voice was missing. We had to wait until 1773 to hear the voice of a Black woman, Phillis Wheatley, through her published poems.

This absence of Black women's voices in the written record is a direct consequence of their degradation by those who claimed ownership over their bodies. Angélique's interrogations and confession form a startling narration of "unsilencing the past," one that "re-tongues" the mouths of Black women and Black people and allows them to shout their narratives of resistance to the high heavens.

When Angélique faced the judges of New France, she ushered in a new tradition in Black women's and Black men's storytelling. She demanded her place in history and made visible the enslaved as a thinking, feeling, intelligent, and complex human. From her lineage would spring such resister-storytellers as Chloe Cooley, John Marrant, Boston King, Peggy Pompadour, Sophia Pooley, Mary Prince, Henry Bibb, Harriet Jacobs, Frederick Douglass, and Ellen Craft.

Acknowledgements

THIS BOOK WOULD not have been possible without the support, commitment, and assistance of a number of people. I thank Dr. Edwin Bezzina, an expert in seventeenth- and eighteenth-century French and French colonial history and jurisprudence, and Adrienne Shadd, an authority on African Canadian history, for their help in translating many documents, including the trial transcripts. Dr. Bezzina was patient and thorough, and I thank him for going beyond the call of duty. To Adrienne Shadd, I offer my thanks for her thoughtful encouragement and many discussions over the years. Heartfelt thanks, as well, to Austin Clarke and Drs. George Elliot Clarke, Nigel Thomas, and Daniel Gay. I am indebted to Dr. Fred Case and Professors Franca Iacovetta, Seth Witherspoon, Bernard Moitt, and Roslyn Terborg-Penn for their review of parts of the manuscript and their expert advice and commitment to advancing the cause of Black history and women's history. Natalie Zemon Davis, professor emeritus of Princeton and renowned scholar of early modern France and women's history, gave helpful suggestions and advice. I thank her.

Many thanks to Father Rolland Litalien, archivist at the Sulpician Seminary in Montréal, for the discussions on Montréal's early history, for photocopying, and for afternoon tea! On my several research trips to Québec, I made many friends who supported the advancement of the book in more ways than one. My deepest gratitude to Pat Dillon, Judge Juanita Westmoreland Traore, Ismail Traore, Shirley Small, Moussa Bakayoko, and Guy and Tanya Giard. Over the course of researching and writing this book, I had two children, and several people helped me and my partner with childcare while I travelled to do research or worked at home. For this I am indebted to the Segree family, Kuya Gwaan, Joanne Atherley, Sharon Allen, Zeinab Warah and her children, the Walker family, and Khetiwe Jorman and her family. And to Hameed Shaqq, Gail Dexter Lord, Patrick Powell, and Maisha Bucham, thanks. They all contributed to the realization of this book.

I would be remiss if I did not express my gratitude to a great historian of New France, Marcel Trudel. For many of us who work in Black history, and certainly in slave studies in Canada, Trudel made our work easier with his research on slavery in Canada and his several publications on the subject. His book *L'esclavage au Canada Français* is a foundational text in Black Canadian history. When I decided to pursue Angélique, I wrote to Professor Trudel and he promptly responded and made some helpful suggestions. His work continues to be an inspiration.

A big thank you to Jean Stephenson and Elaine Genus of Robarts Library, University of Toronto. It is also my pleasure to acknowledge, with great appreciation, my agent, Denise Bukowski, for her support and perseverance, and my editors, Iris Tupholme, Nicole Langlois, and Kate Cassaday of HarperCollins Publishers, for their wonderful insights, patience, and careful edits.

Without the financial support of the Canada Council, the Ontario Arts Council, and the Toronto Arts Council, this book would not have seen the light of day. I thank them very much.

Last but not least, I am indebted to my family, Alpha Diallo, Habiba, Lamarana, and Akil, for their unceasing support, love, and patience. Often, they had to compete with Angélique for my time and attention, and they have come to know her almost as well as I have.

Whatever faults and errors this book may contain are solely mine, and the individuals and organizations mentioned are in no way responsible.

Notes

Preface

1. The Priceville Black cemetery, commonly called the Old Durham Road Cemetery, was ploughed over in the 1930s and turned into a potato patch. Africville, a Black settlement in Halifax, was demolished in the 1960s and 1970s and its residents scattered.
2. The glamorization of the Underground Railroad is one such example of "feel good" history. Canada gave refuge to thousands of enslaved African Americans, and this fact is highlighted over that of Canada's own internal slavery.

Chapter 1: The Torture and Hanging of Angélique

1. Robert Rapley, *A Case of Witchcraft: The Trial of Urbain Grandier* (Montréal: McGill-Queen's University Press, 1998), 186.
2. Ibid., 189.

Chapter 2: Atlantic Origins: The Slave Woman from Portugal

1. See Chapter 9.
2. Robin Blackburn, *The Making of New World Slavery: From the Baroque to the Modern*, 1492–1800 (London: Verso, 1997), 100.
3. Ibid., 107-8.
4. Ibid., 107.
5. Ibid., 101.
6. Ibid., 116.

7. David R. Murray, *Odious Commerce: Britain, Spain, and the Abolition of the Cuban Slave Trade* (New York: Cambridge University Press, 1980).

8. A.C. De C.M. Saunders, *A Social History of Black Slaves and Freedmen in Portugal, 1441–1555* (Cambridge, U.K.: Cambridge University Press, 1982), 62. The discussion on slavery in Portugal is drawn mainly from Saunders's work.

9. Ibid., 77-78. For another example of Black women "insulting" elite White women, see Robert Olwell, "'Loose, Idle and Disorderly': Slave Women in the Eighteenth-Century Charleston Marketplace," in *More Than Chattel: Black Women and Slavery in the Americas*, ed. David Barry Gaspar and Darline Clark Hine (Bloomington: Indiana University Press, 1996), 97-110.

10. Blackburn, *New World Slavery*, 117.

11. Saunders, *Social History of Black Slaves*, 107.

12. The concept of social death is best articulated by sociologist Orlando Patterson in his groundbreaking book *Slavery and Social Death: A Comparative Study* (Cambridge, Mass.: Harvard University Press, 1982).

13. Joseph C. Miller, *Way of Death: Merchant Capitalism and the Angolan Slave Trade, 1730–1830* (Madison: University of Wisconsin Press, 1988).

14. David Birmingham, *A Concise History of Portugal* (Cambridge, U.K.: Cambridge University Press, 1993), 72. The discussion on Portugal's second golden age is drawn from Birmingham's work.

15. A.H. De Oliveira Marques, *History of Portugal*, vol. 1 (New York: Columbia University Press, 1972), 261.

16. The interconnections between Jewish mercantile communities in the Portugese-speaking and Dutch-speaking worlds and in international trade have been well documented. Robin Blackburn makes this point in his discussion on the expansion of the Portuguese overseas trade: Blackburn, *New World Slavery*, 115-16. See also Gérard Nahon, "The Portuguese Jewish Nation of Saint-Esprit-Les Bayonne: The American Dimension," in *The Jews and the Expansion of Europe to the West, 1450–1800*, ed. Paolo Bernardini and Norman Fiering (New York: Berghahn Books, 2001), 255-67; and "'The Brokers of the World': American Jews, New Christians and International Trade," in ibid., 439-513. See also James Homer Williams, *An Atlantic Perspective on the Jewish Struggle for Rights and Opportunities in Brazil, New Netherland, and New York*, in ibid., 369-93.

17. On the Dutch Revolt or War of Independence against Spain, see Martin van Gelderen, *The Dutch Revolt* (Cambridge, U.K.: Cambridge University Press, 1993), 43.

18. On the economic rise of the Dutch, see Blackburn, *New World Slavery,* 185-215.

19. Seymour Drescher, "Jews and New Christians in the Atlantic Slave Trade," in *The Jews and the Expansion of Europe,* ed. Bernardini and Fiering, 450.

20. Wim Klooster, "The Jews in Suriname amd Curaçao," in *The Jews and the Expansion of Europe,* ed. Bernardini and Fiering, 351–68.

21. Birmingham, *History of Portugal,* 59-60.

22. Drescher, "Jews and New Christians," 448.

23. Jonathan I. Israel, "The Jews of Dutch America," in *The Jews and the Expansion of Europe,* ed. Bernardini and Fiering, 335–49.

24. See Klooster, "The Jews in Suriname and Curaçao," 350-68.

25. Blackburn, *New World Slavery,* 212.

26. James C. Boyajian, "New Christians and Jews in the Sugar Trade, 1550–1750: Two Centuries of Development of the Atlantic Economies," in *Jews and the Expansion of Europe,* ed. Bernadini and Fiering, 473.

27. Letter from Beauharnois to Maurepas, in *Documents Relative to the Colonial History of the State of New-York,* vol. 9, ed. Edmund B. O'Callaghan (Albany: Weed, Parsons, and Company, 1856-1887), 1019-20. Also, in 1727, Intendant Dupuy issued an ordinance prohibiting "foreign" merchants from trading or settling in Montréal. Dupuy was particularly incensed about the trading activities of the merchants of Albany, "New England." See ibid., 985-86.

28. Kenneth Donovan, "Slaves and Their Owners in Ile Royale, 1713–1760," *Acadiensis* 25, no. 1 (1995): 21-22.

29. On the colonial trade between the thirteen colonies, Acadia, and Canada, see Donald F. Chard, "The Price and Profits of Accommodation: Massachusetts-Louisbourg Trade, 1713-1744," in *Seafaring in Colonial Massachusetts* (Boston: Colonial Society of Massachusetts, 1980), Faneuil Letter Book, Baker Library, Harvard University.

30. M. Gaucher et al., "Les engagés pour le Canada au XVIIIe siècle," *Revue d'histoire de L'Amérique Française* 14 (1960–61): 250.

31. Jean Lunn, "The Illegal Fur Trade out of New France, 1713–60," Canadian Historical Association *Annual Report* (1939): 40–76.

32. Thomas Elliot Norton, *The Fur Trade in Colonial New York, 1686–1776* (Madison: University of Wisconsin Press, 1974), 121-51.

Chapter 3: The Secret of Slavery in Canada

1. Stephen D. Behrendt, *The Atlantic Slave Trade* [CD ROM] (Cambridge, U.K.: Cambridge University Press, 1999). This database has information on over 30,000 slave ships used in the British trade.

2. James Walker, a historian at the University of Waterloo, discusses how Black history is missing from pioneer history. See James Walker, *A History of Blacks in Canada* (Hull, Québec: Ministry of State for Multiculturalism, 1980), 1-7.

3. Marcel Trudel, *Introduction to New France* (Toronto: Holt, Rinehart and Winston, 1968), 131-33, 138.

4. Hurbert Neilson, "Slavery in Old Canada, before and after the Conquest," *Transactions of the Literary and Historical Society of Quebec* 2, no. 26 (1906): 21.

5. Robin W. Winks, *The Blacks in Canada: A History* (Montréal: McGill-Queen's University Press, 1997), 6.

6. O.M.H. Lapalice, "Les Esclaves noir à Montréal sous l'ancien régime," *Canadian and Numismatic Journal* 12 (1915): 139.

7. See Daniel P. Mannix, *Black Cargoes* (New York: Viking Press, 1962), 65, 67, 243-44.

8. William Riddell, "The Code Noir," *Journal of Negro History* 10, no. 3 (1925): 321-8.

9. Winks, *The Blacks in Canada*, 1.

10. Ibid.

11. Ibid., 6.

12. Ibid., 60.

13. Ibid., 9. See also Marcel Trudel, *L'esclavage au Canada Français: Histoire et conditions de l'esclavage* (Québec: Les Presses Universitaire Laval, 1960), 130. On demography, see Kenneth Donovan, "Slaves and Their Owners in Ile Royale," 3.

14. See Winks, *The Blacks in Canada*, 11.

15. Pierre-Georges Roy, ed., *Rapport de l'archiviste de la province de Québec*, vol. 8 (1921–1922): 113-14. Translated by William Riddell

in "Notes on the Slave in Nouvelle-France," *Journal of Negro History* 8, no. 3 (1923): 323.

16. Ibid.

17. Roy, *Rapport de l'archiviste*, vol. 8, 113. Trans. Afua Cooper.

18. William Riddell, "An Early Canadian Slavery Transaction," *Journal of Negro History* 13, no. 2 (1928): 207. The translation is Riddell's. The original is in French and is taken from Roy, *Le bulletin des recherches historiques* 33, no. 8: 584.

19. Winks, *The Blacks in Canada*, 10.

20. Sigmund Samuel, *The Seven Years War in Canada* (Toronto: Ryerson Press, 1934), 202.

21. Winks, *The Blacks in Canada*, 25.

22. Ibid.

23. Donovan, "Slaves and Their Owners in Ile Royale," 7.

24. William Riddell, "The Slave in Canada," *Journal of Negro History* 5, no. 3 (1920): 276.

25. On the mildness perspective, see, for example, Riddell, "Notes on the Slave in Nouvelle-France," 267; Trudel, *L'esclavage au Canada Français*, 164; and Michael Power and Nancy Butler, *Slavery and Freedom in Niagara, Part One* (Niagara-on-the-Lake, Ont.: Niagara Historical Society, 2000).

26. Lorenzo Greene, *The Negro in Colonial New England* (New York: Columbia University Press, 1942), 256.

27. See Mark J. Sammons and Valerie Cunningham, *Black Portsmouth: Three Centuries of African American Heritage* (Durham: University of New Hampshire Press, 2004), 46.

28. See Bernard Moitt, "Women and Resistance," in *Women and Slavery in the French Antilles, 1635–1848* (Bloomington: Indiana University Press, 2001), 125-50.

29. Neilson, "Slavery in Old Canada," 35.

30. See Dorothy Roberts, *Killing the Black Body: Race, Reproduction, and the Meaning of Liberty* (New York: Vintage Books, 1999), 23-25; Maureen Elgersman, *Unyielding Spirits: Black Women and Slavery in Early Canada and Jamaica* (New York: Garland Publishing, 1999), 21-38.

31. Trudel, *L'eslavage au Canada Français*, 258.

32. Winks, *The Blacks in Canada*, 26.

33. Walker, *History of Blacks in Canada*, 6.

34. See Power and Butler, *Slavery and Freedom*, 18-20; Roy F. Fleming, "Negro Slaves with the United Empire Loyalists in Upper Canada," *Ontario History* 14, no. 1 (1953): 27-30; Donovan, "Slaves and Their Owners in Ile Royale," 21-22.

35. A.F. Hunter, "Probate of Wills of Prominent Men in Public Affairs," *Ontario History* 23 (1926): 337-38.

36. Henry Scadding, *Toronto of Old* (Toronto: Oxford University Press, 1966), 212.

37. The Russells wrote about their slave woman Peggy and her family. Much of Peggy's story is contained in the Russell Papers, a portion of which is Elizabeth Russell's diary, housed at the Baldwin Room, Toronto Public Library. Sections of Elizabeth's diary are reprinted in Edith Firth, *Town of York, 1791–1815* (Toronto: Champlain Society, 1962).

38. Firth, *Town of York*, 243.

39. Ibid., 261.

40. Donovan, "Slaves and Their Owners in Ile Royale," 31.

41. William Riddell, "The Slave in Canada," 267.

42. James Walker, *The Black Loyalists* (Toronto: University of Toronto Press, 1992), 115-44.

43. Winks, *The Blacks in Canada*, 96.

44. Peter Martin, a free Black man, and William Grisley, a White man, witnessed Vrooman binding and disposing of Chloe Cooley. Martin and Grisley related the matter to Simcoe and some members of his Executive Council. See E.A. Cruikshank, ed., *The Correspondence of Lieut. Governor John Graves Simcoe* [hereafter cited as Simcoe Papers], vol. 1 (Toronto: Ontario Historical Society, 1923–31), 304.

45. Henry Dundas was the home secretary in the British government at the time Simcoe wrote to him. Extracts of Simcoe's letter to Dundas appear in Simcoe Papers, vol. 2, 53.

46. For the complete "Act to Prevent Further Introduction of Slaves...," see Power and Butler, *Slavery and Freedom*, Appendix A. The act can also be viewed in *Statutes of Ontario, 1791–1840*, or on the Archives of Ontario Black history website.

47. Riddell, "The Slave in Canada," 324. Henry Lewis, a former slave of William Jarvis, escaped to Schenectady, New York, and wrote to his ex-owner, offering to buy himself. See Henry Lewis to William Jarvis, 3 May 1798, Jarvis Papers, Toronto Public Library.

48. Two censuses of slaves in the Niagara district of Upper Canada were carried out in 1783. The Lower Canadian census was done in 1784. See Winks, *The Blacks in Canada*, 35; Power and Butler, *Slavery and Freedom*, 13-15.

Chapter 4: Bourgeois Slaveholders: François Poulin de Francheville and Thérèse de Couagne

1. *Illustrated History of Canada*, ed. Brown, 156.
2. Hocquart to Maurepas, 25 October 1729, Archives Coloniales, Série C11a, vol. 51, 99-100, Library and Archives Canada (LAC).
3. Francheville to Maurepas, 25 October 1729, Archives Coloniales, Serie C11a, vol. 51, 101-3, LAC. Trans. Edwin Bezzina.
4. Maurepas to Francheville, 4 April 1730, Archives Coloniales, Série C11a, vol. 110, 17-34, LAC.
5. M. Gaucher, M. Delafosse, and G. Debien, "Les engagés pour le Canada au XVIIIe siècle," *Revue d'histoire de l'Amérique Française* 14 (1960–61): 250.
6. Francheville to Maurepas, 21 October 1731, Archives Coloniales, Série C11a, vol. 110, 270, LAC. Trans. Edwin Bezzina.
7. This citation is taken from the document drawn up between Sieur Francheville and his associates regarding the formation of his iron-works firm, Francheville and Company. See Article 15 in "Société formée entre François Poulin de Francheville, Pierre Poulin, François-Étienne Cugnet, Louis-Frédéric Bricault de Valmur, et Ignace Gamelin, Québec, 16 Janvier 1733," Greffe Jacques Pinguet, Archives Judiciaries Québec (AJQ), trans. A.P. Cooper. This is part of the Archives Coloniales series, C11a, volumes 110–12. The copies used for this book came from LAC.
8. Direct reduction of iron ore. Direct reduction is "an archaic technical process permitting direct passage from raw materials (ore, charcoal, flux) to iron, in a hearth or furnace. This process was inexpensive but could produce only limited quantities of iron." Réal Boissonault, *Les Forges du Saint-Maurice* (Ottawa: Ministry of Supply and Services, 1983), 19.
9. The arrival of the Canadian miners was duly recorded in the *American Weekly Mercury*, Philadelphia. The notice states, "We hear from westward, that some French men at Canada, having found

plenty of good iron ore, several of them came lately from thence, and viewed some of our English iron works, with much investigation, they designing to set up works among themselves for the making of iron." See: *American Weekly Mercury*, 20-27 July 1732. The *Mercury* received this information from a Boston paper. The ironworks that the Canadian men examined could have been in present-day Pennsylvania, Virginia, or some other place in the Ohio Valley.

10. Beauharnois and Hocquart to Maurepas, 15 October 1732, Archives Coloniales, Série C11a, vol. 110, 200-02, LAC. The letter bears the signature of the one making the appeal (Francheville) though it is clear that it was the governor and intendant who dictated it.

11. Greffe Pinguet, 16 January 1733, AJQ. Also in the C11a series.

12. "Engagement de Christophe Janson *dit* Lapalme, forgeron, à Françoise Poulin de Francheville, marchand, pour trois années consecutives, pour partir de Ville-Marie et se rendre en la Novelle-Angleterre avec le sieur La Brèche pour faire la visite des forges de fer...," Greffe J-C Raimbault, 22 March 1733, Inventaire de Greffes de Notaires, Archives Judiciares de Montréal (AJM). Also in the C11a series, vol. 110, LAC.

13. Maurepas to Francheville, 21 April 1733, Archives Coloniales, Série C11a, LAC.

14. "Obligation du Francheville de 10 000," Greffe Jean-Claude Louet, 11 October 1733, Inventaire de Greffes de Notaires, AJQ. The contract was signed at the intendant's office at Quebec. Also appears in C11a series, vol. 110.

15. Greffe Adhemar, fils, 22 October 1733, Inventaire de Greffes de Notaires, AJQ. Trans. Edwin Bezzina. Also in the C11a series, vol. 110, 448–49.

16. Francheville to Maurepas, 24 October 1733, C11a, vol. 110.

17. Cameron Nish, *François-Étienne Cugnet, 1719-1751: Entrepreneur et Entreprises en Nouvelle-France* (Montréal : Fides, 1975), 46.

18. Roch Samson, *The Forges du Saint-Maurice: Beginnings of the Iron and Steel Industry in Canada* (Québec: Les Presses de l'Université Laval, 1998).

19. The authors of *Black Portsmouth* also takes issue with this slave-as-status-symbol interpretation by the historians of New Hampshire colonial slavery. They note that this is a "false interpretation" since it "overlooks the capital-producing labor of most slaves in the

region. It overlooks the elite's ownership of farms, wharves, and other loci of productive labour where their slaves were in all likelihood put to work." See Sammons and Cunningham, *Black Portsmouth*, 43–44.

20. Registré de la Curé, Archives de Notre-Dame de Montréal, 27 November 1718.

21. Marie-Angélique was born on 3 October 1719 and died on 28 December 1719.

22. "Donation Mutuelle," Greffes François Lepailleur et Charles Gervaise, 24 February 1727, Inventaire de Greffes de Notaires, AJM. Trans Edwin Bezzina.

23. The *donation mutuelle* functioned as a will. The right to make a will was introduced by the English after the Conquest. See the Clio Collective, *Quebec Women: A History* (Toronto: Women's Press, 1987), 69.

24. Clio Collective, *Quebec Women*, 107.

25. Sépulture de Poulin de Francheville, negociant, Registré de la Curé, Archives de Notre-Dame de Montréal, 30 November 1733.

26. "Obligation de Thérèse de Couagne, veuve de Françoise Poulin de Francheville, au profit de sa Majesté," Greffe Charles-René Gaudron de Chevremont, 19 December 1733, Inventaire de Greffes de Notaires, AJM. Trans. Edwin Bezzina. Also in the C11a series, vol. 10.

27. Greffe Jacques Pinguet, 23 October 1735, Archives Coloniales, Série C11a, vol. 110, 29-42, LAC.

28. "Testament de Dame Thérèse de Couagne de Francheville," Greffe Pierre Panet, 25 February 1764, AJM. Trans. Edwin Bezzina.

Chapter 5: Angélique's Montréal

1. Pierre-François-Xavier de Charlevoix, *Journal d'un voyage: Fait par ordre du oris dans l'Amérique Septentrionale*, ed. Pierre Berthiaume (Montréal: Les Presses de l'Université de Montréal, 1994), 335. Other descriptions of the physical layout of Montréal can be found in Robert Lahaise, *Les edifices conventuels du Vieux Montréal: Aspects ethno-historiques* (Montréal: Hurtibise, 1980), 25; Louise Dechêne, "The Growth of Montreal in the 18th Century," in *Canadian History before Confederation: Essays and Interpretations*, ed. J.M. Bumsted, 2nd ed. (Georgetown, Ont.: Irwin Dorsey, 1972),159.

2. André Charbonneau et al., "The Fortifications of Montréal," in

Opening the Gates of Eighteenth-Century Montréal ed. Phyllis Lambert and Alan Stewart (Montréal: Canadian Centre for Architecture, 1992), 19-30.

3. Dechêne, "Growth of Montréal," 156. Dechêne's article was extremely helpful in constructing the history of Montréal at the time of Angélique. See pages 154-67 for the entire article. Dechêne drew some of her estimates from the 1731 census of Montréal, carried out by the Sulpicians. The census has been edited by Antoine Roy and published as *L'île de Montréal en 1731: Aveu et dénombrement des messieurs de Saint Sulpice, seigneurs de Montréal* (Québec: Archives de la Province de Québec, 1943).

4. Marcel Trudel, *Introduction to New France* (Toronto: Holt, Rinehart and Winston, 1968), 141.

5. *Illustrated History of Canada*, ed. Brown, 159.

6. Dechêne, "The Growth of Montréal," 159.

7. Ibid., 163.

8. Cited in Raymond Douville and Jacques Casanova, *Daily Life in Early Canada*, trans. Carola Congreve (London: Allen and Unwin, 1968), 96.

9. Kathleen Jenkins, *Montreal: Island City of the St. Lawrence*, (New York: Doubleday, 1966), 112-13.

10. See William H. Atherton, *Montreal 1534–1914,* vol. 1 (Montréal: S.J. Clarke, 1914), 347-49; Jenkins, *Montreal*, 107-17; Robert Prévost, *Montréal: A History*, trans. Elizabeth Mueller and Robert Chodos (Toronto: McClelland and Stewart, 1993), 131-47; Trudel, *Introduction to New France*, 189-93.

11. Atherton, *Montreal*, 349.

12. Ibid., 350-51.

13. Alison Prentice, *Canadian Women: A History* (Toronto: Harcourt Brace, 1988), 48-49.

14. Riddell, "The Slave in Canada," 276.

15. See Moitt, *Women and Slavery in the French Antilles,* 57-62; Elgersman, *Unyielding Spirits*, 69-100, 222.

16. Donovan, "Slaves and Their Owners in Ile Royale," 6.

17. Baptême de Angélique, 28 June 1730, Registre de la Curé, Archives de Notre-Dame de Montréal, ANQ.

18. See William Riddell, "The Baptism of Slaves in Prince Edward Island," *Journal of Negro History*, 6 (1921): 307-9.

19. Sammons and Cunningham, *Black Portsmouth*, 47.

20. Orlando Patterson explores the "natal alienation" slaves suffered and the loss of identity they endured as a result of baptism in his groundbreaking book, *Slavery and Social Death*, 54–55.

21. Baptême d'Eustache, fils de Marie-Joseph Angélique, 11 January 1731, Registre de la Curé, Archives de Notre-Dame de Montréal.

22. Sépulture d'Eustache, fils de Marie-Joseph Angélique, 12 February 1731, Registre de la Curé, Archives de Notre-Dame de Montréal.

23. Baptismal records for Louis and Marie-Françoise, 26 May 1732, Registre de la Curé, Archives de Notre-Dame de Montréal; death records for Louis and Marie-Françoise, 27 May 1732 and 23 October 1732, Registre de la Curé, Archives de Notre-Dame de Montréal.

24. See Trudel, *L'esclavage au Canada Français*, 262; Marcel Trudel, *Dictionnaire des esclaves et leurs propriétaires au Canada Français* (Ville LaSalle, Québec: Éditions Hurtibise, 1990) 114; Donovan, "Slaves and Their Owners in Ile Royale," 20–21.

25. André Lachance, *Vivre, Aimer, et Mourir en Nouvelle-France* (Montréal: Libre Expression, 2000), 26–27.

26. Deborah Gray White, *Ar'n't I a Woman? Female Slaves in the Plantation South* (New York: W.W. Norton, 1985), 119-41. Moitt, *Women and Slavery in the French Antilles*, 168.

27. Roberts, *Killing the Black Body*, 33–40.

28. Ibid.

29. Trudel, *L'esclavage au Canada Français*, 178-85. See also Lapalice, "Les esclaves noirs à Montréal sous l'ancien régime," 153.

30. In the American South, "the infant mortality rate among slaves in 1850 was twice that of Whites," says Dorothy Roberts in *Killing the Black Body*, 36.

31. Roberts, *Killing the Black Body*, 39.

32. White, *Ar'n't I a Woman?* 70. See also Adrienne Shadd, "And the Lord Seem to Say 'Go': Women and the Underground Railroad Movement," in Peggy Bristow et al., *We're Rooted Here and They Can't Pulls Us Up: Essays in African Canadian Women's History* (Toronto: University of Toronto Press, 1994), 42-43. For another discussion on Black women's flight from slavery, see Moitt, *Women and Slavery in the French Antilles*, 133-39.

33. Angélique's trial transcripts, 11 April to 21 June 1734, Registre Criminel, IV, ANQ.

34. Jenny Sharpe, *Ghosts of Slavery: A Literary Archaeology of Black Women's Lives* (Minneapolis: University of Minnesota Press, 2003), 141.

35. Lucille Mathurin, *The Rebel Woman in the British West Indies during Slavery* (Kingston, Jamaica: Institute of Jamaica, 1975), 13.

Chapter 6: First Fire, First Flight

1. John Hope Franklin and Loren Schweninger, *The Runaway Slave: Rebels on the Plantation* (New York: Oxford University Press, 1999), 6.

2. For the report of the case against Jean-Baptiste Thomas, see Archives Coloniales, Serie C11a, vol. 64, 1735.

3. Thomas J. Davis, *A Rumor of Revolt: The "Great Negro Plot" in Colonial New York* (New York: The Free Press, 1985), 225.

Chapter 7: April's Fire

1. David Ruddel, *Québec City, 1765–1832* (Ottawa: Museum of Civilization, 1897), 232.

2. Ibid., 235.

3. Phyllis Lambert's "The House and Its Environment," in *Opening the Gates*, ed. Lambert and Stewart, 69.

4. Beauharnois and Hocquart to Maurepas, 9 October 1734, Archives Coloniales, Série C11a, vol. 61, folio 131–39, LAC. Trans. A. Cooper, E. Bezzina.

5. Raymond Boyer, *Les crimes et les chétiments au Canada Français du 17e an 20e siècle* (Montréal: Cercle du Livre de France, 1966), 132.

Chapter 8: The Aftermath

1. Beauharnois and Hocquart to Maurepas, 9 October 1734, Archives Coloniales, Série C11a, vol. 61, folio 131–39, LAC.

2. Jenkins, *Montreal,* 110.

3. Marie-Anne Véronique Cuillerier, *Relation de Soeurs Cuillerier, 1725–1747*, reprinted in *Écrits du Canada Français*, vol. 42, ed. Ghislaine Legendre, 168.

4. Ibid., 169.

5. Ibid., 168.
6. Beauharnois and Hocquart to Maurepas, 9 October 1734.
7. Ibid.
8. Ibid.
9. Ibid.
10. Ibid.
11. Exhibit on Old Montréal, Centre d'Histoire, City of Montréal.
12. Robert Prévost, *Montréal*, 149-50.
13. Ibid., 150.
14. Beauharnois and Hocquart to Maurepas, 9 October 1734.
15. R.E., "Une Cause Célèbre au XVIII Siècle: Le Troisième Conflagration à Montréal, la Procès, la Condamnation et la Mort d'une Négresse Incendiaire en 1734," *Le Canada*, 22, 23 October 1917. Trans. A.P. Cooper
16. News of the fire was broadcasted not only in the colony and France but also in the English colonies to the south. Colonists in New York, Pennsylvania, and New England received word of the terrible fire. One source of information was the Native people who traversed the fluid frontier between New France and the English colonies, as the following extract from a letter printed in a Philadelphia newspaper attests. "We are informed from Canada, by some Indians lately come from thence, that about three weeks ago, one half of the city of Montreal was burnt down to the ground, including the nunnery and several of the most noted merchant houses." See "Extract of a Letter from Albany, dated April 17," in *American Weekly Mercury* (Philadelphia), 18 to 25 April 1734. (The fire did not happen "three weeks ago" but rather one week prior to the report.)

Chapter 9: The Trial

1. Beauharnois and Hocquart to Maurepas, 9 October 1734, Archives Coloniales, Série C11a, vol. 61, folio 131–39, LAC. Trans. A. Cooper and E. Bezzina.
2. The source is Dossier du Conseil Superieur, Angélique's Trial Transcripts, 11 April to 21 June 1734, Registre Criminel, IV: 24-26 P.; Procédures Judiciaires, Matières Criminelles, IV: 237, housed at the Archives Nationales Québec, at both the Montréal and Québec branches.

Foucher's request is also transcribed in R.E., "Une Cause Célèbre."

3. Douglas Hay, "The Meaning of Criminal Law in Quebec, 1764–1774," in *Crime and Criminal Justice in Europe and Canada*, 2nd ed., ed. Louis A. Knafla (Waterloo, Ont.: Wilfrid Laurier University Press, 1985), 77.

4. André Lachance, *Crimes et Criminelles en Nouvelle-France* (Montréal: Boréal Express, 1984), 21–22.

5. William Riddell, "The Slave in Canada," 330.

6. Robert LaHaise, "Raimbault, Pierre," *Dictionary of Canadian Biography*, vol. 2: 541-42.

Chapter 10: The Verdict

1. Peter N. Moogk, *La Nouvelle-France: The Making of French Canada— A Cultural History* (East Lansing: Michigan State University Press, 2000), 64.

2. Ibid.

3. This idea that slaveholders could own and control their slaves' bodies but not their minds is taken from Davis, *A Rumor of Revolt,* 1-2.

4. Ibid., 59.

5. Ibid., 56.

Chapter 11: The Appeal and Final Judgment

1. Yvon Desloges, *A Tenant's Town: Québec in the 18th Century* (Ottawa: National Historic Sites, Parks Services, Environment Canada, 1991), 68. A thorough description of the various neighbourhoods of Québec is given in ibid., 53–77.

2. Raymond Cahall, *The Sovereign Council of New France: A Study in Canadian Constitutional History* (New York: Columbia University Press, 1915), 130.

3. Beauharnois and Hocquart to Maurepas, 9 October 1734, Archives Coloniales, Série C11a, vol. 61, folio 131–39, LAC.

4. Cahall, *Sovereign Council,* 150.

5. Ibid., 155.

6. André Lachance, "Varin de La Marre, Jean Victor," *Dictionary of Canadian Biography*, vol. 4: 749-51.
7. "Daine, François," *Dictionary of Canadian Biography*, vol. 3: 160.
8. Ibid., 160.
9. Dossier du Conseil Supérieur, Procédures Judiciares, Matières Criminelles, IV, 237, ANQ.
10. Ibid.

Chapter 12: The Execution

1. Dossier du Conseil Supérieur, Procédures Judiciares, Matières Criminelles, IV, 237, ANQ.

Chapter 13: Angélique, the Arsonist

1. Marcel Trudel, *L'esclavage au Canada Français*, 227. Trudel has produced a "modernized" version of this book titled *Deux siècles d'esclavage au Québec* (Montréal: HMH, 2004). Boyer, *Les crimes et les châtiments au Canada Français*, 132.
2. Robert Prévost, *Montréal*, 141.
3. Beauharnois and Hocquart to Maurepas, 9 October 1734, Archives Coloniales, Série C11a, vol. 61, folio 131–39, LAC. Trans. A. Cooper and E. Bessina.
4. R.E., "Une Cause Célèbre."
5. Lapalice, "Les esclaves noirs à Montréal sous l'ancien régime," 146.
6. "La justice sous l'ancien régime," *La Patrie*, 11 April 1925.

Epilogue: A Silenced Voice Heard Again

1. Briton Hammon's narrative is published in *Early Negro Writing, 1760–1837* ed. Dorothy Porter (Baltimore, Md.: Black Classic Press, 1995), 522-28.
2. Gronniosaw's narrative, as well as those of Marrant, Cugoano, Equiano, and Jea, is published in *Pioneers of the Black Atlantic: Five*

Slave Narratives from the Enlightenment, 1772–1815, ed. Henry Louis Gates Jr. and William L. Andrews (Washington, D.C.: Civitas, 1998).

3. King's narrative was thought lost to the world until it was discovered in the Provincial Archives of Nova Scotia. It is reprinted in *The Life of Boston King, Black Loyalist, Minister and Master Carpenter*, ed. Ruth Whitehead and Carmelita Robertson (Halifax: Nova Scotia Museum, 2002).

4. Cornel West, "The Ignoble Paradox of Western Modernity," in *Spirits of the Passage: The Transatlantic Slave Trade*, ed. Madeline Burnside and Rosemarie Robotham (New York: Simon and Schuster, 1997), 8.

5. Ibid., 9.

6. *The History of Mary Prince, a West Indian Slave, Related by Herself*, ed. Moira Ferguson (Ann Arbor: University of Michigan Press, 1997); *The Story of the Life of John Anderson, the Fugitive Slave*, ed. Harper Twelvetrees (London: W. Tweedie, 1863); Benjamin Drew, *The Narratives of Fugitive Slaves in Canada* (Cleveland, Ohio: John P. Jewett, 1856; repr. Toronto: Prospero Books, 2000).

7. Jim Henson's book was long out of print and believed lost before it was discovered by historian Peter Meyler and reprinted in *Broken Shackles: Old Man Henson from Slavery to Freedom*, ed. Peter Meyler (Toronto: Natural Heritage Press, 2001).

8. Elgersman, *Unyielding Spirits,* Chapter 2.

9. The Chloe Cooley incident is important because it led to the first antislavery legislation in Canada, as discussed in Chapter 4.

10. George Elliott Clarke, in *Odysseys Home: Mapping African-Canadian Literature* (Toronto: University of Toronto Press, 2002), notes the primacy of Angélique's trial transcripts in African Canadian literature and insists that they be read as a slave narrative.

11. Tituba, one of the "witches" of Salem, was a slave, and her trial records of 1692, which are still extant, give her a forty-year leap on Angélique. However, though fiction writers and storytellers have erroneously portrayed her as a Black woman, Tituba was an Indian. See Elaine G. Breslaw, "Tituba's Confessions: The Multicultural Dimensions of the 1692 Salem Witch-Hunt," in *Race and Gender in the Northern Colonies*, ed. Jan Noel (Toronto: Canadian Scholars' Press, 2000), 119-46.

Sources

Chapter 1: The Torture and Hanging of Angélique

This chapter is constructed from material contained in Angélique's Trial Transcripts, 11 April to 21 June 1734, Registre Criminel, IV: 24-26; and Procédures Judiciaires, Matières Criminelles, IV: 237, Archives Nationales Québec.

Chapter 2: Atlantic Origins: The Slave Woman from Portugal

On Portuguese exploration along the coast of Africa
Blackburn, Robin. *The Making of New World Slavery: From the Baroque to the Modern, 1492–1800* (London: Verso, 1997), 97-125.

Boxer, C.R. *The Portuguese Seaborne Empire, 1514–1825* (London: Hutchison of London, 1969).

On Jewish prominence in Portuguese maritime trade
Blackburn. *New World Slavery*, 115-16.

Marques, A.H. De Oliveira. *History of Portugal*, vol. 1 (New York: Columbia University Press, 1972), 264.

On the build-up of African population in Portugal
Blackburn. *New World Slavery*, 113.

Ortiz, Fernando, and Ivan Van Sertima. *African Presence in Early Europe* (New Brunswick, N.J.: Transaction Publishers, 1993).

Scobie, Edward. "The Black in Western Europe," in ibid., 193.

Saunders, A.C. De C.M. A Social History of Black Slaves and Freedmen in Portugal (Cambridge, U.K.: Cambridge University Press, 1982), 47-59, 87.

On slavery in Portugal
Saunders. *Social History of Black Slaves.*

On the Afro-Catholic fraternities in Portugal and the religious life of the enslaved
Saunders. *Social History of Black Slaves*, 107.
Heywood, Linda M. "The Angolan–Afro–Brazilian Cultural Connections," in *From Slavery to Emancipation in the Atlantic World*, ed. Sylvia Frey and Betty Wood (London: Frank Cass, 1999).

On Manueline legislation concerning slave baptism
Blackburn. *New World Slavery*, 117.

On Portugal's golden age
Birmingham, David. *A Concise History of Portugal* (Cambridge, U.K.: Cambridge University Press, 1993), 65-72.

On the Dutch uprising against Spain
van Gelderen, Martin. *The Dutch Revolt* (Cambridge, U.K.: Cambridge University Press, 1993).

On Dutch dominance in the Atlantic and international trade
Boxer, C.R. *The Dutch Seaborne Empire 1600–1800* (New York: Knopf, 1965).
Israel, Jonathan Irvine. *Dutch Primacy in World Trade, 1585–1740* (Oxford, U.K.: Clarendon Press, 1989).
Postma, Johannes. *The Dutch in the Atlantic Slave Trade, 1600–1815* (Cambridge, U.K.: Cambridge Press, 1990).

On the "second Atlantic system"
Drescher, Seymour. "Jews and New Christians in the Atlantic Slave Trade," in *The Jews and the Expansion of Europe to the West, 1450–1800*, ed. Paolo Bernadini and Norman Fiering (New York: Berghahn, 2001), 447.

On Dutch and French merchants in the fur trade
Norton, Thomas Elliot. *The Fur Trade in Colonial New York, 1686–1776* (Madison: University of Wisconsin Press, 1974).

On the Iroquois role in the colonial fur trade
Lunn, Jean. "The Illegal Fur Trade out of New France 1713–1760," Canadian Historical Association *Report* (1939), 61–76.

On the Schenectady Massacre
Burke, Thomas E., Jr. *Mohawk Frontier: The Dutch Community of Schenectady, 1661–1710* (Ithaca, N.Y.: Cornell University Press, 1991), 68-108.

On the Huguenots in the Atlantic trade
Bosher, J.F. *Business and Religion in the Age of New France, 1608–1763* (Toronto: Canadian Scholars' Press, 1994).

On colonial trade between the thirteen colonies, Acadia, and Canada
Chard, Donald F. "The Price and Profits of Accommodation: Massachusetts-Louisbourg Trade, 1713–1744," in *Seafaring in Colonial Massachusetts* (Boston: Colonial Society of Massachusetts, 1980), Faneuil Letter Book, Baker Library, Harvard University.

Chapter 3: The Secret of Slavery in Canada

On Canadian slavery in Canada
Elgersman, Maureen. *Unyielding Spirits: Black Women and Slavery in Early Canada and Jamaica* (New York: Garland Publishing, 1999).

Riddell, William. "The Slave in Canada," *Journal of Negro History* 5, no. 3 (1920).

Smith, T. Watson. "The Slave in Canada," Nova Scotia Historical Society *Collections* (1899).

Trudel, Marcel. *L'esclavage au Canada Français: Historie et conditions de l'esclavage* (Québec: Les Presses Universitaires Laval, 1960).

Winks, Robin. *The Blacks in Canada* (Montréal: McGill-Queen's University Press, 1997).

On slavery on the Detroit frontier and Acadia
Donovan, Kenneth. "Slaves and Their Owners in Ile Royale, 1713–1760," *Acadiensis* 25, no. 1 (1995).

Lajeunesse, Ernest. *The Windsor Border Region* (Toronto: University of Toronto Press, 1960).

French slavery and colonialism in the New World
Moitt, Bernard. *Women and Slavery in the French Antilles, 1635–1848* (Bloomington: Indiana University Press, 2001).

Mumford, Clarence. *The Black Ordeal of Slavery and Slave Trading in the French West Indies, 1625–1715*, vol. 1 (Lewiston, N.Y.: Edwin Mellen Press, 1991).

On slave occupation, population, and place of residence in New France
Donovan. "Slaves and Their Owners in Ile Royale."

Trudel. *L'esclavage au Canada Français.*

On the decline of slavery across Canada
Winks. *Blacks in Canada*, 99-113.

Chapter 4: Bourgeois Slaveholders: François Poulin de Francheville and Thérèse de Couagne

Biography of Francheville
Jetté, René. *Dictionnaire généalogique des familles du Québec* (Montréal: Les Presses de l'Université de Montréal, 1983).

Nish, Cameron. *Dictionary of Canadian Biography*, vol. 2, "Poulin de Franchville, François."

On the seignerial system
The Illustrated History of Canada, ed. Craig Brown (Toronto: Lester and Orpen Dennys, 1987), 152.

Harris, Cole. *The Seigneurial System in Early Canada: A Geographical Study* (Montréal: McGill-Queen's University Press, 1984).

On Montréal's dominance in the fur trade
Illustrated History, ed. Brown, 152.

On the Treaty of Utrecht and its ramifications for the French regime in Canada
Illustrated History, ed. Brown, 147-50.

On France's reclamation of the areas north and west of the Great Lakes and expansion in the Sioux Country
Trudel, Marcel. *Introduction to New France* (Toronto: Holt, Rinehart and Winston, 1968).

On Francheville's participation in diverse aspects of the fur trade
Greffe Jacques David; Greffe François Lepailleur; Greffe Charles-René Gaudron de Chevremont; Greffe Joseph-Charles Raimbault. Inventaire de Greffes de Notaires. Archives Judiciares de Montréal.

On the first Sioux Company
"René Boucher, sieur de la Perriere," Wisconsin Historical *Collections* 17 (1906): 56.

On the second Sioux Company
"Augustin Mouet, sieur de Langlade," Wisconsin Historical *Collections* 17 (1906): 135.

On the Saint-Maurice mines
Samson, Roch. *The Forges du Saint-Maurice: Beginnings of the Iron and Steel Industry in Canada, 1730–1883* (Quebec: Les Presses de l'Université Laval, 1998).

Biography of Madame Francheville
Jetté, René. *Dictionnaire généalogique des familles du Québec.*
Lachance, André. *Dictionary of Canadian Biography,* vol. 3, "Couagne, Thérèse de Poulin de Francheville."

On the building of the Francheville's house on rue Saint-Paul and information about the neighbours
"Reconstitutions du parcellaire de Montréal." Groupe de recherche sur Montréal et Centre Canadien d'Architecture. This is a reconstitution of Montréal for the year 1725. See also the Montréal census of 1731.

Chapter 5: Angélique's Montréal

On the beginnings of Montréal
Prévost, Robert. *Montréal: A History.* Translated by Elizabeth Mueller and Robert Chodos (Toronto: McClelland and Stewart, 1993), 32-54.

On the various social groupings in Montréal
Moore, Christopher. "Colonization and Conflict: New France and Its Rivals, 1600-1760," in *The Illustrated History of Canada*, ed. Craig Brown (Toronto: Lester and Orpen Dennys, 1987), 157-69.

Trudel, Marcel. *Introduction to New France* (Toronto: Holt, Rinehart and Winston, 1968), 141–45.

On the rhythm of everyday life in Montréal
Douville, Raymond, and Jacques Casanova. *Daily Life in Early Canada.* Translated by Carola Congreve (London: G. Allen and Unwin, 1968), 82-106.

On the administration of New France
Illustrated History, ed. Brown, 122-23.
Prévost. *Montréal: A History*, 98-123.

On the history of the Sulpicians in Montréal
Les Presses de l'Université Laval. *Les prêtres de Saint-Sulpice au Canada: Grandes figures de leur Histoire* (Laval: Les Presses de l'Université Laval, 1992).

Biography of Marie-Joseph Angélique
Trudel, Marcel. *Dictionnaire des esclaves et leurs propriétaires au Canada Français* (Ville La Salle, Québec: Éditions Hurtibise, 1990), 113–14.
Vachon, André. *Dictionary of Canadian Biography,* vol. 2, "Marie-Joseph-Angélique."

On the burdens of domestic work in New France
Elgersman, Maureen. *Unyielding Spirits: Black Women and Slavery in Early Canada and Jamaica* (New York: Garland Publishing, 1999), 71-75.

Neilson, Hubert. "Slavery in Old Canada, before and after the Conquest," *Transactions of the Literary and Historical Society of Quebec* 2, no. 26 (1906): 43-45.

Prentice, Alison. *Canadian Women: A History* (Toronto: Harcourt Brace, 1988), 49.

Riddell, William. "The Slave in Canada," *Journal of Negro History* 5, no. 3 (1920): 324.

On the baptism of slaves in New France
Donovan, Kenneth. "Slaves and Their Owners in Ile Royale, 1713-1760," *Acadiensis* 25, no. 1 (1995): 7.

Biography of Jacques César
Trudel, *Dictionnaire des esclaves*, 103.

Biography of Gamelin
Dumais, Raymond. *Dictionary of Canadian Biography,* vol. 4, "Gamelin, Ignace."

Massicotte, E.-R. "Une chambre de commerce à Montréal sous le régime Français." *Bulletin des Recherches Historiques* 32 (1936): 121-24.

Sulte, Benjamin. "Les Forges Saint Maurice." *Mélanges Historiques* 6 (1920): 5-62.

On birth in New France
Clio Collective. *Quebec Women: A History* (Toronto: Women's Press, 1987), 77-80.

Lachance, André. *Vivre, Aimer, et Mourir en Nouvelle-France* (Montréal: Libre Expression, 2000), 25-28.

On a Black female slave woman's reproductive health
White, Deborah Gray. *Ar'n't I a Woman? Female Slaves in the Plantation South* (New York: W.W. Norton, 1985, 119-41.

Moitt, Bernard. *Women and Slavery in the French Antilles, 1635–1848* (Bloomington: Indiana University Press, 2001), 63-79, 89-99.

On the control and exploitation by Whites of Black enslaved women's reproductive labour

Roberts, Dorothy. *Killing the Black Body: Race, Reproduction, and the Meaning of Liberty* (New York:Vintage Books, 1997), 22-25. (Roberts argues that this control tore apart Black women's lives and fractured the Black family. My discussion about of these issues is drawn largely from Roberts's work.)

Chapter 6: First Fire, First Flight

This chapter is constructed from material contained in Angélique's Trial Transcripts, 11 April to 21 June 1734, Registre Criminel IV: 24-26, and Procédures Judiciaires, Matières Criminelles, IV: 237, ANQ.

Biography of Monière

Dechêne, Louise. *Dictionary of Canadian Biography,* vol. 3, "Lemoine, *dit* Monière, Alexis."

On slave flight and the threat it posed to Whites

Wood, Peter H. *Black Majority: Negroes in Colonial South Carolina from 1670 through the Stono Rebellion* (New York: Knopf, 1974), 321–23.

On France's cosmopolitan army and the soldier in New France

Moogk, Peter N. *La Nouvelle-France:The Making of French Canada—A Cultural History* (East Lansing: Michigan State University Press, 2000), 113–16.

On the collaboration between enslaved people and indentured servants

Beckles, Hilary. *White Servitude and Black Slavery in Barbados 1627–1715* (Knoxville: University of Tennessee Press, 1989).

Davis, Thomas J. *A Rumor of Revolt: The "Great Negro Plot" in Colonial New York* (New York: The Free Press, 1985).

Middlekauff, Robert. *Bacon's Rebellion* (Chicago and New York: Rand McNally, 1966).

Trudel, Marcel. *Deux siècles d'esclavage au Québec* (Montréal: HMH, 2004), 209–10.

On Cugnet's career
Nish, Cameron. *François-Étienne Cugnet 1719–1751: Entrepreneur et Entreprises en Nouvelle-France* (Montréal, Fides, 1975).

Chapter 7: April's Fire

This chapter is constructed from material contained in Angélique's Trial Transcripts, 11 April to 21 June 1734, Registre Criminel IV: 24-26, and Procédures Judiciaires, Matières Criminelles, IV: 237, ANQ; and from a letter detailing the fire and its aftermath from Beauharnois and Hocquart to Maurepas, 9 October 1734, Archives Coloniales, Série C11a, vol. 61, Library and Archives Canada (LAC). Many books on the history of Montréal also deal with the fire. One such publication is Robert Prévost, *Montréal: A History*, translated by Elizabeth Mueller and Robert Chodos (Toronto: McClelland and Stewart, 1993), 140–42, 147–50.

On housing and building construction during this period
Lambert, Phyllis. "The House and Its Environment," in *Opening the Gates of Eighteenth-Century Montréal*, ed. Phyllis Lambert and Alan Stewart (Montréal: Canadian Centre for Architecture, 1992), 69-78.
Moogk, Peter N. *Building a House in New France* (Toronto: McClelland and Stewart, 1977).
Stewart, Alan. "Reconstructing the Eighteenth-Century Town," in *Opening the Gates of Eighteenth-Century Montréal*, ed. Lambert and Stewart, 55-65.

Chapter 8: The Aftermath

This chapter is based on a long letter with attachments of dozens of pages sent by Beauharnois and Hocquart to Maurepas, 9 October 1734, Archives Coloniales, Série C11a, vol. 61, LAC. See also letters to the minister dated 10, 18, and 26 October 1734 and 18 October 1736 [folio 131-39]. Governor and intendant attached to the long letter of 9 October 1734 several memos explaining and outlining how they used the king's financial and material resources to compensate and support the victimized population. The attachments are:

1) a list of the names of all those whose houses were destroyed; 2) an inventory of the supplies from the king's storehouse distributed to citizens and soldiers; 3) a complete description of the destruction done to Hôtel-Dieu, an estimate of how much it would cost to rebuild it, a breakdown of the hospital's debts and revenue, and several letters appealing for financial assistance, from such worthy sufferers as Madame de Ramezay, Sieur Deschaillons, and notary Charles-René Gaudron de Chevremont, all of whom lost their homes; 4) a statement outlining the financial state of the Commissary of the Treasurer of the Marine in Montréal; and 5) the new fire-prevention ordinance that would give Montréal its first fire brigade. A list of the names of those who lost their homes in the fire is provided in the appendices.

On the impact of the fire on Hôtel-Dieu
Cuillerier, Marie-Anne Véronique. *Relation de Soeur Cuillerier 1725–1747*, reprinted in *Écrits du Canada Français*, vol. 42 (1979), ed. Ghislaine Legendre, 167-70.

On the history of Hôtel-Dieu
Olivier Maurault. *L-Hôtel-Dieu: Premier Hôpital de Montréal*, (Archdiocese of Montréal, 1941).

Chapter 9: The Trial

This chapter is constructed from material contained in Angélique's Trial Transcripts, 11 April to 21 June 1734, Registre Criminel, IV: 24-26, and Procédures Judiciaires, Matières Criminelles, IV: 237, ANQ.

On the French legal system, court procedures, and judiciary
Lachance, André. *Crimes et criminels en Nouvelle-France* (Montréal: Boréal Express, 1984), 17-24.

Biography of Raimbault
Lahaise, Robert. *Dictionary of Canadian Biography,* vol. 2, "Raimbault, Pierre."

Chapter 10: The Verdict

This chapter is constructed from material contained in Angélique's Trial Transcripts, 11 April to 21 June 1734, Registre Criminel IV: 24-26, and Procédures Judiciaires, Matières Criminelles, IV: 237, ANQ.

Discussion of law and order, hierarchy, and paternalism in New France, and the king as ruler and lawmaker
Moogk, Peter N. *La Nouvelle-France: The Making of French Canada—A Cultural History* (East Lansing: Michigan State University Press, 2000), 56-66.

Chapter 11: The Appeal and Final Judgment

On the structure, procedures, and rituals of the Conseil Supérieur
Cahall, Raymond. *The Sovereign Council of New France: A Study in Canadian Constitutional History* (New York: Columbia University Press, 1915), 130–67.

Biography of Beauharnois
Standen, S. Dale. *Dictionary of Canadian Biography,* vol. 3, "Beauharnois de La Boische, Charles de, Marquis de Beauharnois."
Trudel, Marcel. *Dictionnaire des esclaves et leurs propriétaires au Canada Français* (Ville La Salle, Québec: Editions Hurtibise, 1990), 276-77.

Biography of Hocquart
Horton, Donald J. *Dictionary of Canadian Biography,* vol. 4, "Hocquart, Gilles."

Biography of Cugnet
Nish, Cameron. *Dictionary of Canadian Biography,* vol. 3, "Cugnet, François-Étienne."

Biography of Verrier
Vachon, Claude. *Dictionary of Canadian Biography,* vol. 3, "Verrier, Louis-Guillaume."

Biography of Varin
Lachance, André. *Dictionary of Canadian Biography,* vol. 4, "Varin de La Marre, Jean-Victor."

Biography of Sarrazin
Rousseau, Jacques. *Dictionary of Canadian Biography,* vol. 2, "Sarrazin, Michel."

Biography of Guillimin
Horton, Donald J. *Dictionary of Canadian Biography,* vol. 2, "Guillimin, Charles."

Biography of Daine
Mathieu, Jacques. *Dictionary of Canadian Biography,* vol. 3, "Daine, François."

Biography of Louet
Biron, Hervé. *Dictionary of Canadian Biography,* vol. 2, "Louet, Jean-Claude."

Biography of Mathieu Leveille
Lachance, André. "Mathieu, le bourreau noir," in *Juger et punir en Nouvelle-France: Chroniques de la vie quotidienne au XV11 siècle* (Montréal: Libre Expression, 2000), 173–81.

On the appeal
Dossier du Conseil Supérieur, Matières Criminelles IV: 237, ANQ.

Epilogue: A Silenced Voice Heard Again

On African intellectuals in Europe
Northrup, David. *Africa's Discovery of Europe* (Oxford, U.K.: Oxford University Press, 2002).

On the idea of progress during the Enlightenment
Mills, Charles W. *The Racial Contract* (Ithaca, N.Y.: Cornell University Press, 1997), 64.

West, Cornel. "The Ignoble Paradox of Western Modernity," in *Spirits of the Passage: The Transatlantic Slave Trade*, ed. Madeline Burnside and Rosemarie Robotham (New York: Simon and Schuster, 1997), 8-10.

On the mental capacity of Blacks as it relates to their personhood
Becker, William H. "The Black Church: Manhood and Mission," in *African-American Religion: Interpretive Essays in History and Culture*, ed. Timothy E. Fulop and Albert J. Robateau (New York: Routledge, 1997), 179–99.

Young, R.J. *Antebellum Black Activists: Race, Gender, and Self* (New York: Garland Publishing, 1995).

On the political act of Black self-making through the creation of literature
Pioneers of the Black Atlantic: Five Slave Narratives from the Enlightenment, 1772–1815, ed. Henry Louis Gates Jr. and William L. Andrews (Washington D.C.: Civitas, 1998), 1-10.

Index

abolitionist movements. *See also*
   antislavery, 294
   in the U.S. north, 102–3
Adhémar, Jean-Baptiste, 219
   verdict on Angélique, 254
Affaire du Canada (fraud), 273, 275
Africa, European exploration of, 25–30
alcohol, controversial trade in, 112, 114, 152
Alva, Duke of, 47
Amherst, General Jeffrey, 139
Amo, Anton Wilhelm, 298
Anderson, John, 299–300
André de Leigne, Pierre (judge), 266, 278
Angélique, Marie-Joseph
   accused of arson, 196, 214
   affair with Thibault, 171–73, 175, 259
   angry behavior of, 7, 128–29, 139, 172–74
   arrival in Montréal of, 23, 66–67, 156
   assumed historically to have been
     guilty, 286
   author's views about her motives and
     behaviour, 286–92
   baptism of, 4, 128, 160–63
   behaviour after the fire, 196–99
   behaviour during the fire, 191–92
   captured and returned to Montréal
     unrepentant, 180–81, 231
   confession of, 6, 18–19
   confronts her accusers, 241–45, 249
   confusion of while testifying, 246
   congé (leave) sought from her mistress,
     171, 175, 221
   defiant acts of, 96, 128–29, 161, 173,
     189–90, 260
   denial of arson, 195–97
   escape from slavery as her primary
     wish, 67, 96, 175, 182, 241
   escapes with Thibault, 173, 179–80, 221
   evidence against her summarized, 252–53
   fear of being sold to Cugnet, 176

fire breaks out in her bedroom at
   Monière's, 178–79
hanging of, 12, 20–22, 283–85
hatred of the French by, 228–29
lack of legal counsel for, 217
lack of status held by, 277–78
legal case against is prepared, 220–31
leisure activity of, 159
motives for arson and escape, 288–92
"New England" residence likely by, 23,
   59–60
origins of, 6–7
Portuguese life of, 23, 32
pregnancies and children of, 7, 163–66
punishments of, 99, 173, 182
pyromaniac tendencies of, 229
relationship with Sieur Francheville,
   128–29, 164–65
residence in low countries, 23
sale price paid for, 87
sent with Thibault to live at Alexis
   Monière's, 177–78
slavery narrative of, 304–6
social isolation and oppression of, 155–56
synopsis of her tragic end, 6
tasks (domestic & agricultural) assigned
   to, 157
testimony of, 221–23, 232–36, 239–40,
   245–50, 279
threats by to "roast" her mistress or
   home, 12, 176–77, 182, 216, 221, 231
timing of her trial and hanging, 217
torture of, 15–19, 282
verdict rendered upon (at Montréal),
   14, 16, 257–59
verdict rendered upon (at Québec),
   279–81
visits Thibault often in prison, 182
Angélique-Denise (slave concubine for
   hangman), 276

Angola, 35
antislavery. *See also* abolitionist movements
    efforts on behalf of, 101, 103–4
    literature of, 294, 298–304
Antwerp, decline of, 49
Arguim, 28
arson, the crime of, 220
asiento (slave trading licence), 30, 55, 83
Azores, 25–26, 30, 32, 34

Baby *dit* Dupéron, Jacques , 93
Baker, Dorinda, 93
baptism. *See also* Angélique, baptism of,
    38–39, 75, 82, 105, 149, 165
Beaucours, Josué dubois Berthelot
    (Montréal governor), 191, 200
Beauharnois de la Boische, Marquis
    Charles de (Governor General), 62,
    110–12, 115, 119–20, 151, 188, 200, 210,
    213–14, 267, 268, 271, 275, 277, 290
    family history of, 266–68
Bégon, Michel (intendant), 72–73, 151, 211
Behrendt, Stephen, 68
Bellefeuille *dit* La Ruine, Louis (hospital
    gardener), 196–97
    testimony of, 242–43
Bennett, Isaac, 98
Benoît, Joseph (physician), 14
Bibb, Henry, 95–96, 294, 302, 306
"Black Atlantic experience", 9, 12–13
Block, Nichus (Angélique's second
    owner), 24, 46, 51, 59–60, 283
blood lines ("polluted"), Portuguese focus
    on, 39–40, 42
Bouffandeau, Jean (priest), 134
Boyajian, James C, 58
Boyer, Raymond, 289
brandy. See alcohol
Brant, Chief Joseph, 93, 96
Brazil, 32, 43–45, 52–55, 57–59
    Catholic slaves in, 39, 43
    Portuguese emigration to, 45
brodequins ("laced boots") torture, 16–19
Brown, William Wells, 294

Buckley, Captain Peter (ship's captain), 64
Butler, Colonel John, 93

Cahall, Raymond, 269
Canada
    as a refuge from slavery, 69
    as a slave-holding nation. *See* slavery
        (in Canada)
Canary Islands, 25, 34
Cão, Diogo, 29
Cape of Good Hope, 29
Cape Verde, 26
capital punishment, methods of in New
    France, 255, 257
Capitein, Jacobus, 298
caravel (ship), development of the, 25
Cartier, George-Étienne, 3
Casa da Mina (office of gold trade), 29
Casa dos Escravos (office of slave trade), 29
the Catholic church. *See also* Christianity;
        the Vatican
    power of in old Montréal, 150
    power of in old Québec, 264–66
Catholicism (slave), nature of, 38
Celestin, Pierre, 73
censitaires (settler tenants), 108, 155
    limitations upon, 117
César, Jacques (slave named as father of
        Angélique's children), 163–65,
        169–70, 283
César, Marguerite (Francheville neighbour),
        131, 191, 219
    testimony of, 227–28, 242
Champlain. *See* de Champlain, Samuel
Charlevoix, Pierre François Xavier, 142
Chartier de Lotbinière, Eustache (vicar-
        general, Québec), 270
children, their status in New France, 130
Christianity. *See also* baptism; the
        Catholic church; Catholicism (slave)
    conversion to among slaves, 297
    rivalry with Islam, 26, 42
Code Noir (regulating slavery),
    applied in Canada, 74–75, 82, 160–61

Colbert, Jean-Baptiste, 118
Compagnie des Indes Occidentales, 112,
    148, 275
Company of One Hundred
    Associates, 71, 153, 155
congé (leave to depart), 171–72, 174–75,
    221
congés (trading permits), 111
Congo, 29, 35
Conseil Supérieur (highest court), 6, 153,
    200, 217, 219, 260–61
    Cugnet's appointment to, 187
    decision of the, 16
    hears Angélique's case, 266, 276–281
    organization of, 264–66
    powers of, 263
Cooley, Chloe (manhandled slave), 101,
    103–4, 304, 306
Couillard, Guillaume, 71
Coutume de Paris (legal code), 16, 260,
    264, 272
Craft, Ellen, 306
Cresques, Abraham (cartographer), 25
Cugnet, François-Étienne (agreed to
    purchase Angélique), 123, 176, 238,
    277–78, 281
    as first councillor of Conseil Supérieur,
    270–71
    social status of, 187
Cugnet, François-Joseph, 193
Cugoano, Ottobah, 296–97
Cuillerier, Sister Marie-Anne-Véronique,
    10, 205–6, 210
Curaçao, 56–57
Cureux *dit* St.-Germain, Louis, 79
Custeau, Catherine (Monière's servant),
    178–79, 219
    testimony of, 237

Daine, François (Conseil clerk & chief
    scribe), 280–81
    personal history of, 274–75
de Barros, João, 31
de Béréy, Jeanne Nafrechoux

    (Francheville neighbour), 131, 219,
    223–24, 227
    testimony of, 238
de Budemon, Pierre Derivon (Thérèse's
    stepfather), 129, 146
de Cavagnial, Vaudreuil, 139
de Chalet, François, 78
de Champigny, Jean Bochart, 72
de Champlain, Samuel, 71
de Chomedey, Paul, 2
de Couagne, Charles (Thérèse's father),129
de Couagne, Louise (Thérèse's niece), 138
de Couagne, Marguerite (Thérèse's niece),
    177, 190, 219, 222, 226–27, 234
    testimony of, 226
de Couagne, Marie-Josephe (sister of
    Thérèse), 160, 177
de Couagne, Suzanne (Thérèse's sister &
    nun), 138, 204
de Couagne, Thérèse. *See* Francheville,
    Thérèse de Couagne de Denonville,
    Marquis (governor of New France),
    72, 75
de Francheville. *See* Francheville
de la Baume, Jeanne (Franceville neighbour),
    testimony of, 228
de la Gorgendière, Fleury (gifted mulatto
    girl), 79–80
de la Vérendrye, Sieur, 146
Delaware, 56
de Léry, Gaspard Joseph Chaussegros, 143,
    200, 211–12, 262
de L'Incarnation, Marie, 8
de Maisonneuve, Chomedey (soldier-
    mystic), 141
de Medeiros, Francisco Mendes, 59
Denys de Saint-Simon, Charles-Paul
    (judge), 266
de Santiago, Miguel Dias, 59
Deschaillons, Madame (Francheville's
    business partner), 114
de Senneville, Hyppolyte, 227
de Souza, Jeronimo Rodrigues, 59
Desrivières, Charlotte, 190, 219, 222,

226–27, 234, 244
Desrivières, Madame (Charlotte's mother), 190, 224, 226
Detroit
    free slave militia at, 103
    frontier and border, 74, 92
    fur trade at, 74, 114, 146
de Vallières, Henry, 136
de Valmur, Louis-Frédéric Bricault, 123
de Vaudreuil, Marquis, 81
Dias, Bartolomé, 29
Domaine d'Occident (Québec), 187
Donovan, Kenneth, 82, 99
Dosquet, Pierre-Herman (Bishop of Québec), 270
Douglas, Frederick, 294, 306
Drew, Benjamin, 300
    collects other slave narratives, 301
du Calvet, Pierre (Huguenot slaveholder), 2, 85
Dundas, Henry, 101
Dutch Republic and empire
    decline of the, 53
    rise of the, 48–52, 57
Dutch Revolt, 47–48
Dutch West India Company, 55–56

Edict of Nantes, 63
Eigersman, Maureen, 302–3
Elliott, Colonel Matthew, 8, 93–96, 99
engagés (contract workers), 170–71
    wishes to escape among, 184–85
England, merchants & traders from, 31, 44
Equiano, Olaudah, 296–97
Eustache (Angélique's son), 163–64

fala de Guiné (Creole language), 38
Faneuil family (of Boston), 63–64
fire, as a threat to colonial towns, 195
Fire, The Great (Montréal, 1734)
    effects following from, 198, 201–13
    events during, 191–95
    introduction to, 6
    losses incurred in, 201–3, 210

First Sioux Trading Company, 115–16
Five Nations members used as fur agents, 65
Flanders. *See also* Flemish traders
    commercial links to Portugal in, 46
    geography of, 47–48
    ravages of wars in, 49–50
Flemish traders, 31, 46
    commercial loyalties of, 50–51
Fort Beauharnois (Lake Pepin), 116, 134
Foucault, François (councillor on Conseil Supérieur), 278
Foucher, François (prosecutor), 16, 215–19, 223, 266
    appeals Angélique's sentence, 257–59, 280
Fox nation, 111–13, 116, 134, 151, 268
Franche-Comté region in France, 170, 184, 187
Francheville, Sieur François Poulin de, 6, 11, 23, 60, 64 , 105–6, 146, 224, 271, 283
    achieves monopoly on iron ore development, 120–21, 124–25
    ancestors of, 108–9
    as Angélique's godfather , 160
    conscientiousness & determination of, 129
    death of, 134, 172
    death of his daughter Angélique, 130
    "donation mutuelle," 131–33
    journey to the Sioux, 133
    marriage of, 129
    mortgages his holdings, 124
    professions and trades of, 107–8, 113–17, 125–27
    relationships to Angélique of , 128–29, 164–65, 172–73, 175
    as a seigneur, 117–18
Francheville, Thérèse de Couagne de, 6, 99, 105–6, 219, 233, 286
    accuses Angélique of arson, 195, 198
    ancestry of, 129
    Angélique's pregnancies and, 163, 165–66
    anger at Angélique of, 173–74
    childlessness of, 133

death and will of, 136–38
"donation mutuelle," 131–33
fears Angélique will burn her house, 177
financial status of upon widowhood, 134–36
forbids Angélique to see Thibault, 182, 186
intention to sell Angélique, 176
lack of control over Angélique, 182–83, 188–90, 259
pays and dismisses Thibault, 183
"professions & trades" of, 135–36
purchase of slaves by, 136
refuses to grant Angélique's *congé*, 172, 174
stops mistreating Angélique, 129
testimony of, 225–26, 249
Franklin, John Hope, 182
Free Blacks, treatment and status of, 41–42, 100
fur trade. *See also* Montréal (old) trade routes for fur
early importance of, 64–65, 114–15, 144–45
French reliance on the Sioux regions for, 111
typical convoy of, 114

Gale, Lorena (playwright), 286
Gama, Vasco da, 29
Gambia, 35
Gamelin, Ignace Jr., 123, 146, 190
owner of Jacques César, 164
testimony of, 237–38
Gatien, François-Lucien (Francheville neighbour), 131
Gaudé, Françoise (mother superior), 204–5
Gaudé, Marie (Thérèse's mother), 129
Gaudron de Chevremont, Charles-René (notary), 14, 219
verdict on Angélique, 253–54
Geer, Allan (historian), 286
Geoffrion, Françoise (servant widow) testimony of, 230, 236, 242
Gervaise, Charles, 131
Ghana, 28, 35
Godard, Jean (miner), 121

Gold Coast (Africa), 28, 35
gold fields
African, 26, 29–30
Brazilian, 43
Grandier, Urbain (brodequins victim), 19
Gray, Robert I.D., 93, 98
Greene, Lorenzo, 87
greffier (court scribe), 217, 272
Gronniosaw, James Albert Ukawsaw, 295
Guadeloupe, 82
Guadron de Chevremont, Charles-René, 211
Guillet de Chaumont, Nicolas-Auguste, 219
verdict on Angélique, 254–55
Guillimin, Charles (councillor on Conseil Supérieur), 274
Guinea, 35
Guyon, Joseph (Francheville neighbour), 131

Hammon, Briton, 295, 299
hangman, difficulty filling the post of, 275
Hegel, Georg, 298–99
Henriques, Manuel Dias, 59
Henson, Jim, 302
Henson, Josiah, 302
Hery, Charles (Thérèse's testator), 136
history, Black Canadian, 7–9, 293–306
Hocquart, Gilles (intendant), 76, 120, 200, 210, 213–14, 271, 277, 290
family history of, 268–69
influence and powers of, 269–70
Hocquart, Jean-Hyacinthe, 268
Hôpital Général (Montréal hospital for the poor), 150
Hôtel-Dieu (original hospital), 3, 11, 136, 138, 150, 171
aftereffects of the fire at, 206–9
engulfed by fire, 191–92, 194, 202–3, 205
history of, 202–4
Hôtel-Dieu (today), 3
Huguenot (Protestant) traders, 62–64, 152, 161
Hume, David, 298

Imperial Act (1790), 91

India, 29
indigenous natives (New World). *See also* Panis
  enslavement of, 70
  genocide of, 34, 113
Inquisition, treatment of slaves under, 42
iron ore, Québec development of. *See also* Saint-Maurice, 119–24
Iroquois, used as fur agents, 65–66

Jacobs, Harriet, 294, 306
Jalleteau, Jacques (Monière's servant), 178, 186–87
  testimony of, 237, 241
Jamaica, 295
Janson *dit* Lapalme, Christophe (iron master), 123
Jarvis, William, 93
Jea, John, 296–97
Jefferson, Thomas, 298
Jewish traders, 32, 46–47, 54–55, 58
Joan of Arc, 257
João II. *See* King João II
"Jupiter" (Peter Russell's slave), 96–98

Kant, Immanuel, 299
Kenya, 29
King, Boston (Loyalist slave), 297, 301, 306
King Charles V (Spain), 30, 47
King João II (Portugal), 28, 32, 45
King João V (Portugal), 43
King Louis XIV (France), 49, 63, 71–72, 75, 152–53, 184, 217, 267
King Louis XV (France), 119, 151
King Manuel I (Portugal), 37–39, 41, 46
King Philip II (Spain), 47
Kirke, David, 71

labour shortage
  in New France, 71–72, 77
  in Québec, 84
  in Upper Canada, 102
La Brèche, Sieur (master forger), 122–23
Lachance, André (historian of New France),
165–66
La Dauversière, Jérôme Le Royer de, 202
La Flamandière, Jean-Joseph (surgeon)
  testimony of, 229–30
Lanctot, Gustave (historian), 148
Langlade, Augustin Mouet de, 117
Langlois, *dit* Traversy, Louis (labourer)
  testimony of, 230–31, 243
Lanoullier, Nicolas (councillor on Conseil Supérieur), 278
Latreille (soldier in Montréal), 5, 21, 171, 247
Leber, Pierre, 73
Lecomte-Dupre, Louis (early slaveholder), 73
legal system, in New France, 217–18
Le Jeune, Olivier, 71, 87, 163
Le Jeune, Paul (Jesuit priest), 71
Lemoine dit Monière, Alexis, 146, 160
  testimony of, 236–37
Lemoine dit Monière, Amable, 190, 219, 227
  testimony of, 245
le Moyne de Longueuil, Charles, 151
Lepage, Louis (hired slave), 78–79
Lepailleur, François, 219
  verdict on Angélique, 254
Lepailleur, Michel, 131
Le Pape Du Lescöat, Jean-Gabriel-Marie, 4, 160
Les filles du Roi (New France), 72
Leveille, Mathieu (slave & hangman), 14, 17–21, 187, 219, 279, 281–85
  history of, 275–76
Lidius, Johann Hendricks (Montreal fur smuggler), 62
liquor. *See* alcohol
Loguen, Jermain, 302
Louet, Jean-Claude (scribe), 275
Loyalists slaveholders immigrate to Canada, 90–91

Madagascar, 70, 73–74, 163
Madeira (island), 25–26, 30, 32, 34
Mali, 26
Mance, Jeanne (nursing nun), 2, 141, 202
manumission, regulation of in New

France, 76
Marché Bonsecours, 2
Marie-Manon (neighbourhood slave girl), 190, 219, 223–4, 233
testimony of, 226–27, 241
Marques, Oliveira, 46
Marrant, John, 295–96, 301, 306
marronage. *See also* slavery, attempted escapes from, 87, 96
Martin, Peter, 304
Martinique, 82, 99, 187, 295
Massicote, E.R. (historian), 258
Maurepas, Comte de (Minister of Marine), 62, 120–26, 209–10, 214
Maurepas, Jean-Frédéric Phélypeaux, Comte de (Minister of Marine), 267, 271
Mauritania, 27
merchant class in old Montréal, 145–47
Michilimackinac, fur trade at, 113–14, 146
Monière, Alexis (husband of Angélique's godmother) 9, 177, 219, 225
Montigny, Sieur Jacques de, 204, 206
Montréal (old), 263
building materials used in, 193–94
as centre of the fur trade, 64–65, 107–9, 112–13, 148
crown limitations on opportunity in, 151–52
deference expected in, 147–48
fires in, 151
fire-prevention actions taken in, 211–13
fortification of, 143
founding of, 141–42, 153, 155
as modern tourist attraction, 1–5
population & social hierarchy of, 143–48
streets and buildings of, 2–5, 142
unhygienic conditions of, 149–50
winter sport in, 149
Moodie, Major John, 300
Moodie, Susanna. *See* Strickland, Susanna
Moriscos (converted Muslims), 40
Morocco, 26
mulatto children, paternity of, 89–90, 164–65
Murray, General James (British Governor in Québec), 84, 88–89, 157

Muslim control of trade wealth, 26

Navetier, Father, 14, 19, 283, 285
"Navigator". *See* Prince Henrique (the Infante) of Portugal
"New Christian" traders. *See also* Jewish traders, 32, 39, 46–47, 54, 56, 59, 160
"New England", original referent of, 61–62
New France
crown administration of, 71–72, 153–55
earliest settlers in, 60, 71, 153–54
non-competitor to French manufacturing, 118–19
population in, 72
New Jersey, 56
New Netherlands, 56–57
French Canadians in, 61
New York. *See also* New Netherlands
English conquest of, 60–61
Normant, Monseigneur Louis, 206
Notre-Dame (Montréal Basilica), 2, 4, 20, 73, 130, 283
nuns in old Montréal, 145, 150

Ojibway nation, 112
Our Lady of the Rosary (Black fraternal order), 37–38

Panet, Pierre, 136, 138
Panis (native North-American slaves), 70, 74, 76, 81, 128
Papineau, Joseph, 104
Parma, Duke of, 48
Pays, Renée (widow), 267
"Peggy" (Peter Russell's slave), 93–98
Pennington, James, 294
Pennsylvania, 56, 62
Pernambuco, Brazil, Dutch conquest of, 52–53
Phélypeaux, Jean-Frédéric (Secretary of State, New France). *See* Maurepas, Comte de (Minister of Marine)
Phélypeaux, Jérôme, 267
Place Royale (Montréal), 12
Poirier, Marie-Louise (Francheville

domestic), 157, 176
Angélique's conflicts with, 233, 235
testimony of, 228–29, 243
Pompadour, Peggy, 306
Pooley, Sophia, 301, 306
Porlier, Claude-Cyprien-Jacques (*greffier*),
16, 219, 223, 244, 257, 285
Portugal
dominance of the slave trade by, 33
empire of, 30, 44
import-export imbalances of, 31, 44–45
initiation of slave trade by, 9, 24, 33
maritime dominance of, 25, 28, 30, 32
poverty in, 45
Poulin family, 108–9, 123
Prévost, Robert, 289
Prince Henrique (the Infante) of Portugal,
his naval empire, 24–28
Prince, Mary, 295, 299–300, 306
Principe, 30, 34
Pringle, Thomas, 300
prison in old Montréal, 215

Québec (old city), 153–55
size and setting of, 261–63
Québec (district/province)
black immigration to, 91
named as such, 81
Québec Act (1774), 91

Radisson, Étienne (Francheville neighbour),
131, 191, 219, 228
testimony of, 224, 244–45
Radisson, Pierre-Esprit, 109, 117
Raimbault, Catherine (Montréal slave
holder), 88
Raimbault, Pierre (Judge), 14, 16–19, 23,
199, 209, 215–19, 260, 266
career of, 220
examines witnesses, 221–25, 232–48
sets execution date, 282
verdict on Angélique, 253, 255–57
Ramezay, Claude de (governor of
Montréal), 130, 151
Ramezay, Madame de (Claude's widow),
210–11
Ramezay, Mother Superior, 204
Raudot, Jacques, 76
Réaume, Charles, 79
Roma, Jean-Pierre, 79–80
Roma, Marie-Anne (godmother to mulatto
half-sister), 79–80
Roy, François (Montréal crier), 196–97
rum. *See* alcohol
Russell, Elizabeth, 93, 96
Russell, Peter, 8, 93–99, 158

Saint Domingue (Haiti), 267
Saint-Maurice
farming & mining around, 117–18
ironworks at, 123–24, 127, 134, 164,
269, 271
Saint-Romain, René Chorel de
(Francheville neighbour), 131
Sancho, Ignatius, 298
San Domingue, 82
Santo Domingo, 295
São Tomé, 30, 32, 34
Sarquint, Sieur Joseph, 136
Sarrazin, Michel (surgeon), 264
personal history of, 273–74
Schenectady Massacre, 66
Schweninger, Loren, 182
seigneurial landownership, 108, 117–18
Senegal, 35
Senegambia, 28
Sierra Leone, 27–28, 35, 63, 297
migration back to, 100
Simcoe, Colonel John Graves
efforts to abolish slavery of, 101–3
Simcoe, Elizabeth, 193
Sioux nation, 111–12
slavery. *See also* slavery ("Atlantic"); slavery
(in Canada)
abolition of. *See* abolitionist movements
attempted escapes from, 40, 76–77,
85–86, 169
Catholicism and. *See also* the Vatican, 38–39
defined, 70
depravity of, 289

family life under, 40–41, 75
gendered nature of, 84
general brutality of, 98–99, 158–59, 168
inciting escapes from, 76
narratives of, 293–97, 301–6
opposition to, 100
perceived "necessity" of. *See also* labour
    shortage, 35
successful escapes or release from, 36–37
White discomfort talking about, 289
slavery ("Atlantic"), 9–12
beginnings of, 24, 27, 29
commercial significance of, 30–31,
    33, 53
Dutch efforts to control, 52–53
England's takeover of, 83
numbers of those affected by, 33, 35,
    43, 56
organization and control of, 29–30
participants carrying out, 34–35, 52,
    56–58, 65–66
transshipment and, 35–36
slavery (in Canada)
after the conquest of Québec, 139
court actions opposing, 104
ended by the British Parliament, 104
first limitations placed upon (1793), 102
forgotten nature and extent of, 68–81,
    105–6
geographical extent of, 74, 77, 92, 100
legal regulation of, 75–76, 81–82, 91
paternalistic aspects of, 76–77, 128, 162
rights allowed under, 78, 82
successful escapes from, 103, 303
temporal extent of, 70–73, 81–83, 104
unsuccessful attempts to limit, 104
widespread ignorance about, 7–8
slaves. *See also* slavery
acts of defiance by, 40–41, 81, 86, 94–96,
    100
alliances with servants, 185–86
brief life expectancies among, 35, 81,
    88, 167–68
desired qualities in when purchased,
    87–88

gifted while still children, 79–80
mandatory baptism of, 38, 41, 75
marginalization of, 41
motherhood among, 168–69
movement of to control rebellion, 188
new cultures created by, 38–39
owners of, 36, 128, 186
petitions for better treatment by, 41
portrayed as non-reasoning inferiors, 299
pregnancies among, 166–67
procurement of, 34–35, 43, 73–74
"respect" demanded from, 37, 40, 172–73
restrictions placed on the movements
    & activities of, 37–40
sales of, 87–89, 97–98
sexual abuse of, 89–90, 168
suicide among, 87
varying treatment of by owners, 82–83
work done by, 33–34, 36–37, 69, 74,
    77–78, 92, 127–28, 157–59, 164, 167
Songhai, 26
sorcery, sinful and criminal nature of, 150
the spice trade, 26–27, 29
Stowe, Harriet Beecher, 302
Strickland, Susanna, 300
Stuart, Rev. John, 93
sugar trade, 44, 51–52
Sulpicians (clerical order), 11, 134, 143,
    145, 150, 160, 197, 203, 206
original powers of, 4, 155
Surinam, 55–57

Talbot, Jean-Jacques (priest), 134
Talon, Jean, 118–20
Taschereau, Thomas-Jacques (councillor
    on Conseil Supérieur), 278
Tétreau, Jean-Baptiste (Francheville
    neighbour), 131
Thibault, Claude (soldier paramour of
    Angélique), 18
affair with Angélique, 171–73, 175,
    221, 259, 283
assumed to be the arson mastermind,
    258
background of, 170

behaviour during and after the fire, 197, 225, 235–36, 250
behaviour on leaving prison, 249–50
captured and jailed in Montréal, 181–82
delays the escape to await his pay, 179, 240
final escape, 288
given a motive for co-conspiracy, 225–26
guilty of contempt of court, 256, 259
hunted after the fire, 217, 230, 244
incriminated by Bellefeuille, 242–43
intractable worker, 171, 176
released and planning next escape, 183–85
sent with Angélique to live at Alexis Monière's, 177, 241
told by Angélique not to work for Alexis Monière's, 178
verdict rendered upon (at Québec), 280
visits Angélique shortly before the fire, 190
Thomas, Jean-Baptiste, hanged for burglery, 185
Thomellete, Marie-Françoise (Francheville servant), 157, 219
testimony of, 231, 244
Togo, 35
torture. *See also* Angélique, Marie-Joseph, torture of; brodequins; hangman
in New France, 6, 15–19, 218–19, 275
trade, marketing and distributing resources for, 31, 44
trade routes
for African gold, 26–28, 30
for furs, 61, 64–65, 111
for ivory, 30
for silk & tea, 30–31
for silver, 51
for slaves. *See* slavery ("Atlantic")
for spices, 26, 30, 51
for sugar & molasses, 30, 44, 51, 58–59
Treaty of Paris (ceding New France to England), 81–82
Trebuchet, François (miner), 121
Tremon, Sieur, shelters Thérèse after the fire, 195, 225
Trois-Rivières, 87, 108–9, 118, 153, 155, 263

Trudel, Marcel (historian), 144, 289
Tubman, Harriet, 301

Underground Railroad, 69, 86
beginnings of, 103
Upper Canada, creation of, 91–92

Vaissiere, Jean (Francheville's agent in La Rochelle), 64
Vallé, Jean-Baptiste, 78–79
Van den Boogaart, Ernst, 57
Varin de La Marre, Jean-Victor (*greffier* & comptroller), 277–78
personal history of, 272–73
Vasco da Gama. *See* Gama, Vasco da
Vatican. *See also* the Catholic church
attempts to discourage trade of Christian slaves, 33
gives Portugal colonizing permissions, 28
Vaudreuil, Phillipe de Rigaud, 110–12
Verrier, Louis-Guillaume (attorney general), 271–72, 279–80
Vieira, Father (Brazilian Jesuit), 55
Volant de Radisson. *See* Radisson, Étienne
voyageurs, 146–47
Vrooman, William (Chloe Cooley's slave holder), 99, 101–2, 304

Wallonia (French Flanders), 60
war, made on "western natives" by Québec, 112–13, 116
The War of Spanish Succession, 42–43, 49, 58, 110
Ward, Samuel Ringgold, 302
West, Cornel, 298
West India Company. *See* Dutch West India Company
Wheatley, Phillis ("slave poet"), 298
Williams, Francis, 298
witchcraft. *See* sorcery

CPSIA information can be obtained
at www.ICGtesting.com
Printed in the USA
LVHW05001815O921
697834LV00002B/148

9 780820 329406